D1605795

SECESSION AND THE SOVEREIGNTY GAME

SECESSION AND THE SOVEREIGNTY GAME

Strategy and Tactics for Aspiring Nations

Ryan D. Griffiths

CORNELL UNIVERSITY PRESS   ITHACA AND LONDON

First published 2021 by Cornell University Press

Library of Congress Cataloging-in-Publication Data

Names: Griffiths, Ryan D., author.
Title: Secession and the sovereignty game : strategy and tactics for aspiring nations / Ryan D. Griffiths.
Description: Ithaca [New York] : Cornell University Press, 2021. | Includes bibliographical references and index.
Identifiers: LCCN 2020052062 (print) | LCCN 2020052063 (ebook) | ISBN 9781501754746 (hardcover) | ISBN 9781501754760 (pdf) | ISBN 9781501754753 (epub)
Subjects: LCSH: Secession. | Sovereignty. | Separatist movements. | Self-determination, National.
Classification: LCC JC327 .G744 2021 (print) | LCC JC327 (ebook) | DDC 320.1/5—dc23
LC record available at https://lccn.loc.gov/2020052062
LC ebook record available at https://lccn.loc.gov/2020052063

For Sharon

Contents

Figures

Tables

Abbreviations

ANC	Catalan National Assembly (Assemblea Nacional Catalana)
AU	African Union
BCL	Bougainville Copper Limited
BRA	Bougainville Revolutionary Army
BRF	Bougainville Resistance Force
CDC	Democratic Convergence of Catalonia (Convergència Democràtica de Catalunya)
CiU	Convergence and Union (Convergència i Unio)
CONIFA	Confederation of Independent Football Associations
CUP	Popular Unity Candidacy (Candidatura d'Unitat Popular)
DIPLOCAT	Public Diplomacy Council of Catalonia (Consell de Diplomàcia Pública de Catalunya)
EOKA	National Organization of Cypriot Struggle (Ethniki Organosis Kipriakou Agonos)
ERC	Republican Left of Catalonia (Esquerra Republicana de Catalunya)
EU	European Union
FAES	Foundation for Analysis and Social Studies
FLNKS	Kanak and Socialist National Liberation Front (Front de Libération Nationale Kanak et Socialiste)
GAM	Free Aceh Movement (Geurakan Acèh Meurdèka)
KDP	Kurdistan Democratic Party
LKS	Kanak Socialist Liberation (Libération Kanak Socialiste)
LTTE	Liberation Tigers of Tamil Eelam
MSG	Melanesian Spearhead Group
NATO	North Atlantic Treaty Organization
OPM	Free Papua Movement (Organisasi Papua Merdeka)
P5	United Nations Security Council Permanent Five Members
Palika	Party of Kanak Liberation (Parti de libération kanak)
PEPERA	Act of Free Choice (Penentuan Pendapat Rakyat)
PNG	Papua New Guinea
PNGDF	Papua New Guinea Defence Force
PP	Popular Party (Partido Popular)
PSC	Socialists' Party of Catalonia (Partit dels Socialistes de Catalunya)

PSOE	Spanish Socialist Workers' Party (Partido Socialista Obrero Español)
R2P	Responsibility to Protect
RPCR	Rally for Caledonia in the Republic
SCC	Catalan Civil Society (Societat Civil Catalana)
SNP	Scottish National Party
TRNC	Turkish Republic of Northern Cyprus
UC	Caledonian Union (Union Calédonienne)
UCDP	Uppsala Conflict Data Program
ULMWP	United Liberation Movement for West Papua
UNFICYP	United Nations Peacekeeping Force in Cyprus
UNGA	United Nations General Assembly
UNPO	Unrepresented Nations and Peoples Organization
WPNCL	West Papua National Coalition for Liberation

SECESSION AND THE
SOVEREIGNTY GAME

1

MANY SECESSIONIST MOVEMENTS, ONE INTERNATIONAL SYSTEM

> **Secession lies squarely at the juncture of internal and international politics.**
>
> —Horowitz 1985, 230

Secession is a common spectacle in world affairs. The high-flying secessionist movement in Catalonia, for example, has disrupted Spanish politics and created a constitutional crisis. On September 25, 2017, the Iraqi Kurds held a referendum on independence that was condemned by the Iraqi government and key regional actors. Bougainville held a referendum in late 2019, and may become the next independent sovereign state. Meanwhile, the breakaway region of Northern Cyprus is locked in a frozen state of division with the Republic of Cyprus, and there is no end in sight. In October 2018, the Morning Star flag of West Papua was brilliantly superimposed upon the Sydney Opera House, reminding the world that there are indigenous peoples who strive for independence in places where such flags are illegal.

One striking aspect of secession is its diversity. Indeed, the settings are often so different that it can seem like we are discussing different phenomena. The parades and public debates on the streets of Edinburgh look different from the Tuareg rebellion of the short-lived Republic of Azawad. The apparent freedom of the people of Artsakh (Nagorno Karabakh) contrasts with the reports of the oppression of the Uighur. The Flemish independence movement consists of political parties that operate in a setting that is a world away, figuratively and literally, from the secessionist-prone regions of peripheral Myanmar or Mindanao. Commensurate with the diversity of settings is a multiplicity of methods. Some independence movements like the Catalan use combinations of electoral capture and civil demonstrations. In contrast, regions that lack the same geographic and political connectivity with their legal home state—regions like Abkhazia—are relegated to a de facto but unrecognized status where defense, deterrence, and diplomacy are critical. Other regions, from West Papua to Western Sahara, are faced with the hard choice between civil resistance and the use of violence.

Is there a strategy to all of this secessionist activity and can we make sense of the tactics we observe? For example, why do some independence movements form political parties that compete in elections when others choose to use extrainstitutional methods like sit-ins, strikes, or even armed insurgency? Put differently, why do some follow the precepts of Mahatma Gandhi as opposed to Che Guevara? Are violence and nonviolent civil resistance both useful tactics, and why do some groups choose one rather than the other? What role does normative persuasion play, and why do some movements appeal to principles regarding human rights when others are keen to showcase their ability to govern effectively? Whom are these arguments intended to persuade? Indeed, what are the obstacles to obtaining sovereign statehood, and what is the process by which it can be obtained? We need a theoretical framework to explain the purpose behind secessionist behavior.

There is considerable value in understanding the strategy and tactics of secession because they have far-reaching consequences. Secession has been the motivating force behind roughly half of the civil wars since 1945.[1] I estimated that there has been an average of fifteen secessionist conflicts per year since the end of World War II,[2] and Barbara Walter has argued that secessionism is the "chief source of violence in the world today."[3] Bougainville won a peace agreement in 2001, after more than ten years of civil war that destroyed most of the infrastructure on the main island and killed as many as 20,000 people (10 percent of the population). In 2013, a teacher in Buka told me that the Bougainville government faced a daunting challenge in training and educating the lost generation that came of age during the war. There were over sixty secessionist movements as of 2017, and these groups were surprisingly networked and aware of the various ways that sovereignty can be obtained. Several scholars have conjectured that the practices surrounding recognition may create unfair outcomes and perverse incentives, convincing some that violence is the surest way to gain independence.[4] If the strategy of secession promotes violence, it would be useful to understand not only why, but also when and where, so that proper policies can be established to save lives.

However, violence is not the only concern because, in one way or another, secession is always disruptive. As the Catalans know, it is a phenomenon that is felt from the parliament to the playground. In recent years, the issue of independence has been the master cleavage in the Catalan parliament and the cause of the constitutional crisis and imposition of direct rule in 2017. The divisiveness that follows can affect children. A friend of mine shared an experience he had when his five-year-old enrolled in a public, Catalan-speaking school in Gràcia, a neighborhood of Barcelona. His son was accustomed to saying his name using the Span-ish pronunciation and was somewhat resistant to being addressed by the Catalan form. This led to some teasing by fellow students who eventually nicknamed him *la facha* (colloquial for "the fascist") because of his association with Spain. The children were probably unaware of the historical significance of the term and had merely imbibed this terminology in the context of the independence movement. But the significance was not lost on the boy's mother and father, who could each point to parents and grandparents who had suffered the persecution of fascist re-gimes in Spain and Portugal. After failing to have the issue properly addressed by the teachers and administration, the parents moved their son to a different school. The father, a Portuguese immigrant, identified that incident as the moment when his wife, a Catalan who was proud of her language and culture, turned away from Catalan nationalism.

Sometimes the social sorting that attends secessionist activity is hardened into militarized boundaries. The island of Cyprus was once composed of a majority Greek-speaking population that lived side by side with the Turkish minority. The ethnic conflict of the 1960s and 1970s led to a tragic and often violent unmixing of the two populations as the Turks moved north and the Greeks moved south, and the boundary between them became hardened as the UN-sponsored demili-tarized zone known as the Green Line. To this day there are built structures, old neighborhoods, and the former international airport inside the buffer zone, der-elict and crumbling. They are frozen in time, like the conflict itself, and the break-away region of Northern Cyprus is stuck in a perpetual liminal state between reintegration and full sovereign statehood.

In the end, secession is a challenge to the state, a form of rebellion. Even at its most constructive, the activity that follows is disruptive. The debate around Scot-tish independence has divided families and polarized society. What would the social costs have been had the nationalists won the referendum in 2014? Seces-sionism is transformative, it is a fact of international life, and it is a phenomenon of great importance that we do not fully understand.

The Argument

This book is about the strategy and tactics of secessionist movements, and the game they play with states and the international community to win their sover-eignty. I argue that the strategy of secession is shaped by the international recog-nition regime, and further contextualized by the setting in which any given secessionist movement operates. Let me define two key terms. First, a secession-ist movement is a "self-identified nation inside a sovereign state that seeks to separate and form a new [recognized] sovereign state," signified in the post-1945 era by joining the United Nations (UN) as a full member.[5] Second, the international recognition regime is the evolving body of international legal norms, rules, and principles that determine when an applicant nation has the right to withdraw from an existing state and become a recognized independent sovereign state. I contend that at the strategic level, all contemporary secessionist movements are alike. Their settings may look different, but the strategic playing field is the same. All of them need to compel and persuade their home state and/or the international community to recognize them. The single biggest obstacle to any secessionist movement is its home state, because the international recognition regime assigns a great deal of weight to the interests of that state. Where the home state is reluctant to negotiate or is repressive, secessionists can go around it and attempt to enlist the support of the international community. This is the sovereignty game, and it applies to the entire diversity of movements from Abkhazia to Artsakh, Scotland to Catalonia, and West Papua to Bougainville.[6]

To secure their strategic goal, secessionist movements engage in two categories of tactics: compellence and normative appeal. Compellence is the use of assets to compel the home state and/or international community to make a change.[7] It is direct action designed to increase the costs of not complying with secessionist demands. In this book I model three specific tactics of compellence: electoral capture, nonviolent civil resistance, and violence. Normative appeal includes a different set of tactics that are designed to showcase the grievances and demands of the aspiring nation and either change preferences on the issue or bring into the game previously uninvolved parties. I identify and examine a set of specific normative appeals: earned sovereignty, decolonization, the right to choose, inherent sovereignty, and human rights. Overall, compellence and normative appeal are analytically distinct because compellence is about incurring costs while normative appeal is about changing preferences.

Although all movements use compellence and normative appeal in pursuit of independence, they do so in different combinations that are shaped by local factors such as regime type, the strength of the state, and the degree to which the secessionist region is integrated with the home state. These factors coalesce around six identifiable kinds of movements: democratized, indigenous legal, weak combative, strong combative, decolonial, and de facto. These six kinds are not ideal-types but rather clusters of characteristics, not unlike peaks on a topographical map, that I have observed through an analysis of all contemporary movements. Secessionists are generally pragmatic and choose tactics that are made available by their setting.

The quote by Donald Horowitz at the beginning of the chapter underscores the fact that secession sits at the intersection of international and domestic politics.[8] Presently, there is only one international system, one UN that secessionists aim to join, and one sovereignty game. To win sovereign statehood an aspiring nation has to conform to the rules given by the international recognition regime. That regime creates the perception of pathways to independence, and there is thus an outside-in character to secessionist strategy that changes over time as the international system changes.[9] However, it is the internal, domestic environment that conditions the tactical choices for any given movement. In sum, all secessionist movements maneuver on the same strategic playing field, but their tactics vary according to local conditions.

Framing the Study

This book makes a number of important contributions to our understanding of secession. First, it brings together three research areas that are usually treated separately: the work on de facto states,[10] the scholarship on secessionist political parties in advanced democracies,[11] and the study of secessionist conflict.[12] These three research areas constitute a kind of compartmentalization in the field because the relevant scholars are normally dialoguing within and not across groups. The work on de facto states looks at how unrecognized but empirical states endure in the international system, and the work is typically conducted by international relations scholars, sociologists, and geographers. The research on secessionist political parties merges with the study of electoral politics and federalism. The work on secessionist conflict blends with the civil-war literature. Yet many movements are discussed in more than one literature or move back and forth between them over time—the boundaries between them are hardly impermeable—and all of these movements are united by the fact that they are playing the same strategic game.

My theoretical framework clarifies the behavior of diverse secessionist movements and accurately predicts the tactics they adopt. Whereas much of the generalist secession literature centers on whether the movement becomes independent,[13] I focus on what they do to achieve independence.[14] This is a neglected area of research, and a vital one given that secessionist behavior is destabilizing and sometimes violent. Furthermore, my theory integrates the work on secession with the research on social movements,[15] civil war,[16] rebel diplomacy,[17] and international law.[18] I then test the implications from the theory through case studies and using original data on the tactics used by 136 secessionist movements between 1946 and 2011. Surprisingly, no one to my knowledge has put forth a strategic theory that cuts across these different literatures for how secessionist movements seek full sovereign recognition and has generated the necessary data to test that theory.

My theory is meant to explain the strategy and tactical behavior of all independence movements, and it encompasses the literatures on secessionist democratic parties, de facto states, and secessionist conflict. Nevertheless, there are elements of the larger picture that receive less attention. Although I do discuss the countersecession strategy of states in chapter 3, and in the case studies, the primary focus is on the movements themselves.[19] Similarly, I treat my independence movements as unitary actors. But as I discuss in chapter 11, these movements are often divided and/or subject to fragmentation, and there is a marvelous literature on this topic.[20] For example, as Phil Roeder notes in a recent book,[21] secessionist leaders are not only interacting strategically with the home state, they are also playing a more internal game as they attempt to win over the hearts and minds of their platform population. These are important parts of the larger picture, and I do address them at select points throughout the book, but they are not central elements of my analysis for reasons of parsimony.

The payoff that comes from controlling the scope of the study is that I can examine other crucial dynamics. For example, I bring in the "international" and show not only how it shapes the strategic playing field but also the very process by which a secessionist movement joins the club of sovereign states as a full UN member. I specify the UN application process and explain why most of the strategic/tactical maneuvering takes place prior to application. Essentially, by controlling the scope of the study and focusing less attention on the dynamics within secessionist movements, I can focus more attention on their relationship with the home state and the international community.

My theoretical framework facilitates a close examination of tactics. I can analyze the choice between different compellence methods like electoral capture, nonviolent civil resistance, and violence. Relatedly, I can investigate the use of different normative appeals. In the qualitative chapters I can explore the degree to which actors think these options work, and the conditions under which they actually choose between them. I can ask secessionist leaders why they choose their tactics and then test my hypotheses in a large-N format.

Finally, by theorizing the conditions that produce different kinds of movements, I can draw conclusions about the tradeoffs that come with them. For example, one of the downsides to becoming a de facto state movement is that, despite the apparent freedom and autonomy, the aspiring nation is relegated to a liminal, halfway position where full independence will be even harder to achieve. The reason is simple; complete separation from the home state removes the levers of compellence, and it is therefore harder for the secessionists to force a change. In contrast, the institutionalization of an independence movement transforms its tactics and makes it less violent, although not more successful. As I discuss in the conclusion, there are tradeoffs to each kind of movement, but there are overall benefits to institutionalization for secessionists, states, and the international system.

Methodology

In this book I utilized a standard mixed-methods approach.[22] First, my research relied on substantial fieldwork and over 100 interviews with representatives of secessionist movements, countersecessionist groups, including state officials, and members of international organizations.[23] Fieldwork was conducted in Artsakh, Bougainville, Catalonia, the Cook Islands, Iraqi Kurdistan, the Murrawarri Republic, New Caledonia, Northern Cyprus, Palestine, Scotland, and West Papua. In addition to the interviews I held in these regions, I also interviewed representatives of these and other groups at different locations, such as conferences, homes-in-exile, political events, or simply over the phone. In this way, I have spoken to representatives of a number of other independence efforts including (but not limited to) Kosovo, the Principality of Snake Hill, Somaliland, the Texas Independence Movement, Tamil Eelam, Tibet, and Western Sahara, as well as the International Monetary Fund, the UN, and Independent Diplomat (a for-profit consulting firm). My approach to interviews was somewhat journalistic, and using what amounted to a snowball approach I typically interviewed representatives whenever and wherever I could. As such, there is some imbalance in the interview coverage of these different groups, but in my view that is inevitable given the diverse settings. For example, my interviews in Catalonia benefitted from a six-month sabbatical in Barcelona where I gradually formed networks on both sides of the issue. In contrast, my interviews with West Papuans were either done furtively on location, because conversations on self-determination there can land one in jail, or outside the country with exiled leaders. The end result is a large volume of information-rich interviews that sit at the core of this book.

Second, I conducted case studies of six secessionist movements: Catalonia, the Murrawarri Republic, West Papua, Bougainville, New Caledonia, and Northern Cyprus. In each case I tracked the development of the movement, examined its strategic and tactical choices, and compared it against my theoretical predictions. Third, I conducted a large-N study of 136 secessionist movements between 1946 and 2011 utilizing a combination of datasets. These include an update of the data on secessionist movements that I created for my 2016 book *Age of Secession: The International and Domestic Determinants of State Birth*.[24] For the tactics of compellence, I used the dataset on secessionist methods created by Louis Wasser and myself.[25] Data on the tactics of normative appeal were created specifically for this project using content analysis of pronouncements by movement leaders, supporters, participants, and third-party observers.

My theoretical framework and research design have inductive and deductive origins. When I first started doing interviews in 2009, I began to develop a picture of secessionist activity. I gradually combined this inductive approach with research in international law and international relations to form a more unified theory of secessionist strategy. Chapter 3 is the product of these inductive and deductive origins, and it is here that I provide a theoretical sketch of my six secessionist kinds. These kinds are not ideal-types, but rather clusters of characteristics that I observed over time. I then moved to conduct case studies—and further fieldwork—of six secessionist movements that best represented these kinds. After confirming my theoretical predictions in these studies, I then moved on to a broader large-N study of all secessionist movements since 1945.

Finally, I should note that I am neutral on the matter of any particular independence movement, for both personal and professional reasons, and that my analysis should not be taken as an advocation either way.[26] These are complex issues, and for rhetorical and argumentative purposes in the book, I will try to specify what is at stake for those seeking independence and for those aiming to hold their state together. Although it is quite natural to sympathize with an individual or group during fieldwork, and to be accused of being a supporter of a group by its opponents who deem that group illegal,[27] my goal has been to treat these matters objectively as a social scientist.

Plan of the Book

The organization of the book follows a narrative arc from the general to the specific and back to the general. The first two chapters provide a conceptual and theoretical treatment of the sovereignty game. Chapter 2 focuses on sovereign states, secessionist movements, and the international recognition regime. Here, I clarify the concepts and use original data to show temporal patterns since the early nineteenth century. I detail the framework for understanding how the recognition regime has evolved since the eighteenth century. Using the literature on sovereignty and international law, as well as interviews with UN officials, I specify the admission process for becoming a recognized sovereign state, and the perceived pathways it creates. In chapter 3, I articulate the strategy of secession. I explain how secessionist movements need to compel and persuade their home state to give consent and/or bring the international community into the contest. I use information drawn from interviews to show that secessionists are well informed about the dynamics of secession. I explain the logics of compellence and normative appeal, I explicate the different tactics within these two logics, and I argue that the choice of tactics depends on local conditions that cluster around six kinds of movements (democratized, indigenous legal, weak combative, strong combative, decolonial, and de facto). In the final sections of the chapter, I discuss a prominent hybrid case, Iraqi Kurdistan, and I examine the counter-strategy of states.

It is in the middle of the book that I zoom in to investigate six case studies that are representative of the six secessionist kinds. Each case relies on fieldwork and interviews. I discuss the development of the movements, their strategy and tactics, and the outcomes. The stories are often quite personal. I use original maps, discuss the flags used by each movement, and I give the chapters an additional ethnographic character. The title for each chapter is drawn from symbolic themes that are resonant in the design of the movement's flag. The sequencing of these chapters is organized around the structural relationship between the independence movements and their state. Catalonia and the Murrawarri Republic are highly institutionalized movements, arguably the most integrated with the state. The next two movements, West Papua and Bougainville, are examples of less institutionalized movements and the dynamics that result. New Caledonia provides a more composite example, set apart chiefly by its ability to appeal to decolonization. Finally, Northern Cyprus is an example of what happens to an independence movement that is completely sundered from the home state.

I will offer a brief summary of the case studies. Chapter 4 is about Catalonia, an exemplar of the democratized movement. Using a substantial number of interviews, I discuss the tactics that the Catalan secessionists have used, and I highlight the possibilities and limitations of a fully institutionalized movement. Chapter 5 is about the Murrawarri Republic, a little-known aboriginal independence movement in Australia. Like the Catalans, the Murrawarri are using the institutional/electoral features of the state to seek their goal, but they are stressing a different normative appeal that rejects the application of *terra nullius* when their lands were originally claimed by Great Britain. Chapter 6 focuses on the long-running independence effort in West Papua. It is an example of the weak combative type. Chapter 7 discusses Bougainville, an example of a strong combative movement, where there is greater symmetry between the capabilities of the two sides. Given the high price that Bougainville paid to win an autonomy agreement and legal referendum—roughly 20,000 people died in their ten-year civil war—this chapter presents another kind of cautionary tale. It also offers a critique of the international recognition regime by showing how violence can be a useful tactic. Chapter 8 is about New Caledonia, an example of a decolonial movement. I track the development of the movement since the 1960s and follow the different tactics it used at different points in time. Chapter 9 tells the story of the independence effort in Northern Cyprus. It showcases the tactical options that are both available and unavailable to de facto state movements, and it provides a cautionary tale for what happens when a secessionist region is separated from the rest of the state.

It is in the final chapters of the book that I zoom out again to take in the strategic and tactical dynamics of secession from a wide angle. In chapter 10, I provide a large-N quantitative analysis of secessionist tactics. Using data on 136 secessionist movements between 1946 and 2011, I examine the statistical relationship between the six kinds of movements and their tactics of compellence and normative appeal. In chapter 11, I identify the causes and consequences of bad strategy and poor tactics. Here, I distinguish three sources of error. These are the problem that all secessionists possess incomplete information about the dynamics of recognition, the phenomenon of wishful thinking, and the fact that secessionists typically have multiple objectives and multiple internal factions. In chapter 12, I conclude with a theoretical and prescriptive analysis of the future of sovereignty game. I highlight several past configurations of the international recognition regime, and I identify three potential future configurations that focus on remedial rights, primary rights, and state consent. I discuss the comparative statics of each configuration—that is, the expected frequency of secession, conflict, and the fitness of new states as a result of the regime. I then argue for the merits of a regime that emphasizes consent-based democratized secession in which independence movements have formal institutional access (voice), but where the conditions for political exit are nevertheless hard to reach. The overall benefits of this configuration would be to reduce conflict both within and between states.

STATES, SECESSIONIST MOVEMENTS, AND THE INTERNATIONAL RECOGNITION REGIME

A State is, and becomes, an International Person through recognition only and exclusively.

—Oppenheim 1955, 125.

To understand the sovereignty game, we must first map out the strategic playing field. What is the process by which an independence movement becomes a sovereign state? Are there rules that guide the behavior of secessionists and, if so, how are those rules formed? In this chapter I provide answers to these questions. I define states and secessionist movements, and I outline their relationship to one another. I then describe the international recognition regime, which I define as the evolving body of international legal norms, rules, and principles that determine when an applicant nation has the right to withdraw from an existing state and become a recognized independent sovereign state. I explain how and why the regime works, how it has evolved over time, and highlight the competing normative demands that sit at the heart of the regime. I specify the resulting pathways to independence for secessionist movements.

Sovereign States

When I discuss sovereign states in this book I refer to those entities that possess international recognition. In the period since 1945, this is nearly always signified by full membership in the United Nations General Assembly (UNGA). There are some exceptions. Switzerland did not join the United Nations (UN) as a full member until 2002, but few would question its prior status as a sovereign state. Taiwan lost its full membership in 1971 when its legal sovereignty was transferred to the People's Republic of China, but it still possesses many of the benefits of sovereignty. As I elaborate below, full UN membership is regarded as the gold standard of contemporary sovereign statehood.

Rather than delve into the rich literature on the concept of the state,[1] I will identify two dimensions of statehood that are important for my theoretical framework. One dimension pertains to the inwardly focused function of the state and its ability to provide political order. The other dimension is outwardly focused and calls attention to recognition by other states. Robert Jackson and Carl Rosberg named these dimensions when they distinguished between "empirical statehood"—Does the state function?—and "juridical statehood"—Is it legally recognized?[2] Stephen Krasner made a similar distinction with his terms "domestic sovereignty" and "international legal sovereignty."[3]

This distinction is relevant for my purposes because the two dimensions do not always go together. On one hand, there are functional states like Northern Cyprus and Somaliland that provide political order and yet are unrecognized. These are typically referred to as de facto states,[4] and in this book I treat the de facto state as a kind of secessionist movement. On the other hand, some states possess international sovereign recognition but lack functional statehood in the internal sense. Although the term has become controversial, "failed state" is often used to describe these entities. Despite their shortcomings, I nevertheless treat these entities as sovereign states. It may seem strange to regard failed states as members of the club that secessionist movements aspire to join. After all, secessionists do not aim to become failed states. But seen from the perspective of the strategic playing field, it makes sense to include states like Somalia because, despite its weakness, it remains a member of the club and has been able to block the independence bid of its own breakaway region, Somaliland. State failure does not prevent a recognized sovereign state from playing the game.[5] However, as I discuss in the chapters to come, that failure can shape the tactics of secessionists who will readily cite it as a reason for why they deserve their independence.

There are currently 193 recognized sovereign states, the member states of the UN. The top trend line in figure 2.1 graphs the number of sovereign states in existence in each year since 1816.[6] One of the notable features of the graph is the proliferation of states in the postwar period; from sixty-five states in 1945, the set expanded by a factor of three. This period of proliferation over more than seventy years has been called the Age of Secession.[7] Another notable feature is the concave pattern of the number of states over time. There were 135 states in 1816 and roughly that number for the next forty-five years before a culling process began that reduced the set by more than 60 percent.[8] The next half-century from roughly 1860 to the eve of World War I was the time of imperialism, state expansion, and the final enclosure of the international system.[9] The low point in this process of political aggregation was reached in 1912 when the international system was com-

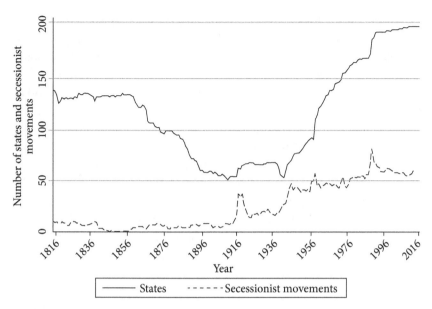

FIGURE 2.1.   Number of sovereign states and secessionist movements (1816–2017)

posed of only fifty-one states, an historical low point without precedent.[10] If the interwar period was one of instability with respect to the life and death of states, the post-1945 era has been dominated by state birth.

The trend line in the number of states is a function of what we might call the death rate and the birth rate. Much like a human population, states are born and states die. State birth occurs when an aspiring group becomes a sovereign state,[11] and state death happens when a sovereign state loses that sovereign status.[12] In the early nineteenth century these two rates were approximately equal, and there was a rough equilibrium at just over 130 states. That equilibrium was upset in the second half of the 1800s as the death rate exceeded the birth rate. The interwar period reached a new equilibrium, albeit one that began with a bump in state birth and ended with a surge in state death. Finally, the post-1945 period has been characterized by an asymmetry in the two rates. The rate of state death has gone down just as the rate of state birth has increased.

This discussion may give the impression that we have a foolproof method for identifying sovereign states over time. We do not. As many scholars have discussed,[13] and as I elaborate in the remainder of this chapter, the criteria for being recognized as a sovereign state has changed over the centuries. Such criteria are as much the product of international diplomacy as they are of clear legal thinking, and they are often disputed. One prominent example is the 1933 Montevideo

Convention on the Rights and Duties of States, in which nineteen North and South American states gathered to establish the criteria for statehood. According to Article 1 of the Convention, "The State as a person of international law should possess the following qualifications: (a) a permanent population; (b) a defined territory; (c) government; and (d) capacity to enter into relations with other states."[14] These criteria focused on the functionality of the state. Moreover, according to Article 3, "The political existence of the state is independent of recognition by the other states." If these alone were the criteria for sovereign statehood, then de facto states like Somaliland would count. Indeed, as I discuss in chapter 12, the sovereignty game would be substantially altered. But these are not the key criteria in the post-1945 international system—whether they were in the 1930s is another matter. My analysis of the contemporary sovereignty game begins with the establishment of the international order following World War II, and, accordingly, I conceive of sovereign states as full members of the UN.[15]

Secessionist Movements

I define a secessionist movement as a "self-identified nation inside a sovereign state that seeks to separate and form a new [recognized] sovereign state."[16] This is a broad definition that includes both the violent and nonviolent cases, occasions of decolonization and dissolution, and instances of de facto statehood. Using the identification criteria from my 2016 book and updating the data through 2017,[17] I can showcase the number of movements per year since 1816—shown in Figure 2.1 by the dashed line. On average, there have been twenty-five movements per year. However, unlike the trend in the number of states, the overall pattern is not concave but generally increasing. Secessionism was rare in the nineteenth century, though not completely absent. There was a sharp spike in secessionist activity following World War I—the so-called Wilsonian moment[18]—followed by a trough in the interwar period. It has been quite common in the post-1945 period, with an average of fifty-two movements per year. There was a high point of eighty-one movements in 1991 that coincided with the communist breakup. As of 2017 there were sixty active secessionist movements in the world.

Now that I have introduced the concept, let me address some qualifications. First, in this book I treat secessionist movements and independence movements as synonyms, and will therefore talk about independence or secessionist movements pursuing secessionist aims. I define secessionism as "the formal demand for independence of a nation from its existing sovereign state."[19] Following Peter Radan, I define secession as "the creation of a new state upon existing territory previously forming part of, or being a colonial entity of, an existing state."[20] I am using these terms in a broad manner that will be familiar to political scientists and some legal scholars. But some may object because secession is a contested term, and some restrict its usage to illegal, violent, and/or noncolonial cases.[21] Indeed, the use of the term by participants in the sovereignty game is sometimes political and strategic. For example, I once spoke on a panel about Western Sahara and used the term secession. Afterward, one of my copanelists, a spokesperson for the Polisario Front, said that they were not a secessionist movement, as the Moroccan government claimed, but a nation seeking independence from Morocco. A related example is West Papua, where the independence movement seeks to get back on the UN List of Non-Self-Governing Territories (the decolonization list). But in the eyes of the Indonesian government, West Papua was decolonized when the Dutch departed in 1962 and is merely an illegal secessionist movement. These terms are politically loaded. I use the concept of secession, and the independence movements seeking secession, in a general sense that includes all attempts.

I do of course recognize that that there are differences in the type of movements within this broad set. Part of my project is to show how those differences inform tactical choices. Nevertheless, I do exclude the classic cases of decolonization in my analysis because, for emerging states like Nigeria, independence was mostly uncontested by the metropole, and the pathway to decolonization obtained a high level of international support. Moreover, the heyday of decolonization is over. As figure 2.2 shows, the number of overseas independence movements has declined precipitously since the 1970s and the vast majority of contemporary movements do not fit the classic understanding of a colonial movement.[22] What I retain for the study are the marginal cases like West Papua, Somaliland, and New Caledonia, where the principle of decolonization has some resonance and yet independence remains elusive.

One fascinating aspect of secessionism is its recursive nature. When figures 2.1 and 2.2 are viewed in tandem, one can see that the number of secessionist movements has generally increased since 1945 even as the number of states has tripled. The simple reason for this pattern is that there is a high replacement rate. New movements are arising to replace many of those that secede, in the way that Abkhazia arose within Georgia, or Biafra within Nigeria. Some secessionist movements have, at least for now, ended their efforts without success and dropped out of the data, such as Moheli or the Tigray nation. But clearly, there are enough new movements to replace the successful cases.

This possibility of movements-within-movements is one of the reasons for the concern over contagion. As former UN general secretary Boutros Boutros-Ghali put it: "If every ethnic, religious or linguistic group claimed statehood, there would be no limit to fragmentation, and peace, security and economic well-being for

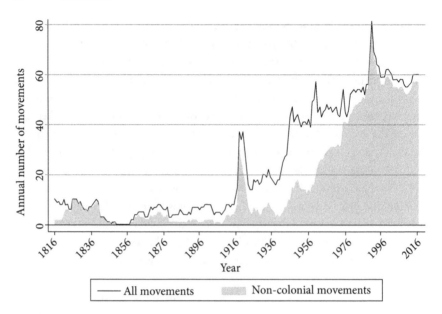

FIGURE 2.2.   Colonial and noncolonial independence movements (1816–2017)

all would be ever more difficult to achieve."[23] In a kind of back-of-the-envelope calculation, Ernest Gellner famously estimated that there are 8,000 potential nations in the world.[24] However, such estimates cannot be exact because national identity is ultimately a fluid category.[25] I recognize a difference between the Catalan nation claiming independence and, say, the Principality of Hutt River. Or to push the comparison to the point of seeming absurdity, I accept that there is a difference between the Kurdish nation and five people in a bar claiming nationhood. But there is no bright line separating these endpoints. Given time, Hutt River could grow to become a viable, believable, and even deserving secessionist movement. In the end, the closest thing to a fundamental (or atomic) unit in the study of secession is the individual.[26] Periodically, individuals organize into groups, self-identify as a nation, and declare independence.

Another qualification pertains to the difference between a full-blown secessionist movement and a less ambitious self-determination effort that seeks a form of local autonomy that falls short of full independence. As Philip Roeder discusses, there are numerous examples of this latter category, including the Cordillera Campaign of the Northern Philippines and the numerous groups that have bargained for federal statehood in India.[27] Both are forms of self-determination campaigns, but secessionist movements demand more from the state—they demand full independence. Groups do sometimes move back and forth between these categories as they increase and later decrease their demands. Some scholars have

created useful datasets that include nonsecessionist, autonomy-seeking movements because they want to understand how these groups modify their demands
in relation to circumstance.[28] However, given that my objective is to study secessionist strategy, it makes sense to exclude those who do not openly seek independence. Although I do discuss the development of secessionism in the case studies,
my analysis focuses on the behavior of secessionist movements once they have
formed.

The International Recognition Regime

There is an old and quite intriguing debate in international political legal theory
regarding state birth.[29] Do states exist prior to recognition and simply declare that
they are sovereign? Or, as the quote at the start of the chapter from Lassa Oppenheim suggests, do states come into being by virtue of the collective and constitutive judgment of the international community? In broader terms, do states
first make themselves and then make the system? Or does the system make states?
These contrasting views are known as the declaratory and constitutive theories
of statehood, and they provide high-level legal or theoretical explanations for the
transition from aspiring statehood to full statehood.[30] I contend that, for the most
part, the constitutive theory of statehood is correct. To be sure, the answer does
depend on various factors. For starters, it depends on how you define the sovereign state. If you write into the definition that states be internationally recognized,
as I have, and thus exclude state-like polities that lack recognition, then it follows
that the constitutive theory will be the more relevant. However, the answer also
depends on the time period in question. For as I discuss, the current international
recognition regime is highly constitutive, but it was less so in the past.

Admission into the Sovereignty Club

A fascinating aspect of the contemporary sovereign state system is its club-like
characteristics. I mean this as more than just an analogy. The most salient feature of a club (or good good), and that which delineates it from a public good, is
excludability; members can set up rules for admittance into the club.[31] The reason members would choose to exclude is that the good in question is only nonrival up to a point. In that sense, a club good sits between the two extremes of
private (excludable and rival) and public (nonexcludable and nonrival) goods:
"For a pure public good the addition of one more member to the club never de-
tracts from benefits of club membership . . . [for] a pure private good, say an ap-
ple, crowding begins to take place on the first unit."[32] Thus, a club good is one in

which members have the ability and incentive to limit membership beyond a certain threshold.

The set of sovereign states has all the features of a club good. First, being in the club has value. As Jackson stated, sovereign states behave like a club where "membership has its privileges."[33] These privileges include, first and foremost, the sovereign right to conduct your own affairs. The value of that right is both practical and symbolic, but it is always stressed in my interviews with secessionist groups. Membership in the club also imparts a legal identity to its members with which they can enjoy a surprisingly large set of benefits, including admittance to major international organizations, access to formal financial aid, and the ability to use international mail and conduct commerce with foreign banks.[34] For example, the de facto state of Somaliland has been largely cut off from international trade and banking because of its nonsovereign status.[35] Finally, sovereign recognition provides states with a form of territorial security that is backed by international law. There are benefits to being in the club.[36]

Second, the club members have incentive to control admission because the good is nonrival only to a point. Although crowding does not necessarily begin with each additional state, and the state system could arguably increase in number and remain efficient, the current members have posited numerous explanations for why membership should be limited. One concern is that additional states will dilute the vote share and political influence of existing members in key organizations like the UN. Unease over this matter arose as the prospect of decolonization promised to bring into the UN a substantial number of states that often held anti-Western sentiments.[37] A different issue pertains to viability: Are microstates truly viable, or will they constitute a drain on international resources?[38] This was the issue of "Lilliputian" states,[39] one that was openly discussed at the highest levels of the UN.[40] Was it equitable to admit the Maldives in 1965, a state with fewer than 100,000 people at the time, and give it the same voting rights as the United States?

The biggest reason for limiting admission is arguably the problem of uncontrolled fragmentation.[41] All of the Earth's landmass outside of Antarctica is plugged into the sovereign state system. As such, any new state constitutes a subtraction in territory from at least one existing state. If there truly was open and unclaimed land—*terra nullius*—then new states could be formed by the movement of people rather than borders, but in an enclosed system new states require the movement of borders instead of people. This is why the admittance of new states creates an open-ended and potentially existential problem for existing states. After all, who are the eligible applicants? How are they defined and delimited? How can the club members support secessionist efforts when doing so may set a precedent that leads to their own territorial dismemberment? Just as aspiring nations have incentive to join the club, existing members have incentive to control admission.

Third, the club members have the ability to control admission. In procedural terms, the defining feature of joining the sovereignty club is obtaining a full seat in the UNGA.[42] More than just a marker of legitimacy, this provides the state with a seat in the global parliament and a corresponding legal identity that is useful for a range of economic and diplomatic reasons. As James Ker-Lindsay writes: "UN membership has come to be regarded as nothing less than the 'gold standard' of international legitimacy."[43] The UN membership process requires that the Security Council must approve applications before they are submitted to the General Assembly. Nine of the fifteen members (60 percent) have to vote in the affirmative without any "no" votes from the five permanent veto-holding members (P5): China, France, Russia, the United Kingdom, and the United States. The P5 are the true gatekeepers to the club. An application that is approved by the Security Council is then subject to a vote in the General Assembly and has to secure a two-thirds majority. Once admitted applicants have declared that they will abide by the UN Charter, they can join the club of sovereign states

At first glance the admission process would appear relatively harmonious. James Crawford notes that only five applicant states met with any objection between 1963 and 2005.[44] The United Arab Emirates was approved in 1971 with only one dissent (South Yemen). Belize was approved in 1981 even though Guatemala dissented. Oman was approved in 1971 with opposition from South Yemen, Cuba, and Saudi Arabia. Kuwait was initially vetoed by the Soviet Union in 1961 and had to wait to two years to gain admission. Likewise, Bangladesh was initially vetoed by China in 1972 and had to wait until 1974 for full admission.

But this apparent consensus is misleading because applications are usually brought before the Security Council only when they are uncontroversial. Applicants are screened in two ways. In formal terms, representatives from the UN Secretariat and Office of Legal Affairs will initially review applications to determine if the applicant counts as a state.[45] That determination is made by reviewing the activities of the applicant—e.g., whether it is a member of prominent international and regional organizations—and by consulting other states for their view. In practice, the applicants that are screened at this stage are usually considered too small and/or unviable. The UN does not release records of screened applicants, but one example is the Principality of Snake Hill, a breakaway region in Australia that declared independence on September 3, 2003. Consisting of roughly 200 people and 1.6 square kilometers of territory, its story is chronicled on its website and in an April 2012 article in *The Atlantic*.[46] In a personal interview on October 18, 2013, with the Snake Hillian leaders, Princess Helena and Princess

Paula, I was shown formal correspondence from the UN and told that its application for UN membership had been rejected.

There is, however, an earlier informal type of screening that occurs when potential applicants dialogue with key actors—to the extent that they can—to gauge how they would vote. An application that is not screened by the UN Secretariat and Office of Legal Affairs is put to the Security Council and voted on formally and publicly. A rejected application at this stage would constitute a setback for many aspiring nations. As a result, there is a self-selection process whereby prominent and potentially successful groups like the Catalans withhold their application until they know that they have the necessary support on the Security Council. For the most serious applicants, most of the action takes place before an application is tendered.

Overall, the members of the sovereignty club have incentive to exclude and the ability to do so. And yet, new states are admitted. South Sudan joined the club in 2011, and Bougainville may join in the near future. In fact, the post-1945 period has been characterized by state proliferation. Clearly, the sovereignty club has a mechanism for controlling admission, an exclusion mechanism, or as I call it, the recognition regime.

The Evolving Recognition Regime

The international recognition regime is an evolving process that consists of legal norms, rules, and principles that determine when an applicant nation has the right to withdraw from an existing state and join the club of sovereign states. As critics will point out, states are a key decider in these affairs, particularly those states in which an independence movement is located. Moreover, strong states are in a better position to prevent secession and pursue their preferred outcome. As I discuss below, there is a conservatism in the recognition regime, and the international system more generally, that is biased toward sovereign states. Nevertheless, states are influenced in their positions regarding independence movements, both foreign and domestic, by the recognition regime.

I argue that that the recognition regime is the product of the collision between two normative traditions: sovereignty norms that emphasize the right of states and liberal norms that stress the right of individuals.[47] As Wayne Sandholtz and Kendall Stiles argue, norms are continuously evolving phenomena, and the character and strength of a given norm at any moment is determined through persuasion, in relation to power, and via the dialectic between sovereign and liberal rights.[48] It is in the normative contest between these two traditions that, for example, norms emphasizing human rights (e.g., humanitarian intervention, anti-genocide, the responsibility to protect) conflict with the right of sovereign states to manage their own affairs.

Much of international relations over the last few centuries is made sensible from this normative vantage point. In the sovereign tradition, rights accrue to the state or, in older times, the person who embodied the state.[49] This tradition is quite old, dating from at least the seventeenth century in Europe. In the liberal tradition, rights accrue to the individual. More of an upstart, this tradition can point to intellectual forefathers such as John Locke, but its force in international life was not really felt until the American and French revolutions.[50] Importantly, these traditions, and the specific norms they encompass, evolve in relation to one another and come into conflict at various friction points.[51] For example, the 2011 intervention in Libya is viewed by many as a victory for the Responsibility to Protect (R2P) over the sovereign right of states to resolve domestic disputes. However, that sort of liberal intervention has remained out of reach in Syria partly because great powers like China and Russia have defended Syria's sovereign right to manage its internal affairs.

This is a useful framework for understanding the recognition regime. Arguments against the recognition of a given secessionist movement are usually made by defending the sovereignty of the larger state from which it wants to exit, citing the right of states to manage their internal affairs and/or preserve their territorial boundaries. Arguments for recognition are more varied, but they are usually grounded in the liberal tradition, emphasizing the right of individuals to determine their political fate and/or be free from persecution. Of course, the actions and interests of strong states influence the normative tension, just as their behavior is shaped by it.[52] This normative tension is quite fluid and, as I show below, the interpretation of the related norms has changed over time.

One can trace the international recognition regime through several periods, with each representing a particular solution for limiting admission to the sovereignty club. The first encompassed the European-based system during the eighteenth century, if not earlier, and existed until the American and French revolutions. The sovereign tradition was dominant during this time and, as a result, states followed a practice that I call recognition by consent. Foreign leaders—usually monarchs—were expected to support other leaders and deny recognition to breakaway regions unless they received the blessing of their sovereign. As the American revolutionaries learned, recognition was difficult to achieve in the absence of British consent. Only the French were willing to break the taboo, largely for strategic reasons, and they were criticized for it.[53] The problem for the Americans was that the ideals they invoked in their declaration of independence were somewhat novel.[54] They were liberal in orientation—indeed, they were radical—and they were not grounded in a commonly accepted system of thought regarding the right of individuals to statehood.

This changed after the Napoleonic wars with the advent of the norm of self-determination. Broadly speaking, self-determination upholds the right of a nation to control its political destiny. When nations possess their own state—the state and the nation are congruent—then the interest of the nation is identical to that of the state. It is for this reason that observers will sometimes refer to the sovereign right of a state to self-determination.[55] But such congruencies are rare given the multinational character of most states and the malleability of national identity. And, as we know from Gellner, there are many more nations than states.[56] It is when minority or stateless nations call on the right of self-determination that it conflicts with the sovereign right of the larger state. Ultimately, self-determination is liberal in orientation, covering the right of individuals to organize and identify as conationals, but its interpretation has changed with time.[57]

During the period running from the Concert of Europe until World War I, self-determination came to be regarded as a negative right. The international community was obliged to not interfere, leaving the aspiring nation to pursue its independence on its own. However, should the nation prevail over its sovereign and establish de facto statehood as a self-determined fact, the international community was expected to recognize its sovereignty and admit it into the sovereignty club. This approach to recognition was led by Great Britain and the United States, who operated from a position of principle—leaders such as Lord Castlereagh, George Canning, and John Quincy Adams held this view of self-determination—and one of strategy—their primary opponents were the conservative European monarchies who sought to maintain the traditional international order. Crawford calls this the Canning Test:

> Third States were expected to remain neutral during such a [secessionist] conflict, in the sense that assistance to a group that had not succeeded in establishing its independence could be treated as intervention in the internal affairs of the State in question, or as violation of neutrality.... But on the other hand international law was prepared to acknowledge political realities once the independence of a seceding entity was firmly established and in relation to the territory effectively controlled by it.[58]

This is what Mikulas Fabry refers to as the practice of de facto recognition. Beginning with the secessions in Latin America, breakaway nations were generally granted recognition once they could establish statehood as a self-determined fact.[59] The development of self-determination as a negative right had created an opportunity for internal nations to become independent by their own hand.

The convulsions of the world wars produced normative change in two important ways. First, the Wilsonian moment at the end of World War I led to "a shift
in the understanding of self-determination from a negative to positive international right."[60] In describing this shift, Fabry uses Isaiah Berlin's distinction of
positive (freedom to) and negative (freedom from) liberty.[61] If the negative right
meant that nations were entitled to become free by their own effort and without
external intervention, the positive right obliged the international community to
assist national aspirations. Under the first interpretation, third parties were expected to do nothing and grant recognition only once the breakaway region had
established a de facto state. Under the second interpretation, third parties were
obliged to take a more active role and assist such efforts even when they had not
prevailed over their sovereign, and perhaps had little chance of ever doing so. That
shift in interpretation dramatically altered the exclusion mechanism for the sovereignty club. If the earlier approach could be summed up as "wait and see the
outcome," the latter became a question of "who counts?"[62] Crawford argues that
self-determination is an "overtly political principle."[63] The difficulty of identifying the qualifying units brings politics into the decision-making process.

The second important normative change was sovereign in orientation. The de-
struction of the world wars gave rise to a prohibition against conquest and an
emphasis on treating sovereign borders as inviolable. Boaz Atzili calls this the border fixity norm, saying, "conquest and annexation of one's neighbor's land,
commonplace in the history of the state system, is no longer on the 'menu of options' for post–World War II leaders and states.[64] Others have referred to the
same prohibition as the norm of territorial integrity; the most salient feature of
the norm is the preservation of sovereign borders.[65] According to Tanisha Fazal,
the norm resulted in the near disappearance of formal territorial conquest after
1945.[66] If, however, the norm was created to prevent external aggression, it has
been remarkably effective at blocking internal fragmentation.[67] Treating the existing territorial grid as sacrosanct presents an obstacle to conquerors and secessionists alike.

This double normative movement produced a recognition regime defined
largely by the sharp tension between sovereignty and liberalism, one that has characterized the international system since 1945. On one hand, there is a value
placed on sovereign boundaries as a means to maintain territorial stability. On
the other hand, there is an emphasis on helping minority nations to achieve self-
determination. The solution for adjudicating these competing demands was to
develop criteria for which nations should count, a difficult and evolving task.
Fabry refers to this as constitutive recognition because it requires that the relevant international actors agree on what criteria should be used to determine who
counts.[68] In the time of de facto recognition that decision was easier because it

was effectively pinned to the outcome of the contest between the secessionists and their government. However, in a constitutive regime where such contests are unnecessary and even discouraged, the community of states has to take a more active role in determining who should have a right to the fullest expression of self-determination: an independent state.

Pathways to Independent Statehood

Since 1945 the question of who counts has been answered in a series of ways that amount to pathways to independence.[69] To be sure, the clarity and power of these pathways vary, but all of them are aspects of the strategic playing field. The first and most prominent pathway is via state consent (see figure 2.3). This is where the central government permits the secession and recognizes the aspiring nation (e.g., Montenegro). It is an uncontroversial move insofar as it requires little from third parties—the decision has been worked out domestically—and it is no different in form from earlier periods. In practice, it is quite rare for the international community to gainsay the recognition of a breakaway region by its central government. One of the most commonly given examples is the refusal of third party states to recognize the independence of the Bantustans out of a concern that South Africa was merely creating client states and perpetuating a form of apartheid.[70] Another example is Manchukuo, the recognition of which was denied by

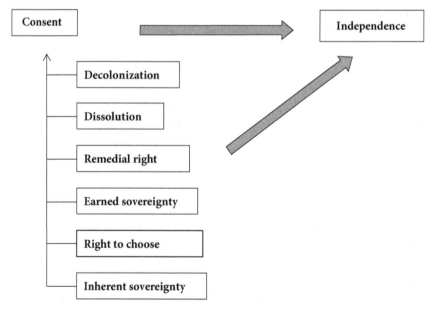

FIGURE 2.3. Pathways to independence

international actors because it was thought that Japan was merely creating an il-legal puppet state.[71] These exceptions notwithstanding, state consent is an uncon-troversial path. It is, however, the process of getting states to concede that can become quite political and strategic, a matter I examine in the next chapter.

It is in the absence of consent that the other pathways rise in importance. How-ever, these pathways are less sure because the state remains an obstacle by retain-ing its home state veto. The remaining pathways are grounded in arguments for why the territorial integrity of the state should be overturned in special circum-stances. They are normative arguments for why the full right of self-determination should be applied here and not elsewhere. They place an obligation on the inter-national community to assist a self-determination effort in select circumstances, and put pressure on the home state to give its consent. Figure 2.3 can be read verti-cally as the gradual development in international thinking on the subject over the post-1945 period. The pathway of decolonization is the most accepted; the bottom pathways regarding inherent sovereignty and the right to choose are more controversial. They are early-stage pathways that may or may not gain acceptance in the future, but nevertheless shape the behavior of secessionists in the present.

Decolonization is the expansion and application of self-determination to col-onized peoples, a process that transformed the world map. The instantiation of self-determination in the UN Charter had been suggestive—people have a right to self-determination—but exactly which people had not been worked out. That began to change as the pressure of decolonization intensified in the early post-war period. In 1960, two resolutions were passed in the UNGA: Resolution 1514, known as the Declaration on Granting Independence to Colonial Countries and Peoples, and its annex, Resolution 1541.[72] Several years later, in 1966, the princi-ple of self-determination was developed further with the United Nations Cove-nant on Economic, Social, and Cultural Rights, and the United Nations Covenant on Civil and Political Rights. Collectively, these confirmed the right to self-determination for both colonized and noncolonized peoples, with one crucial distinction: colonized peoples had the right to full independence while noncolo-nized peoples could pursue greater autonomy within their host state. But how does one differentiate between colonized and noncolonized peoples? This is one of the thorny questions that has attended decolonization and, in form, it is merely a more specific formulation of the original question: Who counts?

The answer in this case was to stress the colonial boundaries of overseas em-pires via the principle of *uti possidetis juris* (as you possess).[73] The reason was that administrative boundaries provided a clear solution to where borders should be drawn—an imperfect one to be sure, but one that was better than all the other pos-sibilities. Steven Ratner says that *uti possidetis juris* is an example of an idiot rule—"a simple, clear norm that offers an acceptable outcome in most situations."[74] The principle had its origins in Roman law and had been applied to the Latin American secessions in the early nineteenth century. It mattered not that the colonial boundaries of Africa were often less than a century old, that they had often been constructed along lines of longitude and latitude by European statesmen who could only speculate on what these regions consisted of, and that the resulting administrative blueprint correlated quite poorly with the ethnic composition of the continent. The application of *uti possidetis juris* was a solution, and there was precedent for using it, but the results often seemed arbitrary and unfair. The fortunate were simply those who were seen to command first-order administrative units of saltwater empires, a distinction that elided minority nations in large continental states like Russia, China, and the United States, and the numerous colonized peoples of Africa and Asia, who were disadvantaged by the colonial administrative map. Jackson estimates that the legal emphasis on administrative boundaries via *uti possidetis juris* reduced the number of acceptable independence claims in Africa from 400–500 to 40–50.[75] There was no bright line separating the nations that qualified for decolonization, such as Uganda, from those who did not, like Buganda, Tibet, Chechnya, or Lakotah. The sorting mechanism has its critics.[76]

Crucially, the importance placed on colonial units via the principle of *uti possidetis juris* has created some ambiguity. Colonial units were combined and divided over time and the status of some units is debatable. As a result, many contemporary independence movements seem to fall, or come close to falling, under the ambit of decolonization. Eritrea stressed its colonial history separate from Ethiopia when it argued for its right to independence. Somaliland has emphasized the fact that its colonial history was different from the rest of Somalia. East Timor successfully argued for a colonial history that was different from the rest of Indonesia. Although West Papua has adopted the same strategy, it has so far failed to obtain international support. Essentially, the pathway of decolonization continues to shape the strategic playing field, a subject I return to in the next chapter.

The next pathway is that of dissolution, a solution that was used during the Yugoslav and Soviet breakups. Like decolonization, this was in part a legal solution meant to create a conceptual distinction between cases of dissolution and other forms of secession. According to Tomas Bartos, "the [Badinter] Commission preferred to view the Yugoslavian situation as one of dissolution, refusing to set a precedent for the secession of national groups within existing States."[77] That is, the Badinter Arbitration Committee decided that Yugoslavia was in the process of dissolution. This removed the home state veto of the Yugoslav government, and nullified the obstacle that its territorial integrity would otherwise present to the emerging breakaway movements.[78] Of course, the Yugoslav government saw things differently and fought a losing battle to retain its territory. Meanwhile, the labeling of the Soviet breakup as a case of dissolution was less controversial because Moscow permitted it.

The application of dissolution raises at least two problems. The first is how to differentiate dissolution from other forms of secession. There is no bright line separating the two categories. After all, the Yugoslav government in Belgrade was quite capable of fielding an army to oppose the secessionists, and the Soviet government surely could have if the will had existed. Yet, contemporary Somaliland is routinely denied recognition on the grounds that its secession is illegal, even though the Somalian state is far weaker and more dissolved than the Yugoslav and Soviet cases. The distinction between secession and dissolution is at best a matter of degree—the ethical merits of the distinction are debated in the legal discourse[79]—and it is a fine example of the difficulty in limiting membership to the sovereignty club.

Second, once a state is designated as "dissolved," the question becomes, "Who counts?" Which groups within the former Yugoslavia and Soviet Union had the right to self-determination via dissolution? Once again, the solution was to focus on administrative lines and categories via the principle of *uti possidetis juris*.[80] The application of the principle was now being used to award independence only to first-order administrative units (republics), and this disqualified many groups such as the Kosovars, Chechens, and South Ossetians. Although the extension of the principle beyond colonies signaled a shift in application, and the Badinter Commission was criticized for it,[81] the logic is clear: administrative lines and categories provide a blueprint, regardless of their provenance.

Although they had existed as rhetorical arguments for some time, the next two pathways came into focus during the Kosovo crisis of the late 1990s. A second-order administrative unit in Yugoslavia, Kosovo lacked the same right to independence as first-order units like Croatia.[82] After fighting a bloody secessionist civil war against Serbia in the 1990s, Kosovo was placed under United Nations administration. After consultation with Western powers, Kosovo declared independence in 2008 and, as of February 9, 2019, has been recognized by some 102 countries.[83] However, Serbia still refuses to recognize Kosovo and, as a result, neither will Russia.[84] Given that it anticipates a rejection of its application for UN membership by the Security Council, Kosovo has not yet applied.[85]

The uncertainty that surrounds Kosovo has bolstered two interpretations of how independence can be obtained. To be sure, these paths are controversial and not at all entrenched. Yet, they provide hope for secessionists and even feature in the tactics they adopt. The first interpretation focuses on the notion that there is exists a remedial right to independence—that is, the right to secession in the face of human rights abuse by the state. Although this right has been advanced mostly by political philosophers,[86] there is some reference to it in international law, however oblique. The 1970 Declaration on Principles of International Law Concerning Friendly Relations contains a savings clause specifying that self-determination should not subordinate the territorial integrity of a "government representing the whole people belonging to the territory without distinction as to race, creed or colour."[87] Some have interpreted this clause as support for a remedial right. Similar language was used at the 1993 United Nations World Conference on Human Rights, and in the 1998 Canadian Supreme Court case on Quebec secession it was held that a remedial right did not hold because the Canadian government had behaved properly.[88] The concept of remedial secession has essentially lurked in the background of international affairs for over four decades, and it came up indirectly in the US decision to recognize Kosovo. Although it highlighted the ethnic cleansing and human rights abuses, the United States shied away from invoking the remedial right and instead called Kosovo a special case that "cannot be seen as a precedent for any other situation in the world today."[89] This perceived pathway to independence informs the decisions and strategies of secessionist movements.[90]

The second interpretation was that of earned sovereignty. This interpretation did not in any way contradict the first interpretation focusing on remedial rights. It basically shifted attention to a subsequent moment when a breakaway region, and de facto state in particular, attempted to establish its credibility as a functional state. The lesson from Kosovo at the turn of the millennium, one that was taken to heart in regions such as Abkhazia and Somaliland, was that good governance and democratic values established standards that warranted status as a sovereign state—"standards before status."[91] To a small extent, this perspective resurrected the concept of de facto statehood that was stressed in the nineteenth century. It was vaguer, and there was no equivalent to the Canning Test, but, as we will see, it has continued to shape the hopes and tactics of secessionist movements.[92]

The final two pathways are the most controversial of all. The first focuses on the right of a people to choose their political fate. Choice theory, also known as primary rights theory, stresses the right of human beings or groups of human beings to secede from the larger state according to a democratic process.[93] There is some variation in terms of how groups are delimited, how minorities within minorities are dealt with, and how referenda should be held, but the overall approach is quite liberal in orientation. Although this argument has some resonance in democratic societies, it has little official support among national governments. As critics point out, the implementation of a right to choose independence is difficult given that it would create fragmentary pressures within states, even strong states that are meeting the social contract. The 2014 Scottish referendum on independence was in some respects an example of choice theory in action, but, of course, the British government agreed to hold the referendum. As the Catalan nationalists know, choice theory is far harder to put into practice when governmental consent is absent. Nevertheless, secessionist movements like the Quebecois do invoke the right in their independence bid, partly as a way to challenge the democratic legitimacy of the home state.[94]

The last pathway is what I call inherent sovereignty. In many ways it is a hybrid of the other pathways, though it perhaps most resembles decolonization as a form of argument. The substance of the appeal is that indigenous peoples in colonized lands were illegally subjugated. As Australian aboriginals argue, they were brought under British rule without any formal treaty or declaration of war. Rather, the land in question was declared *terra nullius* (empty land) and therefore open for seizure. However, as legal cases like *Mabo v. Queensland* (no. 2) have confirmed, the land was, in fact, occupied by aboriginal peoples. Therefore, *terra nullius* was incorrectly applied and the sovereignty of the inhabitants was never relinquished and is inherent.[95] Although this issue is slowly being worked out in domestic legal systems like Australia's, it is far from obtaining traction internationally for a simple reason: all nation-states are built upon some narrative of original and legitimate occupation, but few of these narratives would withstand full scrutiny. Nevertheless, this pathway, like the others, shapes the strategic playing field for independence movements.

The international recognition regime is a work in progress. Its constitutive nature in the post-1945 era has required the club of states to work out who should gain admittance, and that has yielded different pathways into the club.[96] As Crawford put it, "secession is neither legal nor illegal in international law, but a legally neutral act the consequences of which are regulated internationally."[97] The regulators are by and large the club members, who often possess diverse and conflicting interests. The resulting playing field is what Jackson originally called the sovereignty game, which is composed mostly of instrumental rules—"precepts, maxims, strategems, and tactics which are derived from experience and contribute to winning play."[98] Although there is a vagueness and fuzziness to that game, it nevertheless promotes hope in numerous stateless nations that they can win it and gain their sovereignty.[99]

3

A THEORY OF SECESSIONIST
STRATEGY AND TACTICAL VARIATION

Sovereignty is a crown on the head of the healthy that only the sick can see.

—Professor Jamal Ameen, Erbil, May 24, 2017

I heard the above statement when I attended a conference in Erbil in May, 2017. The conference was titled "Iraqi Kurdistan at a Crossroads," and it brought together Kurdish political leaders, businesspeople, and intellectuals, as well a number of foreign diplomats, journalists, and academics. The purpose of the conference was to discuss the ways in which Iraqi Kurdistan could become an independent sovereign state. The speaker, Professor Jamal Ameen, University of Kurdistan-Hewler, made the comment at an opening lecture. When I asked him to elaborate later that day, he told me that he was paraphrasing a quote from health science and had merely substituted "sovereignty" for "good health," and was drawing an analogy between human health and the health of states. By implication, aspiring states like Iraqi Kurdistan see and desire the health of sovereignty. How do they go about obtaining it?

In this chapter, I advance a theory of secessionist strategy and tactical variation. I argue that the strategy and tactics of secession are shaped by the international recognition regime and further contextualized by the setting in which any given secessionist movement operates. At the strategic level, all movements are the same. They are united by the fact that they are all seeking to join the same club of sovereign states, and to join it they need to compel and persuade their home state and/or the international community to recognize them. To do so, they engage in two categories of tactical behavior: compellence and normative appeal. Compellence is the use of assets to coerce the home state and/or international community; it is direct action designed to increase the costs of not complying with secessionist demands. Normative appeal includes a different set of tactics that are designed to showcase the grievances and demands of the aspiring nation and either change preferences on the issue or bring into the game previously uninvolved parties.

Although all movements use compellence and normative appeal in pursuit of independence, they do so in different combinations that are determined by local factors such as regime type, the strength of the state, and the degree to which the independence movement is de facto independent. These factors coalesce around six identifiable kinds of movements: democratized, indigenous legal, weak combative, strong combative, decolonial, and de facto. The conditions in each type favor different tactical options. In terms of compellence, these include electoral capture, nonviolent civil resistance, and the use of violence. In terms of normative argumentation, these include the appeal to earned sovereignty, decolonization, the right to choose, inherent sovereignty, and human rights. Importantly, these local conditions, and the kinds of movements they give rise to, shape the ability of movements to follow one or more of the different pathways to independence that were outlined in the previous chapter. All secessionist movements maneuver on the same strategic playing field, but their tactics vary according to local conditions.

This chapter proceeds as follows. I begin by elaborating the strategy of secession. I discuss the conditions for a strategic theory, I outline the strategic playing field for secessionists, and I explain their tactical behavior. Next, I look at conditions within states to identify secessionist kinds and lay out testable hypotheses for the study. Finally, I consider a prominent hybrid case, Iraqi Kurdistan, and I expand on the countersecession strategies of states.

Strategy of Secession

What explains secessionist behavior? Why do some groups use violence and talk about human rights when others compete electorally, engage in nonviolent civil resistance, and/or appeal to norms regarding the right of a people to choose independence? Is there even an underlying strategic purpose to this behavior? I contend that secessionism can be modelled in strategic terms. The conditions for a theory of strategy include identifiable actors, an objective, rules of the game, knowledge of the game, and resources that can be directed toward achieving the objective.[1] The actors in this, the sovereignty game, are independence movements, states, and the international community, and the objective is to become a sovereign state. As discussed in the previous chapter, the rules of the game are provided by the international recognition regime, which effectively creates perceived pathways to independence that shape strategic and tactical behavior.

It is important to point out that independence movements are not isolated actors operating without knowledge of the larger strategic playing field. On the contrary, they observe one another and are often quite networked. For example, the Catalan secessionists sent political strategists to Scotland in mid-2014 to gather tactical knowledge from the Scottish National Party (SNP) about how to target their independence message to different segments of the population.[2] Moses Havini, the Bougainville diplomat-at-large during the 1990s, stated in a personal interview that during that time he befriended, and learned from, Xanana Gusmão, the East Timorese independence leader, as they pitched their respective causes to the international community.[3] Bayan Sami Abdulrahman, the former Kurdish regional government representative to the United Kingdom (and current representative to the United States) stated that she used to hold weekly knowledge-sharing lunches in London with the representatives of Quebec, Flanders, and Catalonia.[4] In 2018 I attended a workshop on self-determination in West Papua where one of the guest speakers was a member of the Kanak and Socialist National Liberation Front (FLNKS) of New Caledonia. Although much of the networking is bilateral in nature, forums like the Unrepresented Nations and Peoples Organization (UNPO)[5] provide opportunities for members to share experiences. Finally, advice on how to obtain sovereign statehood can also be acquired through diaspora networks, in-house legal counsel, nongovernmental organizations, and consultancies like Independent Diplomat.[6]

One fascinating aspect of the society of independence movements is its status differentiation. Whereas small, low-profile, and potentially farcical movements like the Principality of Hutt River appear keen to network with all other movements, prominent groups like the Scots limit their formal associations for diplomatic reasons. It is well known that the SNP severed formal relations with the Catalan secessionists in the months prior to their independence referendum in September, 2014. The reason was simple: a formal relationship with Catalonia might have created obstacles to gaining membership in the European Union (EU) and United Nations (UN).

In a more general sense, knowledge of the strategic playing field has an influence on secessionist behavior. In her research on the topic, Reyko Huang found that secessionist rebels, "for whom international recognition is essential for attaining independent statehood," are more likely than other types of rebels to engage in international diplomacy.[7] Similarly, Tanisha Fazal concluded that secessionists were more likely than other types of civil-war combatants to conduct their actions in a manner that is consistent with international law.[8] The reason for these patterns is straightforward: aspiring club members need to behave properly if they wish to join the club.

That said, secessionist movements do not possess perfect information. As I discuss in chapter 11, knowledge of the game varies among actors, and many of them engage in wishful thinking. Moreover, the game itself is imperfectly specified. The recognition regime is, after all, an evolving set of norms and rules, and individual states have substantial latitude in their response to secessionist demands. This is not chess, where the rules are perfectly and explicitly delimited. A better analogy is poker, given the importance of bluffing and reputation building, but even there the rules are ultimately fixed. The sovereignty game is more open-ended that that. The playing field is fuzzy, but coherent enough to shape the play.

The final component of a strategic theory of secession is the specification of how resources are used tactically to achieve the objective. That is, given what we know about the international recognition regime, what do independence movements actually do? At the strategic level, there are two general approaches an independence movement can take when attempting to gain international recognition, and most movements use both at the same time. As figure 3.1 illustrates, the first is where the movement persuades the central government to give its consent by removing the home state veto.[9] The second takes the form of an end run where the movement goes around the home state to convince key actors in the international community to take up its cause and either apply pressure on the home state or simply recognize the independence movement.[10] For example, South Sudan was able to remove the home-state veto and get the Sudanese government to consent to its independence. Meanwhile, Bangladesh (East Pakistan) won international recognition in the absence (at least initially) of Pakistani consent. Most movements combine these approaches, but much ultimately depends on the disposition of the home state. Where it is reticent and unwilling to negotiate, the end run becomes more attractive.

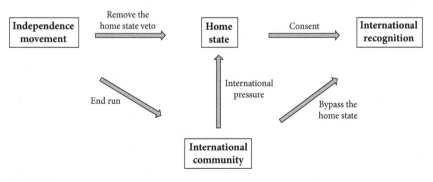

FIGURE 3.1. Strategy of secession

When considering the end run it is important to note that the target audience can vary depending on the independence movement. Although all movements will eventually need to get the support of the Security Council, and the Permanent Five (P5) in particular, the process of securing international support often begins in the region.[11] For the Catalans, EU support is crucial, and I was reminded of this in most of my interviews with Catalan secessionists. Likewise, I attended two conferences in Erbil on the independence of Iraqi Kurdistan, and there the key international actors included Turkey, Iran, and the United States (a kind of informal regional actor); conference attendees often speculated whether and under what conditions the United States would abandon the One Iraq policy.[12] The African Union (AU), one of the strongest regional organizations where secession is concerned, is known for its reluctance to open Pandora's box by recognizing a breakaway region.[13] Yet winning its support remains a prime goal for movements like that in Somaliland.[14] Overall, the importance of the region appears to be variable. Secessionists in Africa and Europe will be hard put if they do not win over the AU and EU, respectively. But for secessionists in Oceania, like Bougainville, there is no analogous regional gatekeeper.

How then does a secessionist movement get the home state to remove its veto and/or win support from the international community? They do so by engaging in two categories of tactical behavior: what I am calling compellence and normative appeal.[15] These categories are analytically distinct. Compellence is about using assets in a directly confrontational way to force a change. In contrast, normative appeal is aimed at preferences. Here, independence movements make an emotive appeal to the population of the home state and the international community. Whereas the purpose of compellence is to make certain preferences costly, normative appeal means to change those preferences. These categories can be roughly mapped onto to Steven Lukes's three faces of power: direct action, agenda setting, and belief shaping.[16] Compellence is mostly about the first face; it is direct political action. Normative appeal is largely about the third face; it shapes beliefs and preferences. As I detail below, the second face is not completely absent, because by choosing certain tactics (e.g., nonviolent civil resistance), secessionists can limit the options for state response.

Secession is about change: a change in sovereignty, an alteration of borders, and a transformation of regional power dynamics. To realize that change, secessionists need to compel the central government and/or international community to recognize them as an independent sovereign state. As Thomas Schelling explained, compellence is a type of coercion aimed at forcing a target to do something that they would not otherwise do.[17] It depends on the credible promise that pressure will increase and punishment will follow if the actor does not comply. To bring about the desired change, the movement may engage in a set of tactics ranging from the use of outright violence to electoral capture to nonviolent forms of civil resistance that put pressure on the target. Suicide bombings by the Tamil Tigers were acts that aimed to influence Sri Lankan state policy. The partial capture of the Catalan parliament was viewed as a means to force the Spanish state to negotiate. The self-immolation of Tibetan monks is partly a form of protest that is designed to put pressure on the Chinese state. I maintain that different movements will choose different compellence tactics depending on their setting. Importantly, as I discuss below, de facto state movements are an outlier in this regard because they are typically sundered from the home state and cut off from the standard levers of compellence. Their success at getting out from under the state has come at a price, a kind of tactical dead end.

The second category of tactics used by secessionists is to make a normative appeal to the hearts and minds of target populations. These appeals conform to the pathways discussed in chapter 2. As the case of East Timor demonstrated, the appeal to human rights can have a strong effect. Similarly, the bloody conflicts in Kosovo and Bangladesh were instrumental in raising international support that paved the way for independence. A different approach is to appeal to liberal democratic norms of legitimacy and argue for the right to choose. The Catalans have repeatedly demanded that the Spanish state give them a referendum on independence, as the United Kingdom did with Scotland. Interestingly, nearly all secessionist movements engage in forms of showmanship and paradiplomacy to portray themselves as viable and functional states.[18] This is most evident in the case of de facto states like Somaliland and Artsakh, which try to show that standards have been reached in the hope of one day achieving the status of independence. But numerous groups develop diplomatic wings, tap diaspora communities, and participate in international organization for stateless nations like the Confederation of Independent Football Associations (CONIFA).[19] It is clear from a visit to the government-funded Catalan National History Museum in Barcelona that this is a nation trying to establish its credentials as a once and future sovereign state.

Compellence and normative appeal can be used in tandem and often complement one another. For example, during its civil war with Papua New Guinea (PNG), Bougainville's leadership relied on its Sydney-based representative, Moses Havini, and his Bougainville Freedom Movement, to bring its cause to a global audience.[20] His efforts were conducted at the same time as secessionist forces fought the PNG army. Military leaders like Francis Ona and James Tanis attempted to compel the PNG government to negotiate by increasing the costs of noncompliance.[21] Havini's diplomatic efforts gradually changed the preferences of the international community about the Bougainville conflict. Changing preferences can ultimately have a coercive effect on the home state because increased pressure is brought to bear through diplomatic channels, boycotts, embargoes, and so on. Although the end result is the same—convincing the home state and/or international community to make a change—the logic is different insofar as it directly targets preferences, even if costs are subsequently incurred as a result.

Secessionist movements come in all shapes and sizes. At close range the realities of Scottish nationalism look rather different from Karen nationalism. But seen from a wide angle, all secessionist movements are playing on the same field. To get recognition as sovereign states, they need to get their home state and/or the international community to make a change. To use Sidney Tarrow's language, there is a local/parochial and international/cosmopolitan nature to secessionist movements.[22] There are numerous local factors that define them, but their playing field is international. Therefore, at a general level the strategy of secession is modular; it can be picked up and deployed by a diverse set of groups and, importantly, these groups watch and learn from one another. Their tactical choices are then calibrated and contextualized by local conditions. I now zoom in to examine this tactical variation.

Tactical Variation

Although secessionist movements display considerable heterogeneity, there are identifiable kinds of movements—what we might call secessionist kinds. This set of kinds is broad in scope and it encompasses three literatures that are usually treated separately (see figure 3.2): the work on de facto states,[23] secessionist political parties in advanced democracies,[24] and secessionist conflict.[25] These three

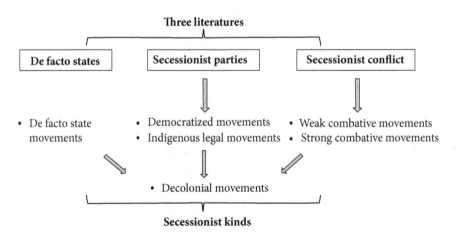

FIGURE 3.2. Secessionist kinds and the wider literature

research areas are fairly compartmentalized, and the scholars working in them are normally dialoguing within and not across groups. Yet many movements are discussed in more than one literature or move back in forth between them over time. And all of them are playing the same sovereignty game.

Analysis of the six kinds of secessionist movements is useful for predicting tactical variation based on local conditions such as regime type, the strength of the state, and the degree to which the region is already de facto independent. Importantly, I am not theorizing a typology in the sense that George and Bennett discuss, where the types are mutually exclusive.[26] Rather, these six kinds represent clusters of characteristics that I have observed through an analysis of all contemporary movements. But there is hybridity, and some movements demonstrate composite characteristics and move back and forth between kinds as local conditions change. As I discuss below, Iraqi Kurdistan represents an interesting hybrid case. Nevertheless, these kinds coalesce around specific conditions that generate predictable patterns of tactical behavior. More generally, when taken as a whole we can see the trade-offs that come with type. For example, becoming a de facto state is a kind of victory for self-determination, yet it reduces the set of tactical options for winning sovereign recognition. Similarly, democratized movements have all the benefits of operating in a modern democracy, but winning a decisive majority in competitive elections can be difficult.

The sequence in which I introduce and examine the six kinds of movements, both here and in the chapters to come, follows from their structural relationship with the home state. I begin with one of the most integrated kinds, the democratized movement (see table 3.1). Democratized movements take place in highly institutionalized or democratic polities; examples include prominent movements like the Québécois and the Catalans. At the macro level they employ the same general strategy as the others: they take aim at the home-state veto and use the end run. However, their tactics differ in accordance with the institutional environment. Their main tactic of compellence is electoral capture—that is, using the democratic institutions of the state to pursue independence. Such movements often commit to nonviolent action as a means to build legitimacy and limit the response options of the state. Their primary normative appeal is that an identifiable nation should be able to choose its political fate via a democratic process. Although these efforts are largely aimed at getting the home state to give consent to independence, the end-run approach is nevertheless part of the game. For example, as I discuss in chapter 4, the Catalan secessionist leadership has attempted to get external governments to apply pressure on Madrid to negotiate.

Democratized movements can create robust organizations.[27] They maneuver in developed societies and typically create formal political parties, and at times several competing parties. They operate under the very nose of the state and are

TABLE 3.1. Tactical variation by kind of secessionist movement

SECESSIONIST KIND	COMPELLENCE	NORMATIVE APPEAL	EXAMPLE
HIGH INSTITUTIONAL			
Democratized	Electoral capture	Freedom to choose	Catalonia
Indigenous legal	Electoral capture	Inherent sovereignty	Murrawarri
COMBATIVE			
Weak	Nonviolent civil resistance	Human rights	West Papua
Strong	Violence	Human rights	Bougainville
DECOLONIAL	Varied	Decolonization	New Caledonia
DE FACTO	n/a	Earned sovereignty (Standards before status)	Northern Cyprus

not clandestine. They usually have deep intellectual, financial, and community support. Although these movements have much going for them and are often the envy of other secessionists, the democratic process commits them to a struggle to win over the majority of the electorate. As the SNP has discovered, that is no easy task, especially in an advanced democracy where the opportunity cost of exit can be high.

Indigenous legal movements are the next secessionist kind. This is a small set, but one with identifiable characteristics, and one that could become more visible with time. It includes the Hawaiian sovereignty movement, the Lakotah, and the Murrawarri Republic, among others. This type of movement represents a variation on the democratized movement because they both occur in, and depend on, a highly institutionalized setting. In fact, they both use the same compellence tactics, which is that they pursue their goal using the institutional environment to compete electorally. The key difference has to do with their normative appeal. To be sure, indigenous legal movements also appeal to the right to choose, as most movements do, especially those in democratic societies. But they have another normative card to play: they can appeal to historical injustices regarding the fate of indigenous peoples in settler societies. To some degree all secessionist movements are networked, but the indigenous legal type share a vocabulary regarding inherent sovereignty. Since these nations were not included under the ambit of decolonization, their legal representatives have typically challenged the legality of their forced inclusion in states like the United States and Australia, arguing that *terra nullius* was incorrectly applied. Their sovereignty was never relinquished and is inherent.[28] As Fred Hooper, chair of the Republic of Murrawarri, put it: "*terra nullius* was a fiction, we declared that we were always independent of Australia," in reference to the March 30, 2013, Murrawarri declaration of independence.[29]

In normative terms, indigenous legal movements challenge the very constitutional basis on which they were originally included in their home state. This is a fascinating argument, and it is one that can probably be found in any movement. It was, after all, central to the argument for decolonization. Even in Scotland and Catalonia, where the relationship between the two referent populations (the natives and the colonists) is both blurred and ancient, I met individuals who questioned the legal foundations for union. The problem with this argument in general is that it is usually quite difficult to identify first nations and separate them from the groups that came later. It is harder still to generate an international consensus around those differences. Although this was achieved with decolonization—international law distinguished the colonizer from the colonized—many other colonized groups, from the Native Americans to the peoples of Eastern Siberia, were excluded. The indigenous legal movements, for whom decolonization did not apply, represent a kind of second attempt, a decolonization part II, to say that their subjugation was illegal. As I discuss in chapter 5, democratic settler societies like Australia are willing to listen.

The next two kinds are the weak and strong combative movements. Together they account for more than half of the secessionist movements since 1945. They are located in weak democracies or nondemocracies, and are usually less institutionally integrated with the home state. This set includes the Uighur and the Karen, among others. Given their interconnectivity and potential for friction with the state (i.e., non–de facto status), and their weakly or noninstitutionalized settings, they are often the location of violence and suppression. As a result, I contend that their chief normative argument will typically focus on the right to independent statehood in the face of human rights abuses by the state. That is, they will pursue the pathway of remedial rights and appeal to the hearts and minds of their audience. Although other normative arguments may be present, their setting simply raises the probability that the human rights argument will be utilized.

The difference between the two types is the strength of the movement relative to their home state.[30] There is a developing literature that argues persuasively for the strategic logic of nonviolent civil resistance, and a central theme in that literature is that this tactic can overcome the asymmetry that normally exists between social movements and national governments.[31] As one leader of the United Liberation Movement for West Papua (ULMWP) told me, "violence does not work for us because the Indonesian state is too strong; nonviolence is the answer."[32] I posit that secessionist movements are more likely to choose violence as they approach parity with the government, as Bougainville did in the 1990s when it was able to fight the PNG forces to a "hurting stalemate."[33] The United States Confederacy chose violence, in part, because it thought it could win. Secessionist movements will blur these lines, sometimes employing both tactics or alternating between them, but I argue that the choice of tactic will correlate with the relative strength of the movement. Nonviolent civil resistance can be an effective weapon, and it can blunt the ability of the state to respond with force, but it is the weapon of the weak.

The fifth secessionist kind is what I call the decolonial movement. The defining feature of decolonial movements is their ability to appeal to the norms surrounding decolonization. Relative to the other normative arguments discussed in this book, decolonization is usually a winning hand, one that is recognized by UN resolution.[34] Indeed, it was by utilizing this argument that many former colonies, from Angola to East Timor, were able to mount an end run on a reluctant home state. Some of the movements in this study, like Western Sahara, are on the UN list of Non-Self-Governing Territories (the "decolonization list"), and their independence is blocked by the home state. Others, like West Papua, are currently excluded from the list for diplomatic reasons and the fact that there is some ambiguity about determining who counts for decolonization.[35] Importantly, the compellence tactics of decolonial movements vary considerably, because their settings can vary. Somaliland is a de facto state movement, West Papua is a weak combative movement, and New Caledonia is currently pursuing independence through the institutions of the French state. They occupy diverse settings but share a common normative appeal.

The final kind is the de facto state movement, a set that includes Abkhazia and Somaliland, among others. These are the least institutionally integrated. They are functional, breakaway regions that are denied international recognition. In each case, their home state has withheld its consent and successfully persuaded the international community to respect its territorial integrity. On one hand, these are success cases because they have won their independence on an empirical basis and effectively exited the larger state. For many movements like the Uighur, that alone would be a victory. On the other hand, their success at establishing de facto statehood has come at a cost. The secessionists have prevailed and established a state in empirical terms but, as a result, reduced or minimized their points of contact with the home state. They cannot engage so easily in forms of civil disobedience or terrorism or electoral competition precisely because they have broken off and are typically separated from the home state by a militarized border, such as the line separating Artsakh from Azerbaijan. Instead of a complex situation of dual and overlapping sovereignty, the two sides are clearly separated by linear boundaries.[36] In other words, they cannot compel the state to make a change because they have little direct leverage.[37] Instead, they have to settle for defending the border and deterring the home state from attacking. In an interview, Masis Mayilian, the foreign minister of Artsakh, told me that Artsakh has little direct leverage over Azerbaijan and is forced to focus on deterrence.[38] Overall, de facto state movements develop a status quo bias that can end in a half step (or local maxi-mum) between reintegration and full independence.[39]

Although de facto state movements can look passive and biased toward the sta-tus quo where compellence is concerned, they are ardent practitioners in the art of normative appeal. These groups have strong incentives to appear state-like and engage in as much diplomatic behavior as possible. They cannot appeal so easily to norms regarding human rights or abuses by the state because they have so little contact with the state. Instead, they try to appeal to the normative argument that good governance and democratic values establish standards that warrant status as a sovereign state. Essentially, they argue that they have earned their sovereignty—see the pathways listed in figure 2.3. They would pass the Canning Test, and if this were the nineteenth century they would likely be recognized.[40] To some ex-tent this becomes a waiting game and it is no surprise that these movements can endure in a frozen status for decades, locked in a diplomatic contest with the home state, waiting for a favorable geopolitical change. In an interview, I asked Ashot Ghoulian, the speaker of the Artsakh National Assembly, if he saw a potential opening for international recognition. In response, he shrugged his shoulders and said that perhaps recognition would come with a "tectonic change" in world politics.[41]

Overall, these six kinds capture variation on the international strategic play-ing field. I contend that it is useful to study them as a set, because most seces-sionist movements will exhibit characteristics of more than one kind. Just as the Catalans have contemplated civil resistance alongside their electoral efforts, some groups like the Polisario Front wonder whether a return to violence would get them further than continued nonviolent civil resistance.[42] The Kanak secession-ists of New Caledonia have used civil resistance and violence at various points, and it is only in the last twenty years that their efforts have been exclusively insti-tutional. There is now a robust research effort to understand the strategic and tac-tical choices of social movements and rebel groups.[43] My theory contributes to this literature by specifying the relationship between the strategic setting of se-cessionists movements and their tactical choices.

A Hybrid Case: Iraqi Kurdistan

Let us examine a prominent hybrid case in light of this framework. The Iraqi Kurds have had a troubled relationship with the central government since the birth of the state in the 1930s. There have been several Kurdish independence efforts over the years, both in Iraq and in the neighboring states of Turkey, Iran, and Syria, which hold sizable Kurdish minority populations.[44] The secessionist move-ment in Iraqi Kurdistan received world attention when it held an independence referendum on September 25, 2017, and won a reported 93 percent of the votes.[45] Although the Iraqi government and key international actors have thus far denounced the referendum, the future of the breakaway region is uncertain.[46] How can we understand the strategic environment of Iraqi Kurdistan in light of my framework?

At the strategic level, the Kurdish strategy for seeking independence has the same profile as all the others. It has to get Baghdad to remove its home-state veto and permit Iraqi Kurdistan to become independent. In the absence of that consent, the Kurds can do the end run by attempting to bring the international community and key actors into the game, to either apply pressure on Baghdad and/or circumvent its wishes entirely. The key actors in this case are the Iraqi state, the United States and the other P5 members, and powerful neighbors like Turkey and Iran, states that have a particular interest in the Kurdish cause given their own minority Kurd populations. If Baghdad can be persuaded or compelled to remove its home-state veto, then the path to Kurdish independence is almost certainly open. Circumvention is a second possibility, but a more problematic one given that states like Russia and China may refuse to recognize Kurdish independence, out of respect for Iraqi sovereignty, and thus block the Kurd's admittance to the UN.

To win sovereign recognition, the Kurdish leadership will have to engage in compellence and normative appeal. However, how it does that in more specific terms is largely a function of its particular conditions. Iraqi Kurdistan is an interesting mix of three kinds of movements. First, it is partly a democratized movement. There are democratic institutions in Iraqi Kurdistan and Iraq in general. However, the institutions are fragile and the state can be classified as a weak democracy or anocracy. Second, there is a de facto character to Iraqi Kurdistan given that it functions in a fairly distinct manner from the rest of the country. It is much more integrated into Iraq than, say, Artsakh is with Azerbaijan. But there nevertheless exists a fractured sovereignty that is roughly delimited by an internal border and guarded by Kurdish military forces, the Peshmerga. Third, Iraqi Kurdistan resembles a strong combative movement given the relative strength of the Peshmerga in relation to the Iraqi military.

Iraqi Kurdistan sits at the intersection of these secessionist kinds, and this has implications for its tactics. Democratized movements like Catalonia seek independence through electoral capture, demonstrations, and nonviolent protests. They simultaneously make normative appeals regarding the right to choose. Kurdish political parties like the Kurdistan Democratic Party (KDP) are clearly seeking their objectives through electoral means, and the movement in general has appealed to the norm of self-determination, as it did when it proclaimed the "natural right of the nation of Kurdistan to decide on its political and administrative path in a referendum."[47] Whether these tactics will ultimately bear fruit turns on the extent to which the democratic process in Iraq is honored. The reaction to the independence referendum on September 25, 2017, suggests that Iraq and key regional actors are unprepared to respect the outcome. However, that could change with time, especially if Iraq becomes increasingly democratic.

Iraqi Kurdistan is also a partly de facto state, and there is an important tension here with its democratized characteristics. Should its separateness increase to the point that the Kurdish region is fully sundered from Iraq by some protected border, then its ability to seek electoral capture and other forms of compellence will fade away as it loses connectivity. If this occurs, then Kurdistan's direct force tactics will change from compellence to dissuasion as it comes to focus on deterrence and defense.[48] In that scenario, the Kurdish leadership would continue to showcase its functionality and institutional standards as part of the argument about why they deserve statehood. The consequence of that outcome is its stickiness and status quo bias, and the danger that the region will just endure in a midspace between reintegration and full independence.

However, should its separateness decrease and should its democratic institutions wither, Iraqi Kurdistan will look more and more like the strong combative type. In many ways, a de facto state is just an extreme form of a strong combative independence movement, one that has won a separate sovereignty and is strong enough to keep it. In contrast, strong combative types are more closely engaged with the state and characterized by overlapping ethnic distributions and zones of control. This can be a dangerous scenario as it raises the probability that violence will be employed not only by the state, but also by the secessionists as a form of compellence.

Overall, the independence effort in Iraqi Kurdistan shows an interesting blend of secessionist kinds. The Kurdish leadership is working though democratic institutions and proclaiming its right to choose even as it showcases its state-like credentials and engages in forms of diplomacy with sovereign states.[49] It combines elements of the de facto and democratized movements with the potential perils of the strong combative kind. Admission to the sovereignty club is a fuzzy process, shaded by luck, and the right constellation of events could suddenly persuade Baghdad to open the gate and/or bring the right actors over to the Kurdish cause.

Bringing in the State

Home states are the primary obstacle to secessionist ambition, and key players in the sovereignty game. How do they respond to the efforts of independence movements?[50] The overall strategy of states is in many ways the mirror image of the strategy of secession. At the strategic level, states defend the perimeter by maintaining the veto, resisting pressure to remove it and weakening attempts by secessionists to compel and persuade others that their cause is righteous. Although states use different tactics depending on context, there are features that are common to all countersecession efforts. Chief among them is the appeal to territorial integrity. The international system is ultimately state-centric, and sovereign states are the key actors and club members. The default solution for any independence claim is to maintain the status quo, and it is therefore incumbent on aspiring states to prove that their self-determination demands supersede the need of the state to maintain its territorial integrity. In the normative collision between self-determination and territorial integrity, and liberalism and sovereignty more broadly, secessionists have numerous cards to play (decolonization, human rights, etc.), but states have the ace: the principle that sovereign territory is inviolate.

Nevertheless, states often need to do more than simply stand behind their territorial integrity. States engage in tactical behavior that is shaped by the same factors that influence secessionists: the degree to which the independence movement is de facto independent, the regime type, and the strength of the state. The issue of connectivity is a good starting point for the analysis because de facto state movements interact with their home state in a fundamentally different way from other movements. Their sundering from the state removes their levers of compellence and shifts the aim of the secessionists toward dissuasion. In some respects, states undergo the opposite transformation. Just as they aim to dissuade when secessionists need to compel, they increasingly need to compel as secessionists focus on dissuasion.

Some of the most developed work on countersecession focuses on situations of de facto statehood.[51] In his groundbreaking research on this topic, James Ker-Lindsay identifies the key features of countersecession policy for states like Cyprus and Azerbaijan that face a de facto state movement. Overall, they need to maintain their territorial claim in an unambiguous manner. This is particularly important in the case of de facto state movements, because "silence about an act of secession may possibly be read as de facto acceptance of the loss."[52] This is one of the reasons why Cyprus has been so clear that Northern Cyprus is an illegal state, "an occupied area." For other home states facing different kinds of independence movements, such as Indonesia in its contest with West Papua, it is less important to be so explicit. Indeed, it may even be counterproductive if it draws attention to a struggle that the state is keen to suppress. But for home states facing a de facto state movement, the separation is more visible, more internationalized, and ultimately more diplomatic in nature. Home states need to prevent the recognition and, indeed, the gradual legitimization of a breakaway region.[53] This can take place in small ways as the breakaway region finds itself isolated and blocked from regional organizations. It can also be done through highly visible means, like, for example, Security Council Resolution 541, the 1983 decision that called on states to respect Cypriot sovereignty and not recognize Northern Cyprus.

Although Tamil Eelam lost any pretentions to de facto statehood when it was reconquered in 2009, its diaspora community fielded a football (soccer) team at the 2018 CONIFA World Cup in London. In a personal interview, the Tamil Eelam manager stated that their purpose was "to play football as a nation, to keep the message alive that they are a nation, a message of self-determination."[54] In an example of a state's attempt to delegitimize secessionist behavior, the Sri Lankan government responded to Tamil Eelam's intended participation with a letter to CONIFA. "'Tamil Eelam' does not exist," it wrote, "nor has it existed in Sri Lanka, either *de facto* or *de jure*."[55] Moreover, the letter stated that the Liberation Tigers of Tamil Eelam (LTTE) was a terrorist organization "that was brought to an end in May 2009." By including the Tamil Eelam team, CONIFA will "promote and support divisive, separatist tendencies as well as violence in many countries including Sri Lanka." This is standard geopolitical language attempting to delegitimize a previously secessionist region by evoking the term "terrorism" and raising the specter of secessionist contagion.

I have argued that de facto state movements can become frozen and reach a kind of equilibrium between reintegration and full statehood. The primary reason for this balance is that the breakaway region is strong enough to hold the state at bay (often because it has a patron) but not sufficiently powerful to either defeat the state militarily or coerce its international recognition. When faced with this stalemate, home states do more than attempt to dissuade the region from gaining further recognition, they try to tip the balance back in their favor. Doing so requires acts of compellence. As the Northern Cypriots have learned, Cyprus has attempted not only to isolate them, but also to make it difficult for them to continue with the status quo by making their independence bid costly. Where possible the home state may even attempt a military solution. Azerbaijan began (and later abandoned) an offensive against Artsakh in April 2016, and Sri Lanka brutally conquered the semi–de facto state of Tamil Eelam in 2009. A key feature of the de facto state movement is that both sides aim to make a change—neither is satisfied—and home states are much more likely to engage in compellent acts.

The tactical dynamics of secession change when the breakaway region is integrated into the larger state. The next separating factor is the institutional structure of the state, because, as stated above, movements in democratic settings are more likely to use the electoral process and appeal to the right to choose. States, for their part, are more likely to respond in kind: to defeat secessionist parties through elections and referenda, and to deny minority nations the right to choose. Here, countersecessionists often put forward arguments about legality and stability. They may claim that secession is unconstitutional,[56] as the Spanish government has done in reference to Catalonia, and they may accuse the secessionists of causing polarization, division, and instability. Of course, a key feature of the sovereignty game in societies like Canada and Spain is the fact that both sides generally avoid using violence. Indeed, it is often explicitly ruled off the table. As long as that remains the case, countersecession tactics will mirror the tactics of democratized movements.

To be sure, there is variation in the way that democracies respond. The British government decided to permit a Scottish referendum. In contrast, the Spanish government has thus far withheld a referendum for Catalonia on constitutional grounds, but has fought the secessionist cause electorally. Both governments have vied to win hearts and minds—that is, to maintain a decisive majority of antisecessionists in the breakaway region—but even here we can see variation. In the run-up to the 2014 Scottish referendum, the British government first relied on scare tactics by saying that Scottish independence would make Scots worse off. It was really only in the final days that the government switched to the opposite approach of appealing to common ancestry and Anglo-Scottish bonds. To the dismay of many observers, the Spanish government has often been slow to appeal to the same bonds of affinity between Catalonia and the rest of Spain. I suspect on a somewhat conjectural basis that the smart move in these cases is for the government to avoid scare tactics, which tends to polarize society and bolster the secessionist cause, and appeal instead to common bonds. French president Emmanuel Macron used this approach effectively when he visited New Caledonia in May 2018.[57]

Countersecession tactics in nondemocratic and/or underinstitutionalized states typically have a different character. Where the state is relatively strong, suppression is a common response. It is illegal to fly the Morning Star flag in West Papua. Indeed, when I attended a workshop there on nonviolent forms of self-determination, I was told to travel without any documents or computer files that referenced West Papuan independence and to bring common holiday gear like a mask and snorkel so that I would not attract attention. Like China with the Tibetans and the Uighur,[58] Indonesia suppresses the self-determination cause in West Papua.[59] For states like Myanmar or Papua New Guinea, where capacity is more limited, and breakaway regions in the periphery are relatively stronger, the government is forced to accept a kind of informal autonomy. Both types are conflict-prone; it is the relative balance between the two sides that changes.

States facing weak and strong combative movements aim to dissuade. They defend what they can, and aim to deter secessionists from advancing their aims via the threat of punishment. The form of the punishment can vary from detainment, incarceration, and assassination, to direct military engagement.[60] Importantly, these states will defend their territorial claim and fight on the diplomatic front, but there is some variation here. Stronger states that can suppress an independence movement will often maintain a kind of silence on the issue, but weaker states that are fighting harder to control the breakaway region are often forced to engage the international community.

The sovereignty game is created by the interaction between states and aspiring states set against the background of the international recognition regime. Although my theory focuses on secessionist action, the actions of the state are an important part of the dynamic. In a sense, they complete the dynamic because the predicted tactics for each secessionist kind develop in relation to the characteristics, capabilities, and tactics of the home state. These tactics are in many ways the mirror image of the tactics used by secessionists. In fact, we can anticipate state behavior based on the kind of movement, a matter I return to in the case-study chapters.

At the strategic level all secessionist movements are the same. They need to make a change in order to become an internationally recognized sovereign state. The surest way to win recognition is to get the consent of the home state. In the absence of that consent, secessionists do what amounts to an end run to get the international community to either apply pressure on the home state or bypass it completely and recognize the aspiring nation. That strategy is shaped by the formal and informal rules and principles that guide recognition. It is at the tactical level that secessionist movements vary because different local conditions favor different tactics of compellence and normative appeal. As the recent events in Catalonia demonstrate, movements in democratic settings will work through the institutional apparatus of the state to force the central government to negotiate. Movements in different, less democratic settings, like West Papua, are more likely to choose civil resistance and/or violence, and appeal to international norms regarding human rights.

My theoretical model clarifies the intentions and behavior of diverse secessionist movements by highlighting what they have in common and how they vary. Using the model, I can predict the tactics that different movements will use depending on their setting. In each of the next six chapters I take a closer look at a particular independence movement that is representative of the different secessionist kinds. I provide a background for each movement, explain how secessionism developed, and I analyze its overall strategy and tactics. In chapter 10, I zoom out again to test my theory in a large-N format.

4

CATALONIA
Drawn in Blood

> **We can debate the ontology of a rock all we want. But if I throw one at you, you will very quickly comprehend what it is.**
>
> —Ferran Pedret i Santos, at a meeting at the Generalitat de Catalunya on September 12, 2015

The contemporary independence movement in Catalonia provides a fascinating glimpse of what secessionism can look like in a modern democratic society. I attended an event at the Palau de la Generalitat de Catalunya on September 12, 2015, at which representatives of the main political parties discussed the issue of Catalan nationalism. The colorful line quoted above regarding rocks and their ontology was made as an analogy with nationalism by Ferran Pedret, a former minister in the Catalan parliament and a member of the antisecessionist Socialists' Party of Catalonia (Partit dels Socialistes de Catalunya, PSC). Pedret is against independence not because he denies the existence of the Catalan nation, but rather because he sees nationalism as a dangerous source of political fragmentation and discord. The author of two books, or political pamphlets as he calls them, Pedret hopes for a federated world government in the "Kantian sense," one where diverse groups can achieve recognition.[1] Meanwhile, Quim Arrufat, the representative of the Popular Unity Candidacy (Candidatura d'Unitat Popular, CUP), a radical left-wing pro-independence party, stated that he supported secession not because he supports nationalism, which he thinks is dangerous, but because he believes Catalan independence is a means to achieve social justice. Each of the remaining party representatives expressed equally thoughtful opinions on the issue of independence.[2] The Catalan independence debate does not lack a philosophical foundation.

It is useful to begin the case studies with Catalonia, because it is a paragon of the democratized movement, a highly institutionalized form of secessionism. One of the striking differences between a movement such as this and the other tactical kinds discussed in this book is the context. The Catalan secessionist movement is institutionalized, its merits are openly debated, and there is substantial media attention given to the issue. It is truly a public debate, one that I argue is much more likely in advanced democracies. Up close it can appear quite different from the efforts in West Papua, Bougainville, and Northern Cyprus, and yet they are playing the same strategic game insofar as they all need to work through the home state and enlist the international community. It is at the tactical level that the context truly matters, for here a democratized movement is more likely to utilize the political apparatus of the state to achieve its ends—rather than resort to violence—and appeal to norms of democratic legitimacy as it does do.

Background

The traditional Catalan heartland straddles the eastern Pyrenees, combining the coastal regions of the Mediterranean in the northeast of modern Spain with Andorra and the south of modern France (see figure 4.1). The region was inhabited at various points by Iberian tribes, the Carthaginians, the Romans, and the Moors, among others. Catalan is typically grouped together with Occitan, constituting a branch of the Romance language family.[3] Although the regions of Valencia and the Balearic Islands are often claimed as part of the Catalan lands—and indeed dialects of Catalan are spoken there—these areas were conquered in the thirteenth century and are thus extensions from the original heartland.[4] One study done by the government of Catalonia puts the total number of Catalan speakers at 9.1 million.[5] Andorra is the only country where Catalan is the official language.

The coalescence of the early Catalan protostate took place in the wake of the Carolingian reconquest of the region from the Moors. This was the so-called Spanish March, a borderland between the Frankish kingdoms to the north and the Islamic power to the south.[6] The Catalan counts began as vassals to the Franks, but increased autonomy, if not full independence, came as the Frankish power receded. Gradually, the various counties of the Spanish March were consolidated as the County of Barcelona. In the twelfth century it unified via dynastic marriage with the Kingdom of Aragon in a quasi-confederal relationship.[7] For the next two centuries Barcelona flourished as a maritime power in the Mediterranean, acquiring possessions from Sardinia to Athens, setting up diplomatic posts at major shipping ports, influencing the rules and practices surrounding commerce, and effectively rivaling other city-states like Genoa and Venice.[8] The unification of Aragon with Castile in the late fifteenth century introduced a period of Catalan decline, shifting the balance of power into the Iberian heartland and reorienting Spanish ambitions toward the Atlantic and the Americas.[9]

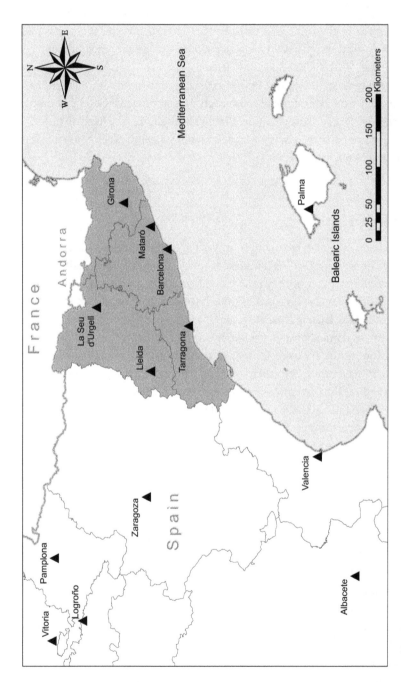

FIGURE 4.1. Map of Catalonia and surrounding territories

This period between the withdrawal of the Franks and the integration with Aragon has formed the basis for a controversial question in the current independence debate: Was Catalonia once an independent and sovereign state? This matters for some because former sovereignty adds historical weight to the cause, in effect supporting the position that Catalan independence would merely be a restoration of the status quo prior to Castilian (or Spanish) domination. The emphasis on this narrative is on display in the Catalan History Museum, an impressive map-heavy exhibition with the stated mission to "preserve, explain and popularise the history of Catalonia as collective heritage and strengthen citizens' identification with the nation's history." [10] One information plaque in the museum says clearly that Count Borrell II of Catalonia achieved de facto independence from the Frankish court of Hugues Capet in 988, and "from that time forth, the Catalan counts ruled with complete sovereignty over their lands."[11] In conversations and interviews I have heard critics on the other side of the debate dismiss these claims as propaganda, arguing that Catalonia was never a state.

Such attempts at an historical reckoning are fascinating to observe.[12] Of course, from the perspective of international law it does not matter if Catalonia was once a sovereign country, but in various ways it may matter in the court of public opinion. For example, a recent article in *The Economist* took a stand on the issue and implied something about Catalonia's credentials by saying: "Unlike Scotland, Catalonia was never an independent nation state."[13] For what it is worth, I do not think the matter can be reconciled without a baseline understanding of the state that can reach back more than 1000 years. In his book *Vanished Kingdoms*, Norman Davies is notably quiet on the matter, calling attention to the contemporary effort to rewrite history, and leaving it for others to determine whether the County of Barcelona was always a vassal and whether or not such vassalage was formal or de facto.[14]

The early modern period was the setting for two events that are central to the Catalan national narrative.[15] The first was the Catalan Revolt (1640–1652), or War of the Reapers as it is often called locally, a rebellion against Spanish authority that took place in the context of the Thirty Years' War. Catalonia's defeat in that struggle is commemorated in the national anthem, "El Segadors" (the Reapers), a stirring and rather violent call to arms against oppression. The second and more important event was the result of Catalonia's role in the War of Spanish Succession, when it chose to back the Habsburg and not the Bourbon claim to the Spanish throne. That decision put Catalonia on a collision course with Castile and France, culminating in the siege of Barcelona and its eventual fall on September 11, 1714, a day remembered as the juncture when Spain stripped Catalonia of its traditional rights and institutions[16] and therefore commerorated in modern times as the Catalan National Day, or *La Diada*. A spectator at a home game for

FC Barcelona, Catalonia's celebrated football (soccer) club, is reminded of this date when the clock strikes 17:14 and the fans chant "Independencia!"

Nationalism subsided after the Catalan Revolt and full incorporation of the region into the Spanish state. Indeed, the embrace of the larger Spanish identity even flourished for a time, especially during the Napoleonic Wars at the beginning of the 1800s. However, in the latter part of the century Catalonia underwent an industrialization process and cultural renaissance that left a lasting legacy in terms of artistic, cultural, and economic development. Known as *La Renaixença*, this was a period in which the city of Barcelona expanded, where a passion for modernist architecture (and art more generally) blossomed, often supported by wealthy industrialists, and when the concept of the Catalan nation began to take hold. This was a high-water mark in the boom-and-bust cycle of Catalan history, and Catalonia entered the twentieth century as a confident nation.

But it was not to last, for in the late 1930s Catalonia once again chose the losing side during a war that engulfed Spain. The Spanish Civil War was a watershed moment in Spanish history, a prelude in many ways to World War II, one that is covered in evocative books like Ernest Hemingway's *For Whom the Bell Tolls* and George Orwell's *Homage to Catalonia*. The war pitted the Nationalists, eventually led by General Francisco Franco, against a coalition of Republicans, communists, anarchists, and regional groups like the Basques and Catalans. It was in the uncertain political climate just before the war that Catalonia reestablished its autonomous government, the Generalitat, and moved in the direction of greater political and social freedom, if not outright independence.[17] Franco's victory ended all of this and began a period of dictatorial rule and suppression of the Catalan language and culture.

The events of the 1930s, the civil war, and subsequent period of Francoist rule loom large in the Catalan imaginary. Evidence of this is everywhere. On a holiday to the remote and picturesque Núria Valley in the Pyrenees, I serendipitously stayed at the hotel where the Catalan Statute of Self-Government was signed in August 1931. Pictures of famous Catalan leaders like Francesc Macià and Lluís Companys adorned the walls, and I realized that the sitting room was a kind of shrine to a country that was nearly born. In a 2015 interview, Pere Aragonès, the current vice president of Catalonia, proudly recounted his ancestry and said that his grandfather had attended Macià's funeral in 1933.[18] Many middle-aged Catalan acquaintances told me that their parents were still uncomfortable speaking Catalan in public, even in the twenty-first century, because it had been outlawed in their formative years under Franco's rule. In the largely pro-independence neighborhood of Gràcia (a section of Barcelona), one can visit the air-raid shelters where citizens sought cover from fascist bombers during the civil war. In the highly acclaimed *Ghosts of Spain*, Giles Tremlett argues that the past is not dead in Spain, despite the Pact of Forgetting (Pacto del olvido) that attended the end of Franco's rule.[19] This is certainly the case in Catalonia.

Franco's death in 1975 paved the way for Spain's democratic transition, a major inflection point in Spanish history. In a short period of time it transitioned from a highly centralized and unitary state under Franco to a constitutional democracy with a quasi-federal structure.[20] As Juan Linz put it: "The Spanish constitution of 1978 represents an effort—and a largely successful one—to provide a framework for a new democracy and a new type of state in Spain."[21] The resulting *estado de las autonomías* struck a balance between the Francoist holdovers who sought to retain the centralized and unitary state and those left-leaning or ethnic subnational groups who advocated a confederal or further decentralized arrangement.[22] The Spanish state decentralized into a democratic state consisting of seventeen autonomous regions, *autonomías*, possessing the constitutional right to self-rule.[23]

Catalonia has generally blossomed since the democratic transition. The Generalitat was restored, and the Catalans have enjoyed a high level of local governance. One important and far-reaching competency is the ability to conduct public-school education in Catalan. Whereas it was previously a somewhat covert language of the home, Catalan is now spoken freely on the streets and on the playgrounds. The dominant political figure during these years was Jordi Pujol, the president of Catalonia from 1980 to 2003. Pujol did not champion the independence cause, but he did bargain for Catalonia's political gains, often playing a kingmaker role in Spanish politics. For example, his conservative Catalan party, Democratic Convergence of Catalonia (Convergència Democràtica de Catalunya, CDC), allied with the broader Spanish conservative party, the Popular Party (Partido Popular, PP), in 1996 to make José María Aznar the prime minister. The agreement was known as the Majestic Pact (el Pacto del Majestic), and a photograph of the key meeting to seal the bargain shows Pujol, Aznar, and several other negotiators including Mariano Rajoy, the man who would later come to embody much of Catalonia's discontent with Spain.[24]

Perhaps Catalonia and Spain were destined to face a secessionist crisis. If so, this was not apparent to many during the first thirty years of democracy. Numerous interviewees who are now pro-independence told me that they were surprised that the secessionist movement took off as it did. Some thought it inevitable, but something that would come much further in the future. As late as 2006, only 14 percent of the population supported independence; in 2014, that number would reach 45 percent.[25] The recent independence drive in Catalonia has created a constitutional crisis in the country. It has shaken the confidence of the Spanish state, and raised difficult questions about when a minority nation should have the right to decide its political fate. For roughly thirty years since the transition to democracy, Catalan secessionism was quiet, dormant, but full of potential. Why did it come to the surface?

The Development of Secessionism

A side effect of the study of secession is an increased appreciation for flags. These highly symbolic banners communicate important nationalist themes. The Catalan independence flag, known as the *Estelada*, is one of my favorites (see figure 4.2). It represents a modification of the traditional Catalan national flag, the *Senyera*. Although both flags are ubiquitous in Barcelona, there is a notable difference between them: the *Senyera* celebrates the Catalan nation but it does not imply secessionism; the *Estelada* does both. The *Senyera* is known by its iconic four red bars across a field of gold. The origin myth for that design refers to a ninth-century battle against the Moors in which Count Wilfred the Hairy of Barcelona was mortally wounded. According to the story, King Charles the Bald dipped his fingers in the blood of Wilfred's wound and drew the four bars across Wilfred's shield. The resulting coat of arms was thus a symbol of Catalan bravery.[26] This is an unusually stirring account for the origins of a flag, the kind one would expect to find in a fictional work like *Game of Thrones*, and a life-size recreation of the event is displayed at the Catalan History Museum. The *Estelada* is a more recent

FIGURE 4.2. The independence flag of Catalonia

flag that dates from the early twentieth century. It incorporates the base design of the *Senyera*, but adds a blue triangle and five-pointed star at the hoist. The lone star (*estrella*) was inspired by the Cuban independence effort against Spain at the turn of the century. Thus, the *Estelada* augments the *Senyera* with a symbol of freedom.

The events in Catalonia starting around 2005 highlight the contingent nature of nationalism.[27] Even if the right conditions exist, it may take a spark to light the fire. The catalyst in this case was the tortured process and related debate over revising Catalonia's Statute of Autonomy.[28] The statute is important because it specifies the limits of Catalan autonomy in relation to the 1978 Spanish Constitution. In 2004, Spain's prime minister, José Luis Rodríguez Zapatero, invited Spain's regional communities, or *autonomías*, to update their statutes if they wished. There is some debate about whether Zapatero promised to accept all updates, but, in any case, the stage was being set. The Catalan parliament quickly drafted a new statute and then submitted it to the Spanish parliament as part of an initial approval process. What followed was a five-year period of increasing acrimony as various actors fought over the wording of the proposed statute. One of the most sensitive elements of the new statute was in the preamble, where Catalonia was defined as a nation. Spanish conservatives from the PP challenged this language by arguing that it contradicted the Spanish Constitution, which recognized the "indissoluble unity of the Spanish Nation." The more nationalist actors in Catalan politics, particularly from Esquerra, were diametrically opposed to any attempts to water down the language.[29] Despite efforts at shuttle diplomacy by various leaders, including the future president of Catalonia, Artur Mas, the controversial aspects of the statute were eventually struck down and/or modified by the Spanish Constitutional Court in 2010. Less than two weeks later on July 10, 2010, more than a million Catalans took to the street to protest under the slogan "Som una nació. Nosaltres decidim" (We are a nation. We decide).[30]

The statute crisis activated a fault line in the Spain-Catalonia relationship. Carme Forcadell, former president of the parliament of Catalonia, told me in an interview that she was not always secessionist but became mobilized during the statute crisis. She said there was no clear threshold, "it was like drops of water being added to a glass."[31] The drops of water could be summed up as a growing feeling of frustration with the Spanish state and shock at the increasing anti-Catalan rhetoric coming from certain political figures and segments of Spanish society. According to Salvador Cardús, an economist and columnist, "the triggering of secessionist feeling . . . has to do with an unrelenting process of humiliation since 2006."[32] In sum, the crisis exposed a fault line and began a process of recrimination. By the time I started conducting interviews in 2015, I was struck by the degree of polarization. I was often told by non-Catalans, especially those who lived elsewhere in Spain, that Catalans are racist snobs, and I was told by many Catalans that the Spanish were uncouth racists.

An interesting and rather tragic feature of the crisis was its rhetorical peculiarity. Article 2 of the Spanish Constitution reads:

> The Constitution is based on the indissoluble unity of the Spanish Nation, the common and indivisible homeland of all Spaniards; it recognizes and guarantees the right to self-government of the nationalities and regions of which it is composed and the solidarity among them all.

There is an ambiguity in the usage of the terms "nation" and "nationalities." According to Cristina Perales-García, a professor of communications, this word choice was adopted during the democratic transition as a way to posit a single Spanish nation and thus please the conservatives, while acknowledging (and thus placating) the national characteristics of the regions.[33] It was a precarious solution that worked as long as it was not challenged.

Various other factors fed the process of polarization.[34] At the societal level, many are convinced of the basic differences between Catalans and Spaniards. For example, I was often told that Catalonia has a greater history of democracy than the rest of Spain. Several interviewees claimed that the Catalan government was the first democratic body in modern Europe, earlier even than that of England. I read a similarly intriguing account in a pro-independence book by Simon Harris,[35] one that would fit nicely with social scientific theories on the relationship between warfare and state making.[36] According to Harris, the territorial characteristics of the Spanish reconquest had long-run implications for the development of democratic institutions. The reconquest was led predominately in central Spain by Castile, which conducted a centuries-long land-based campaign against the Moors. From that project arose a military aristocracy that was resistant to the development of democratic institutions. For Catalonia, however, that north-to-south expansion ended at Valencia quite early on, forcing the Catalans to turn their attention to the sea and expansion across the Mediterranean. The resulting alliance between merchants and the navy checked aristocratic privilege at home and helped facilitate the rise of democratic institutions. This is a fascinating argument to speculate upon, and it may be true, but, perhaps more importantly, it is a popular theory that many believe.

One notable aspect of these purported differences is that they are often advanced by thoughtful and often highly educated individuals. In his book *Disdain, Distrust, and Dissolution*, Germà Bel provides empirical data of the stereotypes and perceptions of difference that many Spaniards have of Catalans.[37] In separate and unrelated interviews, two men (one Catalan and a non-Catalan from Madrid) told me the same story about their experiences in the military

(Spain ended mandatory service in 2001). Both reported that the Catalans kept to themselves socially, far more so than other regional nationalities like the Basques. When pressed for a reason, both men fell back on a commonly held view: the Catalans possess a different sense of humor and socialize differently.

Not surprisingly, economic issues have fed the division. Catalonia is one of the wealthiest regions in Spain, and Catalans often complain that they pay more in federal taxes than they receive in benefits—effectively subsidizing poorer regions across the country.[38] And yet, as Bel points out, there are areas in which federal funding is grossly insufficient, such as the poor infrastructure system in Catalonia.[39] These economic concerns were acutely felt during the Global Financial Crisis, which hit Spain particularly hard. Meanwhile, the Basques have possessed greater autonomy over local taxation since the democratic transition, and recent requests by Catalonia to be given the same rights have been rebuffed.[40]

Collectively, these feelings of frustration, difference, and increasing acrimony generated an environment of secessionist energy. And notably, it was not the elites who first exploited it, but society itself. An important aspect of democratized secession is its grassroots, somewhat bottom-up character. Secessionism is usually an elite-driven project in less developed and less democratic societies like West Papua and Bougainville because the general population is less connected and less educated. Elites can control the discourse more easily, and the state, for its part, can often thwart the independence bid by co-opting the secessionist leadership. The dynamics are different in a region like Catalonia with its formidable civil society organizations and educated, media-savvy citizenry. Here, the leadership can be co-opted by the people and the civic organizations that stand for independence. It is said that Artur Mas, the president of Catalonia from 2010 to 2016, only became a true secessionist in 2012 when the Spanish government failed to meet certain demands and the Catalan National Assembly (Assemblea Nacional Catalana, ANC), a civic organization dedicated to secession, persuaded Mas to join its side.[41]

I was often told during interviews that the strength of the Catalan independence movement flows from three bases. As Vicent Partal, the journalist and founder of VilaWeb, told me, these are civil society, the intelligentsia, and politics—and civil society is the core.[42] When secessionism in Catalonia came from the bottom, it was assisted by two organizations: Omnium and Assemblea. Omnium is an older and smaller organization, dating to 1961, that was originally involved in the promotion of the Catalan language.[43] It became a more political organization in 2010 in relation to the public protests. In September 2015 I attended a two-day public-relations event in which Omnium brought in a number of scholars, journalists, and foreign politicians to introduce them to Catalan culture and history, and showcase the independence effort. The highlight of the event was the public demonstration on *La Diada*, in which over one million people gathered to demand independence. It was an impressive spectacle. Assemblea is a bigger and younger organization that was founded in 2012 with the purpose of obtaining independence for Catalonia. The first president of Assemblea was Forcadell, a charismatic and highly skilled public organizer. A rough division between these sibling organizations is that Omnium stresses outreach while Assemblea focuses on mobilization.

Both organizations (and the movement in general) are assisted by what has been described as a high level of cultural associationalism.[44] Liz Castro, an author and former leader of Assemblea, told me that the organizational bedrock of the independence movement is the neighborhood associations; she said that "these groups are a part of your life and act as civic organizations in the way that Robert Putnam discussed in *Bowling Alone*."[45] The groups have diverse purposes. Some are *casteller* groups, that is, local neighborhood teams that regularly meet to practice and compete in the formation of human towers, a popular Catalan pastime. Others are organized around particular festivals, such as the breathtaking *Correfoc* (fire runs), in which neighborhood teams dress up as devils, carry pitchforks lit with fireworks, and invite others to run through the shower of sparks as the crowd dances to drums. According to Castro, associations such as these provide a ready-made base that can be mobilized for other purposes like independence-related demonstrations.

The second base in the movement is the intelligentsia. Partal maintains that this is vital because it gives the movement the ability to design and articulate political and economic policies, and defend them against opponents.[46] There is no question that the Catalan independence movement possesses a formidable intelligentsia. Whether that is an aspect of Catalan society and not simply the natural outgrowth of secessionism in an advanced democracy, I cannot say.[47] Take, for example, the Wilson Initiative, a collection of six highly successful, pro-independence economists and political scientists who aim to provide information about the value and viability of an independent Catalonia.[48] A fundamental challenge for secessionist movements is uncertainty reduction—how does an aspiring nation become independent and will it be viable? All movements struggle to reduce that uncertainty, but it helps when you have experts on your side. In my meeting with Partal, he showed me and compared the transition documents for the Catalans and the Scottish National Party (SNP).[49] He pointed out that the Catalan document was thicker and more nuanced. It was the product of several highly skilled and very dedicated academics.

The third base is the political structure. With its inclusion, a movement can access and begin to harness the political institutions of the state. Without it, a people-led and intelligentsia-backed movement will grow frustrated and is more likely to use extra-institutional methods. But it is hard indeed for political elites to ignore those forces in a democracy. Such was the case with Catalonia. There had always been true believers, like Oriol Junqueras, the former vice president of Catalonia, and long-running independence parties like Esquerra, but with Artur Mas's conversion to secessionism in 2012, Catalonia now had an advocate in the presidency.

Strategy and Tactics

Catalan secessionism has been one of the most visible and electrifying independence efforts in recent years. Most people seem aware that the inhabitants of a region of Spain called Catalonia are trying to become independent, like the Scots, and perhaps the Kurds, that they organize breathtaking marches in the streets of Barcelona, and that they have political parties vying for power. Although the Catalan independence effort may seem like a unique case, at the strategic level it is no different from any other. The home state, Spain, is the central obstacle to its ambitions. Until it gets Madrid to remove the veto, or at least negotiate, Catalonia is very unlikely to win its independence. Like other movements, it has attempted to do an end run around the Spanish government and enlist the help of the international community. In this case, the key external players are the EU member states, who can apply pressure on Spain to negotiate and/or potentially withhold EU membership from Catalonia. It is at the tactical level that Catalonia truly differs from the other case studies in this book, for here we can see how the context shapes the methods.

Relative to other secessionist kinds, democratized movements are more likely to use the institutional apparatus of the state to pursue their ends, and less likely to use extra-institutional methods, especially violence. Indeed, electoral capture as a compellence tactic seems to crowd out the other options. A good example of this is the Catalan regional election of September 27, 2015, widely held to be a kind of stand-in for an independence referendum. The Catalan and Spanish political landscape had changed rapidly in the years just prior, both in response to the Global Financial Crisis, which shocked the Spanish economy, and as a result of the groundswell in secessionist sentiment. At the national level, two insurgent parties, We Can (Podemos) and Citizens (Ciudadanos), had risen to challenge the traditional two-party system comprising the Socialists (Partido Socialista Obrero Español, PSOE) and the PP. At the regional level, the traditional Catalan conservative alliance, Convergence and Union (Convergència i Unio, CiU), was fracturing over the issue of secession.[50] When President Mas embraced the secessionist cause in 2012, he took elements of his party, Convergència, with him.

Moreover, two additional left-wing parties or coalitions, CUP and Catalonia Yes We Can (Catalunya Si que es Pot), had arisen earlier that year. This was a snap election called by Mas in order to clarify the position of the key parties on the matter of secession. Although the president was apparently a committed secessionist, it was unclear where the Catalan parliament stood.

One fascinating element of the election was the highly sophisticated ground game of the secessionists. Two weeks before the election I was given a tour of the call center for the campaign, where dozens of volunteers were contacting individual voters. In a subsequent interview with one of the heads of the campaign, I was told that they used microtargeting techniques that attempted to segment the population according to preferences.[51] My interviewee and others had been sent the previous year to Scotland to observe the methods of the Scottish National Party (SNP) during the 2014 referendum and learn how to set up a call center (evidently, the first of its kind in Spanish elections). I was told that the campaign took care to not neglect senior citizens, who generally vote but are afraid of independence, and the young, who are keen on independence but less likely to vote.

What did the Catalan secessionists hope to achieve by winning the election, and how exactly would it help them to secure independence? I was in Barcelona during the campaign season and I asked this question repeatedly. The general answer was that by winning a majority in parliament, the pro-independence side could say to the world that the people have spoken and they want independence. It would be a symbolic victory that would feed the normative appeal that they have to the right to decide their political fate. I got the sense in my interviews that some Catalans believed that this alone would be enough, even though the Spanish government said that such a victory would be meaningless.

However, the Catalan leadership saw an election victory as merely one step, albeit a crucial one, on the road to independence. In an interview with a prominent Catalan political scientist, and one of the intellectual advisers to the secessionist movement, I was told that a Catalan government with a pro-independence majority could begin to establish the necessary institutions of statehood—such as setting up a national bank—in a way that could not be shut down by the Spanish government.[52] Indeed, these steps were outlined in the 2014 White Paper on the National Transition of Catalonia.[53] This remarkable 135-page document, published by the government of Catalonia, was produced by the Advisory Council on the National Transition, a group of notable thinkers and scholars. They "held 54 plenary meetings which were captured in the more than 1,300 pages" of eighteen reports that culminated in the White Paper.[54] The document begins with a somewhat philosophical discussion that is reminiscent of the American Constitution and Declaration of Independence.[55] It then lays out the stages from an initial consultation with the Catalan people, to a declaration of independence, to the approval of a constitution, to the organization of Catalonia as a new state, and finally to the formation of its relationship with the international community.

There is a crucial question that sits at the heart of the Catalan independence project, and it is one that is hard to answer: At what point will the Spanish government be forced to react? Like other secessionists, the Catalans need to compel their home state to give them what they want. But if the Spanish government can simply ignore their demands indefinitely, then compellence has failed. Successful compellence requires action, in contrast to deterrence where success is measured by whether the targeted behavior is not acted upon.[56] One of the challenges for secessionists is that it is difficult to know when and at what point the state will concede. Where is the breaking point? This is a question I asked all my interviewees in Catalonia (and in other secessionist regions), and the answer was usually unclear. In the end, actors can only speculate. This is apparent in the 2014 White Paper, where the authors identify steps on the path to statehood that effectively increase the pressure on Madrid. One of the earliest steps would be to hold a consultation with the Catalan people to see if a majority supports a referendum on independence; with a positive outcome, the Spanish government would be obliged to negotiate.[57] If, however, the Spanish government remained silent, then a plebiscite (referendum) could be held; following that a declaration of independence; and following that, the establishment of Catalan state institutions that would replace those of Spain. At some point, Spain would simply be forced to respond, or otherwise watch as Catalonia set up a new country.[58]

The end run is an important strategic element for the Catalans, and the EU loomed particularly large in my interviews given its role as a kind of regional gatekeeper. It was often said that the EU would not allow Spain to ignore Catalan demands and/or that the EU could not ignore them because political conflict in Spain could eventually threaten the economic and social stability of the union. Surely there is a reservation point for EU leaders, and had the financial markets declined rapidly, or worse, had violence erupted in 2015, I suspect that key foreign leaders like Angela Merkel would have pressured Spain to end the standoff. In an interview with Albert Royo, the former secretary general of the Public Diplomacy Council of Catalonia (Consell de Diplomàcia Pública de Catalunya, DIPLOCAT), a public-private consortium that managed the public relations of the independence drive, I was told that external support would be crucial.[59] Royo stated that DIPLOCAT, together with personnel at the Generalitat, had developed networks with politicians throughout the world, but particularly in Europe. He thought there was a red line for EU intervention and, importantly, he intended to cross it. That is, he intended to "create conflict" that would force Europe and Spain to respond.

An interesting aspect of Catalonia's diplomatic wing is its relative youth. There is a substantial and rather powerful group of individuals in their late thirties and forties who had gained experience working in Brussels as part of the EU. In a personal account that resonated with the stories of other interviewees, Royo said that he had previously worked for the European Committee of the Regions, but had gradually come to believe that it was only states, and not regions like Catalonia, that had power in the EU.[60] Therefore, to have real power and real political voice, Catalonia needed to become a state. Along with other personnel like Raül Romeva, Roger Albinyana, and Manuel Manonelles, Royo had developed his networks and his diplomatic and linguistic skills in Brussels.[61] One senior officer in the independence effort told me that these individuals had been recruited because of their EU-honed skills.[62] In a way, these "Brussels Boys" had been brought to the secessionist cause by their dissatisfaction from working with the EU. In another interview, the anthropologist Susan DiGiacomo summed up the reaction by saying: "we thought the EU was a society of nations but it's really a club of states."[63]

Throughout these efforts the Catalan secessionists have alighted on a central normative appeal regarding the right to decide. In the introduction to the White Paper, "Deciding to Win the Future," President Mas stressed that the Catalans have the opportunity to decide their future.[64] Later, in the argument for why their efforts are legitimate, it is stated clearly that the Catalan independence drive is grounded in the principle of "self-determination as a people's exercise of the right to democratically decide."[65] This was far from an abstract philosophical notion in the Catalan debate, it was a concept openly expressed on the street. The slogan for the July 10, 2010, protest was: "We are a nation. We decide."[66] I attended frequent demonstrations in 2015 and 2017, and, in addition to the singing and the dancing and the waving of flags, I saw numerous posters with political messages. Many of them conveyed the basic idea that the Catalans have the right to choose. This messaging on both the street and by the political leadership combined with the intelligentsia to create a rather nuanced discussion rarely seen outside the academy. In an interview with Jaume López, a lecturer at the University of Pompeu Fabra and a former research director at CatDem, a pro-independence think tank, he parsed the difference between the right to self-determination and the right to choose independence.[67] He stated that the Catalans should have the right to negotiate with the state and that, if the state refuses, then the right is elevated to the choice for independence.

The right to choose was the dominant normative argument in the Catalan case. In part, this is because the appeal resonates particularly well in democratic societies. But it must also be said that democratized movements have less to work with. Although I sometimes heard secessionists deploy the language of empire—that

Spain's relationship to Catalonia was imperial—no one seriously suggested that the pathway of decolonization was available. The argument regarding earned sovereignty was similarly ill-fit to the situation given that Catalonia is so thoroughly integrated with the larger state. The appeal to human rights had a bit more traction, but its usage was largely conditional on potentially bad behavior by the Spanish government. Indeed, part of the strategy of generating conflict was to draw out bad behavior. But in the meantime, too little of it was there. Democratized movements appeal to the right to choose not only because it resonates with their institutional setting, but also because they are pragmatic and typically cannot appeal to the other arguments.

A striking feature of democratized secession is that they are often split, tight-run affairs. The SNP narrowly lost the 2014 Scottish referendum, and the No campaign won the 1995 Quebec referendum by the barest of margins. The 2015 Catalan regional election, seen as a consultation on independence, was similarly split. The pro-independence side won 72 of the 135 parliamentary seats (a 53 percent majority), but they won only 48 percent of the popular vote. That discrepancy came down to the fact that seat apportionment favored the rural districts that were relatively pro-independence. Although this was claimed by the secessionists as a mandate to pursue independence, the questionable results checked their momentum. In the aftermath of the election I spoke to numerous secessionists who felt the movement needed to slow down and focus on the building of support. Had the secessionists won an overwhelming majority of the vote—say 80 percent—subsequent events may have gone differently.

Since 2015 the independence effort has been mostly characterized by a kind of grinding uncertainty. A division in the independence parties led to an initial investiture crisis wherein CUP refused to support Mas as the Catalan president. Given Mas's connection to the scandal-ridden Catalan conservative party, Convergència, the left-leaning CUP was prepared to force a new election and undermine the independence effort rather than support Mas.[68] As a result, Mas was forced to step down and the independence forces settled on Carles Puigdemont, a man widely viewed as more committed to independence than Mas.[69] Uncertainty also prevailed at the national level as the two insurgent parties, Podemos and Ciudadanos, successfully transformed the traditional Spanish two-party system into one with four parties of roughly equal representation. This development led to endless speculation about whether the secessionists would fare better under a left-leaning coalition, who were generally amenable to negotiation, or, somewhat counterintuitively, under continued conservative leadership, which was more likely to reject Catalan demands and thereby inflame the issue.[70] Through it all, Prime Minister Rajoy, vilified by the Catalan secessionists, was able to stay in power until June 2018.

The key event in recent years, one that caused a Spanish constitutional crisis, was the October 1, 2017, Catalan referendum on independence. Puigdemont and the hard-line secessionists had doggedly followed the original plan and decided to hold an official referendum. Had Spain decided to permit a Scottish-type referendum, perhaps the antisecessionists would have won the vote and then potentially put the issue to rest. Instead, the government declared that such a referendum was illegal, and calls were made to boycott the event. Not surprisingly, the Yes side took a reported 92 percent of the ballots, a result that would have been far more even had the opposition mobilized its supporters. Of perhaps more importance was the police crackdown at many of the polling stations. When the Spanish National Police and the Guardia Civil attempted to remove voters from the stations, violence resulted and some 1,000 people were reportedly injured. One foreign colleague of mine who served as a neutral observer at a station was violently thrown to the ground by police when they stormed the building.

The weeks following the referendum were tense and the world waited to see what both sides would do. Would the secessionists declare independence as they promised should they win the referendum? How would Spain react? And where was the expected international response? After all, the violent images of the police crackdown had gone viral and it seemed that the secessionist leadership had finally gotten the conflict they wanted. In an interview on October 4, 2017, Royo expressed shock at the Spanish crackdown and disappointment in the tepid European response.[71] It seemed the redline for intervention had not been crossed.[72]

It was in this period that the Catalan leadership looked indecisive. On October 11, Puigdemont made an ambiguous declaration of independence, but then, on account of pressure from moderate voices, immediately suspended it so that negotiations could be held. For his part, Prime Minister Rajoy sought to invoke Spanish Constitutional Article 155, which would suspend Catalan autonomy and impose direct rule for the first time since the democratic transition. Finally, after mounting pressure from hard-line secessionists, who were further motivated when the Spanish government began to arrest Catalan leaders like Jordi Sànchez and Jordi Cuixart on charges of sedition, the Catalan parliament declared independence on October 27, 2017.[73] As a result, Article 155 was triggered and Catalan autonomy was suspended. Within days, Puigdemont and other leaders fled Spain to avoid arrest.

At the time of this writing, the situation in Catalonia has remained relatively static. The population appears to remain roughly split on the issue of independence, but the secessionists retain a narrow majority in the now restored parliament. The leadership on both sides has changed. Puigdemont remains in exile, several Catalan leaders are still in jail, and the new president is Quim Torra, in office since May 2018. Rajoy lost a vote of no confidence the following month, and since that time Spain has been led by the Socialist leader Pedro Sánchez, who has promised to open a dialogue on the Catalan issue.

In many ways, the Catalan experience illustrates the difficulty of winning independence via institutional methods, especially when the target population is split on the issue. To be sure, nonviolent extra-institutional methods have been present. Forcadell writes that the early demonstrations of Assemblea were designed to win over the population and the political establishment.[74] These were explicitly peaceful demonstrations, but they succeeded in their objective. In a personal interview, she lamented that the cost of their success was a kind of takeover of the cause by politicians—i.e., the movement had become institutionalized.[75] There is an interesting tension here given that institutional access may obviate the need for extra-institutional methods. Perhaps extra-institutional methods will become more common in the wake of the constitutional crisis? As a potential sign of this, in December, 2018, two imprisoned Catalan leaders conducted a hunger strike to protest their incarceration.

Although nonviolent extra-institutional methods may accompany institutional methods, violent tactics are far less common. I was always struck by the reaction of my interviewees to the question of whether violence would eventually be used. Everyone felt that violence was off the menu, not even open for consideration. Theirs was a peaceful movement, and there was a clear difference from the violent kind.[76] In his comparative analysis of the Basque and Catalan secessionist methods, Luis De la Calle argued that whereas the Basque leaders were marginalized and more susceptible to the use of violence, the Catalan elites were brought into the political process and their methods were moderated.[77] Institutional access shapes the movement by stressing the ballot over the gun. Of course, the setting could change as the situation deteriorates, the government becomes more oppressive, and institutional access is lost.

Those seeking a complete understanding of Spain's countersecession strategy will likely be disappointed. I was regularly told during interviews with people on both sides of the issue that the strategy of the Rajoy administration was vague and somewhat baffling, that government representatives were notably absent at *La Diada* events, and that Rajoy would say that Catalan secession was against the constitution and then say little else. Some read a "wait and see" strategy into this; others felt that the government was perilously ignorant. One political operative told me that Rajoy was taking advice on the Catalan issue from prominent members of Fundación para el Análisis y los Estudios Sociales (FAES), a conservative thinktank in Madrid. In the end, it was hard to divine a clear strategy, if it even existed. However, this is not so unusual. For a secessionist movement, the purpose is clear, and energy is focused on that purpose. But a central government has many tasks and challenges on its agenda, and secession may be a lesser concern.

That concern may become quite salient in the case of de facto state movements, as we will see in chapter 9 on Northern Cyprus, because the standoff with the secessionists can gradually subordinate other problems. For other kinds of secessionism, the central government may not give the issue the same level of attention.

One element of counterstrategy that was noticeably absent, at least during the Rajoy administration, was a sincere attempt to appeal to the hearts and minds of the Catalan electorate. The appeal to common bonds can dampen the mood and help win over moderate voters, and last-ditch efforts such as these helped the British government win the 2014 Scottish referendum. However, there was very little of this rhetoric coming from Rajoy. I was told in interviews that the reason for this reticence was that Rajoy gained strength within his conservative PP by taking a strong stance—polarization helped fortify his political position. Notably, the Spanish monarchs, first King Juan Carlos and then his son, Felipe VI, did make these appeals, but it was to little effect.[78] It is too early to say, but with Pedro Sánchez in power the message from Madrid may change to one of greater conciliation.

In the contest of democratized secession, much of the countersecession efforts are mounted by opposing elements of civil society and the political parties vying for power. One representative organization is Societat Civil Catalana (SCC), a Catalan civic society formed in 2014 to oppose the independence drive. In an interview, the former SCC President, Rafael Arenas, told me that SCC is dedicated to two missions: (1) To argue that being Spanish is a broad category that can accommodate being Catalan too; (2) To argue that Spain should see the Catalan issue not as a problem, but rather as an opportunity for the development of pluralism.[79] Arenas described himself as part of the rise of the anti-independence silent majority that was trying to "break the spiral of silence." He pointed out that secessionists have a rhetorical advantage because it is easier to mobilize people around the goal of "change" than the goal of maintaining the status quo. Nevertheless, he felt that growing frustration with secessionist methods and the deadlock it created was energizing the antisecession base. An ambivalence, if not outright opposition, to secession is also present in the political parties. Ciudadanos, a center-right party that formed in Catalonia in 2006, has transformed the political landscape across Spain and is now the leading opposition party in the Catalan parliament. Meanwhile, prominent political leaders like Ada Colau, the mayor of Barcelona, have maintained a careful neutrality on the issue of independence. This push and pull of politics, and the public debate that accompanies it, are a core feature of democratized secession.

Catalonia is an example of a democratized movement, a kind of secessionist effort that is particularly integrated with the home state. It demonstrates how secessionism plays out in a highly institutionalized setting. Like all the others, its strategy is shaped by the strictures of the international recognition regime, but its tactical options are contextualized by its domestic setting. Here, violence does not appear to be on the menu of tactical options, and perhaps it will remain that way as long as secessionist energy is channeled through the political apparatus of the state. There are costs that come with this kind of movement, including polarization and political deadlock. But are those costs as great as the repression, violence, and state rupture that often occur in other settings? I return to this question in chapter 12 after reviewing the secessionist dynamics in other kinds of movements.

5

MURRAWARRI

Earth, Sky, and Ancestry

We declared that we were always independent from Australia.

—Fred Hooper, chair of the Republic of Murrawarri, interview, June 27, 2018

"I would like to acknowledge the Gadigal of the Eora Nation, the traditional cus-todians of this land and pay my respects to the Elders both past and present."[1] In the Australian lexicon this statement is an Acknowledgement of Country. It pays respect to the Gadigal, a subgroup of the Eora nation, an aboriginal people that inhabited the Sydney area prior to British colonization. I first heard the acknowl-edgment at the opening of a lecture at the University of Sydney and I heard it many times during my employment there. It has become a kind of cultural practice across Australia, to varying degrees, in which different aboriginal nations are paid respect depending on the locale. At more formal events it is common to ask an Elder of the local community to open the ceremony with a Welcome to Country. I invited an Elder on one occasion: a lecture I helped organize at Sydney Univer-sity on human rights abuses in West Papua at the hands of the Indonesian gov-ernment. It seemed fitting to open a lecture concerned with the marginalization of a nation with the comments of a representative of another marginalized nation.

The demands of secessionist movements are grounded in the belief that the relationship between their land and nation takes precedence over the need of the state to maintain its territorial integrity. Typically, secessionist movements argue that they existed on the land prior to the state that now controls them.[2] As we saw with Catalonia, such claims are quite often open to contestation because of the difficulty of identifying nations historically, the boundaries between nations, and the states that had sovereignty over them. But these claims are more robust in the context of European colonization, which is one of the reasons why decolonization in the postwar period has been relatively successful. No one denies that the Australian aboriginals inhabited the continent for thousands of years before the British came. The question is what to do about that inconvenient truth.

This chapter discusses the secessionist efforts of the Murrawarri Republic, a leading example of the indigenous legal secessionist kind. This is a small set of movements that share certain defining characteristics. They occur in highly democratic and institutionalized states. Like democratized movements, their primary compellence tactic is electoral capture—that is, they use the institutional apparatus of the state to seek their ends. But unlike Catalonia and Quebec, they stress a different normative appeal that calls attention to their autochthonous origins. They were there prior to the colonizing power, their subjugation was illegal, and their sovereignty is therefore inherent. Although many secessionist movements adopt the language of subjugation and colonization, the members of the indigenous legal set are united by a similar setting and shared vocabulary. They challenge the original acquisition of their land on legal grounds, and to some extent they succeed because the states in which they reside are not completely deaf to their argument. Their efforts become quite legalistic, perhaps more so than with other types of secessionism. At the moment they occur in settler states like Australia, Canada, and the United States because their origins are clear and because the relatively accommodating legal and institutional structures of those states have an influence on secessionist tactics.

Background

The Murrawarri Republic is a self-declared region in the interior of Australia that straddles the border between the federal states of North South Wales and Queensland (see figure 5.1). According to the republic's website, the total land area is 81,796 square kilometers, roughly the size of Austria.[3] This is a sparsely populated and arid land. The purported capital, Barringun, is literally a one-store town.[4] It is interesting to note that of the different maps used in this book, the Murrawarri Republic was the hardest to draw. Bougainville and New Caledonia are islands, West Papua comprises two delineated Indonesian provinces, and Northern Cyprus is separated from the rest of the island by a clear demilitarized zone. There is no shortage of maps for each of these regions. In contrast, maps of the Murrawarri Republic are rarer and more controversial.[5] It is not recognized as an internal jurisdiction by the Australian government in the same way that Spain recognizes Catalonia.[6] It is only recognized by the Murrawarri and other neighboring aboriginal groups, though interestingly, a partially drawn map of the republic currently exists on Google Maps.[7]

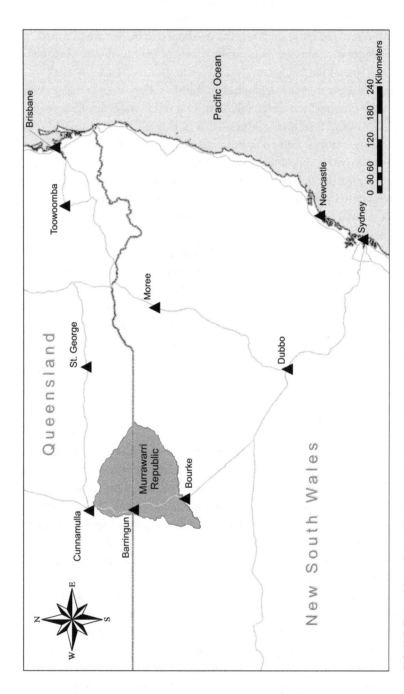

FIGURE 5.1. Map of eastern Australia and the Murrawarri Republic

According to Fred Hooper, the chair of the Murrawarri Republic, the borders of the territory were worked out by talking to elders in the nation and were based on traditional boundaries—rivers, sand ridges, boundary trees—that had been used to demarcate the land of the Murrawarri from other nations.[8] The designated borders overlap two legally recognized federal states, an unusual cartographical feature. Although the map was only recently constructed, it references a region that existed before the Australian map was drawn. It is as though two different images of the world were merged into one.

The Murrawarri people (sometimes spelled Maruwari) are from the Culgoa river region of northern New South Wales and southern Queensland, a part of the Darling River watershed.[9] The name Murrawarri means "to fall (*warri*) with a fighting club (*murru*) in one's hand." The Murrawarri language is a member of the Pama-Nyungan language family, one of the more than 250 aboriginal languages and roughly thirty-one language families of Australia.[10] Fred Hooper claims that the nation consists of about 3,500 people.[11] It is not clear how long the Murrawarri have inhabited the region or even when the concept of the Murrawarri as a people began to take hold. Their history is intertwined with that of other indigenous Australians and that is an entirely oral history (prior to European colonization). It is currently estimated that the early migrants to Australia came between 40,000 and 60,000 years ago. There were as many as a million aboriginals in Australia by the late-1700s but estimates vary widely.[12]

The first British colonization mission to Australia—known now as the First Fleet—landed in Botany Bay on January 1788.[13] It was here that the colonists made their first contact with members of the Eora nation. That contact would ultimately have a transformative and controversial effect on not just the Eora but all of the indigenous peoples across the continent. The gradual removal from coastal territory and introduction of European diseases devastated the population, reducing it to approximately 95,000 in 1901 and some 30,000 in 1930.[14] The Australian aboriginals became a truly marginalized people. They were not even given Australian citizenship until 1967.

The overall trajectory of the colonizer and colonized in Australia is quite similar to other settings around the world, from the Anglo settler states and the countries of Latin America to the French overseas possessions like New Caledonia. In most cases, that trajectory is characterized by an increased attention to indigenous rights, a gathering call for restitution, and a gradual political and cultural mobilization of the native populations. A form of aboriginal cultural nationalism began to take hold in Australia in the 1960s and 1970s and popular culture followed as rock bands like Midnight Oil sang of the historical injustices that aboriginals faced.[15] Since the early 1990s Australians have observed National Aboriginal and Islanders Day Observance Committee (NAIDOC) week, a period each July that celebrates the cultural achievements of native Australians. Not unlike the American debate over the significance of Columbus Day, there is an active wing in Australian society that refers to January 26 not as Australia Day, a national holiday celebrating the landing of the First Fleet, but as Invasion Day. All of this can be seen as a work in progress as Australian society reinterprets its past.

The Development of Secessionism

The Murrawarri flag, created in 2013, is divided into two horizontal stripes (see figure 5.2). The bottom brown stripe represents the earth. It is notable that unlike the Kanaks and Bougainvilleans who chose green to represent the earth on their flags, the Murrawarri associate the earth with the color brown. Having been to all three places, I can say that in each case the color fits the landscape. The upper blue stripe represents "the sky where Murrawarri spirits wait until their return on the falling star, water and the people."[16] The white eight pointed star near the hoist in the upper left corner of the flag symbolizes "the return of the Ancestors spirits on which they return to earth and the eight points on the star represents [sic] the eight clan groups of the Murrawarri Nation and the future provinces that will make up the Murrawarri Republic." In sum, the flag combines geographic

FIGURE 5.2. The Murrawarri independence flag

features—the earth and sky—with a representation of ancestry and politics—an eight-pointed star. The designer, Kylie Gibbon, reports that the idea for the flag came to her as she watched the sun set over the land.[17]

How did this secessionist movement develop and how can it be understood as an example of the indigenous legal kind? For a quick answer, it is useful to visit the splash page for the website of the Murrawarri republic, which says the following:

> The Murrawarri Nation is an old and ancient Nation situated on the continent of Australia. Australia was made up of over 500 different Independent Nations before Capitan Cook placed the British flag on the continent in 1770 and claim to the 150th parallel on behalf of the King of Great Britain under the principle of *Terra Nullius*. The Murrawarri Nation was one of those Nations with our own laws and culture and a governance system to manage our country in harmony with Mother Earth and nature and the environment. Because the High Court overturned the principle of *Terra Nullius* the Murrawarri Nation remains free and independent and ultimate title remains with the Murrawarri peoples and the Murrawarri Nation.[18]

The thrust of the Murrawarri argument for independence is that their land was brought under British control in an illegal manner, a fact that has since been recognized by Australian legal authorities. If they were never properly brought into the state in the first place, then they were never properly part of the state in the years that followed. As Hooper stated in a 2017 interview, in reference to the March 30, 2013 declaration of independence: "we didn't declare independence from Australia. We declared that we were always independent from Australia."[19]

A central component in the Murrawarri argument, and the indigenous legal argument more broadly, focuses on the concept of *terra nullius*. With origins in Roman law, *terra nullius* translates roughly to "nobody's land." James Crawford notes the importance of the concept in traditional law where the acquisition of land is concerned, writing: "Where territory was already occupied or acquitted, cession and conquest became the appropriate modes of acquisition."[20] However, if the land was empty, then it could be claimed without cession or conquest, which are formal processes requiring an interlocutor. *Terra nullius* was utilized primarily during the period of European colonization for reasons that make sense in the context of the times. These were expansive states, competing for territory, and they needed to develop legal guidelines for how territory could be acquired. A state could declare war and conquer the land, or it could acquire it by formal treaty. But where land was empty, as some land surely was, it could be acquired by simple occupation and declaration of title.[21]

The problem was that "emptiness" was to some extent in the eye of the beholder. Crawford flags this problem quite clearly when he states: "The category *terra nullius* was not self-defining nor did practice bear out the positivist assumption that territory was either *terra nullius* or part of an existing state. The category *terra nullius* was a residual one . . . [determining] the level of habitation and political organization was not easy, and it was decided by a small set of European states who possessed bias and incentives to seize land." In numerous cases the concept *terra nullius* was used implicitly or explicitly to claim land where there were inhabitants who were deemed inferior, sparsely settled, and/or insufficiently organized to negotiate as a state.[22] Although the land was not empty, it was sufficiently empty by the standards of the European powers, the ones who decided. This approach can form the legal foundation for territorial acquisition as long as the key parties agree. But what happens when the consensus on the "emptiness" question changes?

Determining that *terra nullius* was incorrectly applied requires two enabling conditions. First, as Crawford says, there is a threshold condition: Can we identify the indigenous people and differentiate them from other populations?[23] This is difficult to do in many, if not most, places because the world map is built upon millennia of human migration, intermixing, and forced removal. German-speaking people are apparently the indigenous inhabitants of Germany, but of course their ancestors both displaced and merged with other prior groups and the borders of the state have been moved overtime. Who is to say that the ancestors of the Eora nation did not violently displace a different people who previously inhabited the coastal region of modern-day Sydney? However, this threshold question is more easily and confidently answered in the context of colonization—there is a clearer breakpoint and the two populations are more easily differentiated. The second condition is that you have a government that is willing to listen, to acknowledge the unfortunate beginnings, even if it shows no sign of rolling back its territorial claims. Both of these conditions are satisfied in the relationship between Australia and its aboriginal nations.

To understand how the somewhat archaic concept of *terra nullius* became a core argument of contemporary Australian secessionist movements, it is necessary to review legal developments in the past few decades between aboriginals and the state. Consonant with the rise of aboriginal nationalism was an increased willingness to fight for land rights, or what is called native title. In the 1971 Gove Land Rights Case, an Australian court acknowledged, for the first time, a preexisting form of aboriginal law but ruled that it was insufficient to grant native title.[24] Although the decision did not invoke the term *terra nullius*, it got at it indirectly by raising the issue of prior and sufficient habitation. The watershed moment came twenty years later with the 1992 *Mabo v Queensland (No. 2)* judgment, now known colloquially as *Mabo*.[25] Here, the Australian High Court ruled that *terra nullius* did not apply where inhabitants were present and, as such, the Meriam people, led by claimants Eddie Mabo, David Passi, and James Rice, had native title to their lands.[26] This decision set a precedent for native title and thrust the relatively obscure concept of *terra nullius* "into Australian consciousness."[27]

Mabo has had far-reaching effects that are still playing out. The Native Title Act of 1993 formalized the recognition of native land ownership by legislation, and it was one element of a much larger legal, academic, and social debate about Australia's history. There were of course two sides to this debate—and beneath it all lay a concern over how far it would go—but the center of gravity had shifted in the direction of reconciliation. As Reynolds put it: "*Terra nullius* was out of step with international standards of human rights—it is inherently discriminatory."[28] This was given a public voice when the conservative prime minister John Howard stated: "We recognize that this land and its waters were settled as colonies without treaty or consent."[29] Although the preceding legal decisions, legislative rulings, and public statements were directed primarily at the issue of property, it was perhaps only a matter of time before claimants pushed the matter an additional step to focus on sovereignty.

The Murrawarri Republic declared independence on March 30, 2013.[30] Hooper stated in a personal interview that the Native Title Act was a token gesture that had not gone far enough.[31] For example, it did not give local nations sufficient bargaining power when negotiating with mining companies. In a different interview, Hooper stated that the Native Title Act was "unjust and unfair legislation" because it limited the ability of aboriginal nations to conduct affairs on their land.[32] But *Mabo* had "overturned the fiction of *terra nullius*," which meant that the Murrawarri had never been a part of Australia. What "needs to be established is a framework of treaties between the government and each of the continent's indigenous nations." The restoration of sovereignty, in practice, would give the Murrawarri and other nations true control over their land.

An interesting aspect of indigenous legal movements it that they are highly networked.[33] According to Gabriele Abbondanza, "27 nations have already requested template documents based on papers released by the Murrawarri's Council."[34] The Euahlayi nation, a neighbor to the Murrawarri, declared independence on July 1, 2013.[35] Similarly, the Wiradjuri Central West Republic declared independence on January 22, 2014.[36] These groups are closely connected through associations like the Sovereign Union, they observe and learn from one another, and they share a common vocabulary. Although the connections are stronger at the domestic level, parallels are commonly drawn with indigenous movements in other similar societies like Canada, New Zealand, the United States, and even Sweden.[37]

Strategy and Tactics

In strategic terms, the indigenous legal type is no different from the other groups studied in this book. They are playing the same game and to win it they need to convince their home state to remove the veto or else gather sufficient international support. However, there is a clear tactical signature to these movements that is quite similar to the democratized type insofar as they utilize the institutions of the state. The key difference pertains to normative appeal; their primary pitch focuses on inherent sovereignty.

The compellence tactics of the Murrawarri Republic are thus far institutional in nature. Like other institutionalized movements, they use the political apparatus in their region—in this case the local aboriginal council. Hooper stated in an interview that they will proceed to build an independent state through normal channels.[38] Not unlike Catalonia, the Murrawarri intend to build a state by writing a constitution, forming a parliament, and laying the essential groundwork for a working government. All of these moves are catalogued on the republic's website.[39]

Meanwhile, extra-institutional methods are not being used. When asked about violent methods, Hooper replied that they are dedicated to nonviolence and that "we have law on our side."[40] When asked about forms of nonviolent civil resistance, he replied that they had considered trying to block bridges and basic access to the land but determined that it was too confrontational and that much of Australia would see that behavior in a negative light. It would be bad publicity. Likewise, he said that they still pay their Australian taxes because proper conduct is an element of the positive picture they want to portray. In a similar vein, Ghillar Michael Anderson, a leader of the neighboring Euahlayi secessionist movement, stated: "Our people are mature and intelligent. . . . We're not picking up guns or throwing Molotov cocktails. We've studied our conqueror's laws, proven how they've broken them and are now turning those laws against them. We will force an issue the Australian government does not want to debate."[41]

It is in the realm of normative appeals that the Murrawarri Republic is different from democratized movements, for its core appeal is presented using the language of inherent sovereignty. This is clear from a visit to its website and in interviews with its personnel, and it has also been communicated in its outreach efforts. Interestingly, the Murrawarri sent their declaration of independence to the Queen of England shortly after it was announced. Their reasoning was that as the monarch of the country that improperly applied *terra nullius*, the Queen owed them an answer.[42] Eventually, they did receive a letter from the Queen's Office addressed to "The Chair of the People's Council of the Murrawarri Republic," stating that the matter would have to be referred to Australian authorities.[43]

Similarly, they wrote to the governor-general of Australia, who replied that they cannot get involved in this matter as it is outside of their competency. Their outreach campaign also includes a letter to the UN about the possibility of getting on the list of Non-Self Governing Territories. At the time of this writing, they had not received a response.

All of this raises a strategic question that sits at the heart of this book: How will these efforts elicit the desired response from the state? As we saw in the previous chapter, the Spanish government eventually cracked down on the Catalan secessionists. But in this case, the Australian government has not responded to the Murrawarri declaration of independence.[44] Perhaps, unlike Spain, Australia can afford to ignore the problem given the relatively low profile of the Murrawarri movement. Indeed, one striking and potentially problematic aspect of the Murrawarri Republic is its near invisibility. Many (certainly everyone in Spain) know about the Catalan independence movement. Its flag decorates countless balconies in Barcelona and its leaders are regularly on the air. In contrast, very few people have heard of the Murrawarri Republic and Australian academics and friends were often surprised when I told them. When I drove through the republic I met an older Australian couple at a roadside stop on the border just north of Barringun. They were traveling in their caravan. When I mentioned Murrawarri and pointed to the capital of Barringun, they showed surprise and said that they had never heard of the movement. There were no signs on the road that referenced the republic and its flag was nowhere to be seen. On the southern edge of the republic along the Darling River is the historic frontier town of Bourke. Among other things it possesses an excellent history museum, the Back O' Bourke Exhibition Centre, that showcases the rich history of Australian settlement. But aboriginals received little mention in the museum. They and the Murrawarri Republic seem like ghosts in that country, old and new.

There are two complementary ways in which the Murrawarri aim to force a response from the Australian government. The first is to use institutional methods to build their political apparatus, develop networks, and increase their visibility. In addition to the outreach efforts listed above, the Murrawarri Republic has signed a treaty with twenty-two other aboriginal nations and is seeking to create interaboriginal trade agreements.[45] Hooper cited the Montevideo Convention criteria (see chapter 2) and said that the republic is following the core precepts and is gradually being dealt with as a nation. The second approach is to build on *Mabo* and pursue the normative argument of inherent sovereignty via legal channels. Through a combination of compellence and persuasion, the state should eventually negotiate.

The Murrawarri secessionist effort has given way to an interesting legal debate. At the center of that debate is whether the victory represented by *Mabo* can be extended from the issue of land to the issue of sovereignty. Thus far, the Australian government has put a wedge between the two issues. As Henry Reynolds writes, although the state "demolished the concept of *terra nullius* in respect to property, it preserved it in relation to sovereignty."[46] The position of the Australian government has been that sovereignty issues cannot be negotiated. For instance, Prime Minister John Howard said: "Countries don't make treaties with themselves, they make treaties with other nations and the very notion of a treaty in this context conjures up the idea that we are two separate nations."[47] This concern was well put by George Newhouse, a well-known human rights lawyer who works on aboriginal issues: "Although I recognize this country has largely failed to acknowledge the role that English colonizers played in Aboriginal dispossession, I am not sure the Declaration of the Continuance of the State of Murrawarri Nation has any meaning in law."[48] In essence, negotiating a treaty is a matter of international not domestic law.

Critics have characterized this position as skirting the issue.[49] By saying that it is beyond the ambit of domestic law, the Australian government is hiding behind "what is known as the act of state doctrine."[50] But a set of scholars and legal authorities have challenged the position that nothing can be done to ameliorate the false foundations of Australian legal ownership of the land.[51] There are ways forward, where the will exists, and indeed one can look to other Anglo-settler countries for examples. Sean Brennan, Brenda Gunn, and George Williams compared the position of Australia with respect to its indigenous peoples with that of Canada, the US, and New Zealand, and concluded that Australia is the most behind. Canada, in particular, has made substantial strides in recent years. In the 1970s it recognized the "capacity of its Indigenous peoples to enter into modern day treaties with its national and provincial governments."[52] Although the Australian High Court may be predisposed to thinking that treaties with domestic nations is beyond their competency, it is not intrinsically so. The success of the inherent sovereignty argument, and the transition from the principle undergirding *Mabo* from a focus on land to one on sovereignty, depends on not just a legal analysis but also political and public will.

One can see from this discussion that the success of the Murrawarri Republic, and the indigenous legal type more generally, depends on the participation of the state. Relative to the other secessionist kinds, perhaps even more than democratized movements, movements like the Murrawarri need to work with the state to achieve their goal. They need to generate sympathy in the domestic population and persuade key actors to take up the issue on legal grounds. It is hard to imagine that success would come from these efforts in more autocratic societies. But even in Australia this will be a hard-fought, somewhat experimental effort. And it may ultimately fail if the Australian High Court, backed by Australian so-

ciety, determines that the permission of independence invites the complete un-
raveling of the state. In an interview, Fred Hooper recognized the challenge ahead
of them and stated that they will push for as much sovereignty as they can.[53]

The Murrawarri Republic is perhaps an unusual addition to this book. It is certainly the least well known of the case studies. But it is an important addition
because it demonstrates a particular configuration of factors. I have described the
six secessionist kinds as clusters of characteristics that I liken to peaks on a topographical map, where the map itself can be thought of as the strategic playing field.
The peak representing indigenous legal movements is quite close to its better-
known high institutional sibling, the democratized movement. They share the
same tactic of compellence, which is to use the institutions of the state. But their
appeal to inherent sovereignty is unique, similar in form to decolonization, a kind
of decolonization part II. While it is unclear that such movements will win their
independence anytime soon, they are out there, and they are gradually being listened to.

6

WEST PAPUA
The Morning Star

> **Member of Independence movement: "How does France respond when the FLNKS holds a congress?"**
>
> **Member of FLNKS: "France doesn't stop it. We're free. They may monitor our activities but they do not attempt to shut us down."**
>
> **Member of Independence movement: "The French Government is very kind."**

West Papua is an example of the weak combative type of secession movement, and it demonstrates what can happen to secessionism in weakly institutionalized settings.[1] It is the location of an independence movement that has existed since the early 1960s, oscillating between tactics of insurgency and civil resistance that are aimed at the home state, Indonesia. Like the other movements discussed in this book, the West Papuan secessionists pitch their cause internationally, citing human rights abuses as well as the freedom to choose and principle of decolonization. But its tactical setting is unlike the other movements. It is integrated with the larger state and yet cannot engage in electoral capture. Unlike Bougainville, it faces a powerful military opponent whom it cannot dislodge from the territory nor fight to a standstill. It is relegated to a peripheral status, diplomatically isolated, where the prospects can seem hopeless.

The Lonely Planet Guidebook refers to West Papua as Indonesia's final frontier.[2] This is an apt characterization because it does indeed have the features of a frontier. It is a vast territory (420,540 square kilometers), roughly the size of California, consisting of mostly unspoilt wilderness and a relatively sparse population of 4.3 million people. Its central cordillera includes a glacier, despite its equatorial location, and its chief peak, Puncak Jaya (4884 meters), is regarded as one of the Seven Summits, and the highest mountain between the Himalayas and the Andes. Flying to West Papua requires a domestic flight from one of the core Indonesian islands of Bali, Java, or Sulawesi. On such flights it is common to see contractors who work for mining and logging companies.[3] The region has the appearance of a police state, at least in the urban zones and/or economically vital locales and, as a visitor, I was struck by the bewildering array of police, military, and paramilitary bases. Not unlike the Native Americans of the nineteenth-century American frontier, the West Papuans are gradually becoming a minority in the face of migration of ethnically dissimilar groups from Java, Madura, and Bali. Like the Native Americans, many West Papuans feel marginalized, suppressed, and the victims of racism.[4]

Background

West Papua is the colloquial name given to the western half of the island of New Guinea—the eastern half being the sovereign state of Papua New Guinea (see figure 6.1). I adopt this usage in the book because it is consistent with the meaning used by those seeking independence. The name Papua references the indigenous inhabitants, the Papuans. Somewhat confusingly, West Papua is also the formal name for one of the two Indonesian provinces of the region of West Papua; the other province is simply Papua. The province of West Papua was divided (and created) from the province of Papua in 2003. Prior to that the region was called Irian Barat (West Irian) and later Irian Jaya. The Indonesian word *Jaya* means "victorious" or "glorious," and Irian is an acronym that stands for Ikut Republik Indonesia Anti Nederland (Join the Republic of Indonesia against the Netherlands).[5] Clearly, the name Irian Jaya has revolutionary overtones—it replaced the former colonial title of Dutch New Guinea—and the transition in name from Irian Jaya to Papua and West Papua tracks the evolution of the Indonesian state from revolution to attempts at inclusiveness.

However, referring to the region by just one name may obscure its rich cultural complexity. West Papua—and the island of New Guinea more broadly—is, by any measure, an extraordinarily diverse place. I have seen various estimates of the linguistic diversity, from as few as 200 languages to 1,000 languages divided over thirty language families.[6] Indeed, several sources claim that it has the highest linguistic diversity of any region in the world.[7] Many of the languages are mutually unintelligible, and the groups that speak them are often small in number and live in remote locations.

Like Bougainville, the territorial unit of West Papua is the product of colonialism and the expansion of the state system. The name New Guinea is a colonial artifact that was given by the Spanish in the 1500s, who saw a similarity in appearance between the indigenous peoples there and the people of the Gulf of Guinea region in West Africa. Likewise, the border separating West Papua (and Indonesia for that matter) from Papua New Guinea is set along the 141st meridian, another example of the imperial application of Cartesian thinking to territory

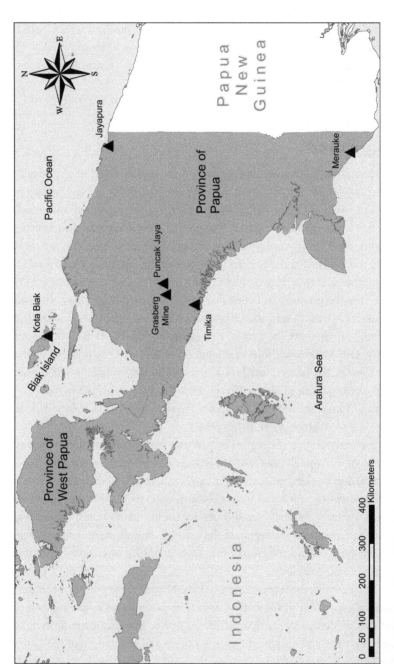

FIGURE 6.1. Map of West Papua

that was largely unknown and unexplored.[8] Indeed, it was not until the 1930s that a trans-island flight revealed that the interior highlands were densely populated by heretofore uncontacted cultures.

The western half of the island became a Dutch colonial possession, Dutch New Guinea, formally a part of the Dutch East Indies. Under a normal application of the principle of *uti possidetis juris*, West Papua would have remained part of Indonesia when it gained independence in 1949. However, the Dutch had in a somewhat informal sense governed West Papua as a separate territory.[9] For this reason, and the fact that the West Papuans did not want to become independent as a part of Indonesia, the Dutch retained the territory until 1963. During these fourteen years, the Dutch East Indies was a standalone colony, one that was on the United Nations (UN) list of Non-Self-Governing Territories. From the West Papuan perspective, it was a colony and had a right to independence given the rules regarding decolonization. But from the Indonesian perspective, West Papua was a traditional part of Indonesia, a part that should never have been sundered in the first place. In the Indonesian national imaginings, according to Benedict Anderson, the folklore of the anticolonial struggle relied on a map stretching from the western tip of Sumatra to the eastern edge of West Papua, a region that few nationalists ever visited but one that all included in the concept of Indonesia.[10]

West Papua was thus a casualty of decolonization, and eventually the Cold War. Its future was a divisive issue on the international agenda from 1949 to 1962, one that was debated in the United Nations. The Indonesian claim to the region was supported by most of the new African and Asian states, the Soviet bloc, and less than half of Latin America. The Dutch side, and latterly the West Papuan claim, was supported by Western states, many of which still retained colonies.[11] The resulting gridlock supported the status quo and, eventually, the Dutch created a West Papuan legislature and began laying the groundwork for independence.[12] West Papua declared independence on December 1, 1961, and within weeks the Indonesian state responded with an attempted invasion, Operation Trikora. Although the Dutch successfully repulsed the invasion, the Indonesians won on the diplomatic front. Indonesian president Sukarno's courting of Soviet support pressured the Americans and Australians to find a solution to the problem that would not alienate Indonesia and risk losing it to Soviet influence. The outcome was the New York Agreement, signed by all sides, which placed West Papua under UN control, administered by Indonesia, with the understanding that the West Papuans would be able to determine and decide their own future.[13]

The next chapter in the saga would serve alongside the 1961 Indonesian invasion and the betrayal of the New York Agreement as a founding narrative in the West Papuan independence struggle.[14] This was the Act of Free Choice (Penentuan Pendapat Rakyat, PEPERA), a plebiscite on West Papuan self-determination

that was held in 1969 in accordance with the New York Agreement. In a cautionary tale on the dangers of referendums, particularly when viewed by one side as
rigged and illegitimate, 1,025 individuals voted unanimously to join Indonesia.
Because of the difficulties in staging a referendum across a vast, multiethnic, and
rather inaccessible territory, these representatives (less than 1 percent) were chosen to stand for the broader population. Inevitably, such a method would invite
biases. Who is available to vote and are they disproportionately urban? How were
they chosen? In this case, the Indonesian authorities handpicked the voters, which
opened the process to substantial criticism. Although the UN-endorsed referendum brought West Papua formally under Indonesian sovereignty, the West Papuans call it the Act of No Choice.[15] Collectively, these events constitute the historical
and conceptual bedrock of the independence struggle.

The Development of Secessionism

The Morning Star flag is the primary symbol of independence. It was first raised
on December 1, 1961, the occasion on which the West Papuans first declared independence.[16] Not unlike the Bougainvillean flag, the Morning Star is a relatively
recent design that was created in the months preceding the declaration. The creator, Nicolaas Jouwe, was one of the early leaders of West Papua, a man who went
into exile in the Netherlands after the 1963 Indonesian takeover. Although he
vowed to never return so long as Indonesian occupation continued, he returned
in 2010 to live out his remaining years.

The flag consists of a wide vertical red stripe at the hoist, a five-pointed white
star set in the middle of the vertical red stripe, and thirteen horizontal alternating blue and white stripes (seven blue and six white) set to the right of the vertical stripe (see figure 6.2). According to one website, the thirteen stripes symbolized
the thirteen planned provinces of West Papua.[17] The color blue represents faith,
white signifies peace, and red denotes courage. However, the star is arguably the
key symbol on the flag. It references the story (or myth) of Manarmakeri, a
messiah-like figure who, according to legend, left West Papua in search of enlight-
enment, embodied in the figure of a person named Kumeseri, also known as the
Morning Star.[18] The legend holds that Manarmakeri will eventually return one
day and bring change.[19] Although the details of the myth vary somewhat, the larger
implication is clear. This is a story of hope and transformation to come, a fitting
and rather stirring message for an independence movement.

The Morning Star is considered illegal by the Indonesian authorities because
it is seen as advocating for independence. In sharp contrast to Barcelona where

FIGURE 6.2. The Morning Star flag

the *Estelada* and *Senyera* are ubiquitous, one has to look hard to find the Morning Star in West Papua. I saw it once at a small market where a vendor was selling handmade bags and purses, and one of the purse designs depicted the Morning Star. I asked a local friend if the vendor would be arrested, and they replied that the West Papuans push the envelope in small, subtle ways such as this—after all, it was a purse not a flag—and that such acts constitute everyday forms of resistance.[20]

The West Papuan movement is, like Bougainville and rather unlike Catalonia or Northern Cyprus, built across a tremendously heterogeneous population. Many of the people claimed by the secessionist movement speak mutually incomprehensible languages. It is one of the many ironies of colonialism and decolonization that they are grouped together—indeed brought together—by the colonial experience. The nation they imagine is the product of that collective experience, one that is typically imagined in Bahasa Indonesian, a non-native language brought to them by the Dutch.

The history of the movement is reminiscent of the other secessionist movements studied in this book. It is full of acronyms, of political and military wings, of groups dividing and recombining over time. The original parent group is the Free Papua Movement (Organisasi Papua Merdeka, OPM), founded in 1965.[21] Loosely included under the umbrella of the OPM are territorially based and often autonomous militant bands, civil resistance groups, and exiled leaders living abroad. In addition, the movement has been bolstered in recent decades by "a plethora of church and NGO-based groups established with a view to seeking independence."[22] The West Papua National Coalition for Liberation (WPNCL) was formed in 2005 from a merger of many such groups. However, the current umbrella organization for the independence struggle is the United Liberation Movement for West Papua (ULMWP), formed in December 2014 with headquarters in Port Vila, Vanuatu.[23]

This is a secessionist struggle with a history of violence. Jason MacLeod writes that the estimated death toll for the 1963–2014 period is approximately 100,000, but notes that the estimates vary widely.[24] Secessionist leaders like Benny Wenda and Jacob Rumbiak put the figure much higher, at about 500,000. Meanwhile, estimates by the Indonesian state are as low as 1,000 during this period. The Uppsala Conflict Data Program (UCDP) documented periods of battle-related violence that stretch across the entire period (see table 6.1), with a noticeable spike in the late 1970s. In addition to the violence, there are reports (disputed by the Indonesian state) of policies of detention, torture, and general tactics of intimidation,[25] as well as the encouragement of pro-Indonesian militias among the immigrant populations in West Papua.[26]

One cause of concern for the West Papuans is the feeling that they are becoming increasingly marginalized on their own land. A chief driver of this process is the Indonesian transmigration program, an attempt by the state to relocate people (often poorer) from densely populated Java and Madura to the less populated and less developed outer islands, such as Sumatra, Sulawesi, and West Papua. Although exact figures are hard to come by, it is estimated that some twenty million Indo-

TABLE 6.1. Conflict data for West Papua, 1946–2016

YEAR	INTENSITY LEVEL[a]
1965	1
1967	1
1968	1
1969	1
1976	2
1977	2
1978	2
1981	2
1984	1

Source: Uppsala Conflict Data Program.
Note: Years with fewer than twenty-five battle deaths are omitted.
[a] 1 = 25–999 battle-related deaths; 2 = 1000+ battle-related deaths[27]

nesians have been relocated in this way. This has dramatically altered the population balance in West Papua. Non-Papuans accounted for approximately 4 percent
of the population in 1971 and 32 percent of the population in 2000.[28] Jim Elmslie
estimates that non-Papuans were a majority by 2010 and would account for
71 percent of the population by 2020.[29] Whether or not this represents an attempt
by the state to transform the ethnic composition of the region, instead of simply
transferring populations to less populous provinces, the native reaction is not
hard to anticipate: they will see this as a form of imperialism that alienates them
from their land.[30]

Some observers of the state of affairs in West Papua have called it "slow-motion
genocide."[31] In addition to the demographic trends, the West Papuans feel marginalized from the economy and relative prosperity that non-Papuans enjoy. West
Papuans are disproportionately poorer and have higher rates of incarceration and
alcoholism. The ethnic, linguistic, and religious differences combine with stereotypes of West Papuan backwardness to perpetuate forms of racism.[32] Not unlike
the marginalized indigenous groups of Australia and the United States, there is a
seeming intractability to the divide that gives rise to despair.

While tragic, the local tensions and related violence are all too common where
the aspirations of an independence movement clash with the desire of the state
to maintain its territorial integrity.[33] Much has been written on the natural resources and potential income that West Papua represents. The Grasberg Mine in
the heart of the territory is a tremendously lucrative project, accounting for some
US$12.1 billion in payments to the state between 1992 and March 2011.[34] But
more generally, Indonesia is a fissiparous state that needs to hold together. It
has faced secessionist movements in Maluku (in 1950), East Timor from 1975 to
2002, and Aceh since 1976.[35] As Barbara Walter documents, the language of the
state regularly evokes the dangers of precedent setting and the need to deter
secessionists.[36]

Although presidents Sukarno and Suharto took a hard line on secession, B. J.
Habibie initially took a more conciliatory position when he came to power in
1998. He permitted a change in name from Irian Jaya to West Papua and he even
briefly allowed the Morning Star to be flown in Jayapura (albeit below the Indonesian flag). Moreover, he permitted East Timor to secede. But reactions to his
policies from the more nationalist elements of the Indonesian state forced him
to harden his position and eventually forced him out of office. "In February 1999,
three weeks after Habibie's concessions to the East Timorese, John Ondawame,
international spokesman for the Free Papua Movement, told reporters 'we would
like to see the Indonesian government's new policy towards East Timor be re-
peated again in West Papua.'"[37] Similarly, the Acehnese secessionists requested a
referendum like East Timor. These demands raised concerns about domino effects

and the danger that Indonesia was "falling apart." In January 2000, Abdurrahman Wahid, Habibie's successor, warned that there should be no efforts toward
independence in West Papua or Aceh.[38]

One of the key historical events in recent times is referred to as the Papuan
Spring—the transition to democracy that began in 1998 following the fall of President Suharto and the accession of Habibie. It was in this period that East Timor
finally gained independence and, at least initially, there were signs that Indonesian society was opening up. However, concerns over too much autonomy, freedom, and indeed fragmentation led to a conservative backlash. The tragic events
in Biak City in July 1998 dashed West Papuan hopes.[39] On July 1 the Morning
Star was raised on a water tower in the city and demonstrators camped beneath
the tower for six days before being dispersed violently by the Indonesian military. Some estimates put the resulting death toll at 200 and there are haunting
stories of abuse and torture that took place in the weeks that followed.[40]

One interesting feature of the tactical setting is the fact that Indonesia is a democracy, and has been since 1999. Although its democratic credentials are questionable in some areas, it has counted as a weakly consolidated democracy in the
relevant indices.[41] Nevertheless, the West Papuans lack the political voice that
the Catalans or Kanaks possess. Flying the Morning Star flag is illegal and
independence-focused demonstrations are routinely broken up by the police or
military. Moreover, they cannot form a viable West Papuan nationalist political
party like Esquerra in Catalonia or FLNKS is New Caledonia. This is because of
the electoral design of the political system that aimed, among other things, to create centripetal pressures and prevent the rise of regional parties.[42] To compete, a
party must open a chapter: (1) in all provinces of Indonesia; (2) in no less than
75 percent of all regencies or municipalities; (3) in no less than 50 percent of all
districts in each of the regencies or municipalities. Essentially, the system favors
large multinational parties and crowds out small regionalist parties. The West Papuans cannot currently engage in electoral capture like their counterparts in more
democratic countries.[43]

In sum, the secessionist movement in West Papua fits the weak combative
model. Except in remote regions of the interior, the secessionists do not possess
de facto control over their territory like the Northern Cypriots. Despite the transition to democracy, key features related to electoral politics and freedom of speech
prevent the secessionist movement from attaining the level of political voice that
one normally finds in a democratized setting. Finally, Indonesia is clearly a strong
state with substantial military and paramilitary forces. As I document below, the
tactics of the secessionists have evolved in relation to their inability to challenge
the state militarily.

Strategy and Tactics

At the strategic level, the West Papuan independence effort is like all other secessionist movements. Its primary opponent and obstacle to independence is the
state. Its strategic behavior takes the dual approach that we have seen elsewhere.
First, it is aimed at getting the Indonesian government to remove the home-state
veto. Second, it aims to bring in the international community to apply pressure
on Indonesia and potentially circumvent its wishes completely by recognizing
West Papuan independence. It is at the tactical level that we can differentiate West
Papua from the other movements in this book.

In terms of compellence, the West Papuan secessionists have gradually evolved
over the course of sixty years from a largely insurgency-based movement to one
that increasingly stresses tactics of nonviolent civil resistance.[44] In a personal interview, one of the independence leaders told me that the movement is in a tran-
sitional phase. Whereas the earlier leadership was often wedded to violent
methods, the newer and younger leaders and participants were generally more
urbanized, more technologically savvy, and less convinced that violence would
work. A number of prominent West Papuan organizations have publicly declared
their commitment to nonviolent methods.[45]

A set of other factors helps explain the transition from violent to nonviolent
methods. One is a realization that the Indonesian state was too strong to fight
militarily. The conflict was too asymmetric and West Papua lacked an outside
sponsor that could provide military aid.[46] According to Octovianus Mote, vice
chair of the ULMWP, a military struggle is not rational because the Indonesian
forces are too powerful.[47] A second factor is the realization that nonviolent methods shifted the movement's center of gravity from a rural project consisting predominantly of men to a more broad-based urban enterprise. The use of violent
methods narrowed the movement and, indeed, it worked at cross-purposes with
other efforts regarding diplomacy and nonviolent civil resistance. According to
Mote, violent methods can be counterproductive because they create bad press
and play into the hands of the hardliners in the Indonesian government.[48]

An interesting aspect of the West Papuan movement is how much it has begun to imbibe the discourse on nonviolent civil resistance. This is an area where
secessionists are particularly influenced by activists, academics, and recent books
like *Why Civil Resistance Works: The Strategic Logic of Nonviolent Conflict*.[49] One
prominent analysis and strategic proposal for West Papua makes the case for why
nonviolence is the better compellence tactic.[50] It forces a dilemma on the state
between choosing suppression, which galvanizes, and permission, which enables.[51]
It strengthens the movement by increasing participation, diversity, unity, and

tactical ability.[52] Nongovernmental organizations like Pasifika are working with the movement's leadership to train local participants in the language and methods of nonviolent civil resistance.

In 2018 I had the opportunity to attend a strategic planning and development workshop for the independence movement. The workshop consisted of roughly twenty-five participants, two organizers, and several international guests like myself. The participants were brought in from all over West Papua and Indonesia. They included former insurgents and political prisoners, several pastors, and a seminarian. A few men and women were wanted by the authorities and were now "underground." Roughly half of the participants had been beaten by the police at one time or another, several claimed to have been tortured, and they all seemed to know people who had been killed by the police, military, or paramilitary forces. The workshop was sponsored by the ULMWP and its purpose was to help organize secessionist leadership, build unity, promote nonviolent methods, and develop a comprehensive strategy for obtaining independence.

Secessionist tactics are shaped by the setting. The Northern Cypriots and Abkhazians possess their own independent, albeit unrecognized state and, for them, life is not so different from state-possessing nations elsewhere. The Catalans and the Scots have fully democratized movements and their resulting political efforts bear a likeness to other forms of formalized political contestation. However, state suppression transforms a secessionist movement in a different way: it makes it a resistance struggle. The workshop I attended was clandestine, and the participants (especially the West Papuans) took great risks in attending. I was advised to not carry any secession-related documents, academic books, and computer files, when traveling to the workshop. The event was housed in a cloistered location, secure with lookouts, and the participants were given a set of backup plans and related alibis to adopt in the event of a police raid. On the one occasion when I ventured outside the venue to purchase gifts, I attracted police attention as a Westerner at a market for West Papuans and my handlers advised me to leave immediately lest the police begin to ask questions. Whereas the Iraqi Kurds can meet in a public venue in Erbil, attended by the media, and discuss their independence drive, the West Papuans have to meet in secret, risking arrest or worse.

At close range I have found all secessionist movements to be inspirational. There is always a sense of hope, enthusiasm for the mission, and a poignant celebration of national identity and culture. But secessionist movements in the form of resistance struggles are truly stirring, and I was unprepared for the level of camaraderie and devotion I found when attending the workshop. The participants would begin each session by joining hands and singing spirituals. They engaged in highly emotional unity-building exercises and forms of ritual. For example, in one exercise they formed a circle, joined hands, closed their eyes, and took turns calling the names of those who have inspired them, alive or dead. With each calling the group would murmur "present" (hadir in Bahasa Indonesian). When the circle was complete, the leader asked "for how long are they with us?" (Untuk berapa lama mereka hadir dengan kita?), and they responded: "For always, for always, for always" (Untuk selamanya, untuk selamanya, untuk selamanya). I was told that this was a way to invite the larger community (the living and the dead) to bear witness to their struggle, and that the practice was borrowed from past Latin American resistance movements.

That event was one of many training workshops that are held periodically in West Papua, in other parts of Indonesia, and abroad. The frequency of these events has increased in recent years as the leadership has gradually come to stress tactics of nonviolence and civil resistance, and has become connected to outside agents and organizations that are willing to assist. In a personal interview with one independence leader, I asked if similar training events were held for the militant wings of the independence effort in West Papua.[53] The answer was no, and the primary reason was that there was no outside organization that was available and willing to train the secessionists in violent tactics. There is no neighboring state or international organization willing to arm the West Papuan independence personnel. There is no modern-day Che Guevara who can sneak into the territory with weaponry, combatants, and the backing of a sympathetic foreign government. In that sense, West Papua is truly on its own. But that is, of course, one of the reasons that it is a weak combative movement; it lacks the local capability and/ or external support to challenge the state militarily on terms that approach symmetry. Nonviolent resistance is a powerful tool, but it is the weapon of the weak.

The tactic of electoral capture was sometimes mentioned in conversations I had with secessionist leaders. Some interviewees felt that this approach was unlikely to pay off given the electoral rules of Indonesia that favor large country-wide parties and exclude small regional parties. In addition, the individuals I interviewed did not have sufficient trust in Indonesian democracy to think that an electoral path à la Catalonia would be open to them.[54] I pointed out that Aceh had won a local autonomy arrangement that permitted a regional party,[55] but respondents felt that such rights gave too little and were, in any case, not something that the Indonesian state was likely to repeat with West Papua.

One foreign interviewee who helped broker the Aceh negotiation stated that the outcome relied on a set of favorable conditions. First, the Free Aceh Movement (Geurakan Acèh Meurdèka, GAM) was more unified and could credibly bargain in the name of the Acehnese. Second, the 2004 tsunami that killed upward of 160,000 Achenese put pressure on all parties to find a solution. Third,

Indonesian president Susilo Bambang Yudhoyono was well disposed toward an agreement, even though it ultimately cost him politically. Overall, achieving this outcome in West Papua would require similar conditions.[56]

In the West Papuan case there are two dominant normative appeals. The primary one stresses human rights.[57] There is a substantial focus in the literature on the practices of the Indonesian state vis-à-vis the West Papuans.[58] The foreign media are either not allowed to visit West Papua or else are heavily censored when they are permitted. The leadership knows that the appeal to human rights is a useful tactic for winning support. Indeed, one aim of the current strategy is to gain sympathy both domestically and internationally. The Indonesian leadership has varied in its position vis-à-vis West Papua. Habibie was initially well disposed toward regional movements in East Timor, Aceh, and West Papua. President Abdurrahman Wahid (also known as Gus Dur) was similarly receptive to West Papuan interests and concerned over human rights issues, but his more conservative vice president and eventual successor, Megawati Sukarnoputri, was willing to give the military greater latitude in its dealings with the West Papuan secessionists.[59] Internationally, the ULMWP is working to develop its diplomatic relations. In 2015, it successfully joined the Melanesian Spearhead Group (MSG) with observer status.[60]

The second common appeal focuses on decolonization. I found in my discussions with participants that they knew that they had once been on the list of Non-Self-Governing Territories. Moreover, they were well versed in the narrative that the Act of Free Choice was really an Act of No Choice and that their right to self-determination had been violated. Indeed, decolonization came up quite frequently, and interviewees would mention the UN Special Committee on Decolonization (C-24) and discuss their chances of getting reinstated on the list of Non-Self-Governing Territories. The method of doing so was via normative appeal—that is, pitching their cause to key states and convincing them that they should count for decolonization. Crucially, as I was told in an interview, human rights are a vital parallel message because they can reinforce the impression that this is a colonized people who should be reinstated on the UN List.

One of the main figures in the West Papuan independence struggle is Benny Wenda. To avoid arrest by the Indonesian authorities, Wenda went into exile in 2003 and has since been based in Oxford, England. Not unlike Moses Havini with the Bougainville independence effort in the 1990s, Wenda functions more or less as a diplomat-at-large. A charismatic individual, he provides a face for the cause and regularly travels to other countries to "educate the world, let them know about the oppression and violence in West Papua, and campaign for its legal right of self-determination."[61] As much as possible, Wenda and his associates stress the ongoing human rights violations in West Papua by disseminating video footage, photographs, and other forms of testimony, such as the short film *Justice for Murdered Children*.[62] Similarly, he communicates the history of the region and about the illegal way in which it was absorbed by Indonesia and removed from the UN List of Non-Self-Governing Territories. The overall aim is to generate support both internationally and in Indonesia.

Can the West Papuan leadership make a persuasive case that the region should be placed on the list of Non-Self-Governing Territories and, laterally, achieve independence via the pathway of decolonization? This is a threshold case. There are two potential arguments here. The first and perhaps weaker argument is that Dutch New Guinea (West Papua) was informally managed in a manner that was separate from the rest of the Dutch East Indies. This is a questionable argument given that informal practices are harder to identify, and ultimately it is the formal jurisdictions that are the subject of *uti possidetis juris*. However, a similar argument was made with respect to South Sudan, so there is some potential valence on the issue.[63] The second and potentially winning argument is to stress the fact that Dutch New Guinea was on the UN decolonization list from 1949 to 1963, and that it was ultimately brought under the Indonesian flag via a questionable referendum. This is the primary decolonization argument that the independence leaders focus on.[64]

In overall strategic terms, the current focus of the secessionists is to force the Indonesian government to negotiate and bring international pressure to bear. The chief tactics include nonviolent civil resistance and normative appeals that focus on human rights, and latterly on decolonization. By shining a light on the human rights abuses in West Papua, the independence leaders hope to build the necessary international support. By committing acts of civil resistance, the secessionists aim to create friction that showcases their cause and generates sympathy. Whether these tactics will work in the end is unclear. The Indonesian state appears intractable and there is no obvious friction point that will compel it to change course. Perhaps increased conflict and imagery of that conflict will turn the tide.

Secession is a form of rebellion, and it can take many forms. I was struck by the following question from a practitioner at a workshop in West Papua on nonviolent civil resistance. The man asked: "What happens if we fail, and what is our responsibility to those we bring into the movement?" This is a question that all secessionists in any setting need to ask. But in a weak combative movement like West Papua, one in which the rebellion is one of resistance, where meetings are clandestine and flags are illegal, where personnel risk their lives by attending a meeting dedicated to nonviolent demonstration, the question is most salient.

7

BOUGAINVILLE
A Nation That Has Come of Age

This is Australia's Vietnam!

—Moses Havini

This chapter is about Bougainville, a secessionist region that has been brought up at various points in the book.[1] Bougainville is an example of a strong combative movement. It is not (was not) institutionally and democratically integrated into the home state of Papua New Guinea (PNG) in quite the same way that Catalonia is with Spain. But it is also not de facto independent like Northern Cyprus. Moreover, as I show below, it cannot make a persuasive argument that it, like New Caledonia, can and should achieve independence via the process of decolonization. It has therefore been relegated to the somewhat residual category of combative movements, where violence and the appeal to human rights are common tactics. Arguably the key difference between it and West Papua was its ability to challenge the state.

The story of Bougainville is instructive. Indeed, it is well matched with West Papua and New Caledonia in regional and geopolitical terms. All three nations are Melanesian, they interact with many of the same states (PNG, Australia, etc.), and they formally and informally dialogue with one another. The stark differences in their outcomes and success call attention to their different tactical settings. And yet given all of this it must be noted that Bougainville is the most likely to get through the sovereignty gate, not only compared to West Papua and New Caledonia, but also with respect to any other contemporary independence movement. Most of the world seems unaware of Bougainville—indeed, even scholars of secession often know little about it—but it is, I conjecture, the most likely candidate for becoming the next sovereign state. What does that say about the sovereignty game? Do strong combative movements have the best chance? Does violence work? I touch on these issues here and return to them in chapter 12.

Background

The region of Bougainville—now formally called the Autonomous Region of Bougainville—consists of a main island (Bougainville), a secondary island to the north (Buka), and a series of much smaller islands (see figure 7.1). The total area is 9,438 square kilometers, about 4 percent of the total landmass of PNG, and the current population estimate is 250,000.[2] The backbone of the island is a volcanic range reaching a height of 2,715 meters, and there are substantial tracts of tropical rain forest. When the US Marines landed on November 1, 1943, the divisional historian wrote that the island was "wilder and more majestic" than any other spot they had encountered in the South Pacific campaign.[3]

The cultural diversity on the island group is striking, and one sign of this is the linguistic complexity. An authoritative account claims that there are sixteen Austronesian languages and nine non-Austronesian (Papuan) languages but notes that such estimates can vary (they are usually much higher) depending on how one differentiates languages from dialects.[4] When I first visited the island in 2013, I met an American musicologist who was writing her PhD dissertation on the varied folk music of Bougainville; she claimed up to fifty languages, many of them quite small and endangered. Although these different language groups have a rough geographic separation, their speakers often come together in the same community where they intermingle and even sort by occupation.[5] Like West Papua, the region is diglossic. Whereas the local Austronesian and Papuan languages form the bedrock, there is a more general secondary level, superimposed above the first, consisting of Tok Pisin, the creole language of PNG. Tok Pisin is essentially the lingua franca of Bougainville. However, in some ways, English constitutes a third level, above the other two. It is one of the official languages of PNG, and it is commonly spoken among the more educated Bougainvilleans.

Like so much of the globe, Bougainville's contemporary status and conceptualization are a legacy of colonialism and the expansion of the state system. The region is named after Louis de Bougainville, the French explorer who sighted the main island in 1768 and named it after himself, despite the fact that the islands had been inhabited for over 30,000 years. In the late-nineteenth-century rush for territory, Germany claimed Bougainville and later added it to its colony of German New Guinea.[6] This was part of the 1886 Anglo-German agreement for dividing the Solomon Islands—Germany got Bougainville and the British claimed

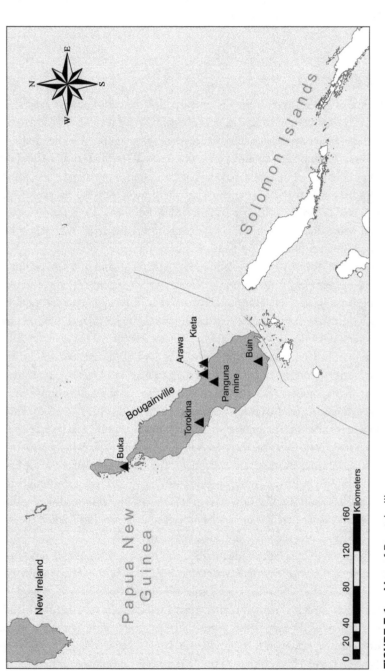

FIGURE 7.1. Map of Bougainville

the rest. Germany lost New Guinea during World War I, along with its other co-lonial possessions, and the region was combined with British New Guinea and converted into a League of Nations mandate under Australian control. Then, in 1975 PNG became an independent country via the pathway of decolonization. Three years later, the Solomon Islands gained their independence in the same manner. It is on account of these historical developments that Bougainville is now formally a part of PNG, a region some 600 kilometers to the west, and not the Solomons, the island chain they are a part of and the nation with whom they share a cultural affinity.

For all its good intentions, the project of decolonization used a least-bad so-lution when determining who should count for independence. The principle of *uti possidetis juris* relied on the colonial map and sovereignty was awarded to first-order administrative units of overseas empires.[7] As a result, regions such as Bougainville and West Papua found themselves, unfortunately and accidentally, decolonized into a country that was somewhat foreign and contrived. In a move that was also made by numerous other peoples—from the Karen to the Buganda to the West Papuans—the Bougainvilleans saw the writing on the wall and tried to preempt the process. They declared independence on September 1, 1975, as the Republic of the North Solomons, two weeks before PNG declared independence on September 16.[8] Technically, they declared independence from Australia, but that is not how the world saw it. Rather, this was a PNG problem that should have been worked out domestically in the newly emerging state, even though the Bou-gainville leadership had signaled its concerns to the UN as early as 1962.[9] One of the first acts of the government of the now sovereign state of PNG was to suspend the provincial government of Bougainville and send troops to occupy the islands.

I coded two temporal movements in the secessionist data used in this book. The first Bougainville movement existed from 1975 to 1976, beginning formally with the September 1 declaration. The movement and related crisis ended in mid-1976 when the first prime minister of PNG, Michael Somare, reached an agreement with the Bougainvillean leadership under John Momis. Both men were fairly moderate—indeed, they knew each other—and an Organic Law was passed that created the North Solomons Provincial Government, an arrangement of devolved gover-nance.[10] That arrangement kept the peace for a time, but it did not last. A second more violent and far more consequential iteration of secessionism began in 1988.

The Development of Secessionism

The Bougainville independence flag was created in a nationwide competition in 1975. The winning design was created by Marilyn Havini, an Australian woman

FIGURE 7.2.   The Bougainville independence flag

married to Moses Havini.[11] There is a strong design element to the Bougainville flag and it is particularly rich in detail and symbolism (see figure 7.2).[12] The blue background field represents the sea. The central symbol, the upe, is a headdress worn by young men during an initiation ceremony that serves as a rite of passage to adulthood. The red and white stripes on the upe represent leadership (to be worn by chiefs) and gender equality (in some traditional ceremonies men wear one red strip in their hair and women wear two). According to the designer, the central position of the upe implies that "the Bougainville PEOPLE [emphasis in original] are now mature and have 'come of age' to be recognized as a political identity.[13]

The green patterned band around the upe symbolizes the kapkap, a traditional symbol of authority made of mother-of-pearl and turtle shell. Although the kapkap design would normally vary by tribe, the design in this case is meant to denote: (1) the outlying reef of sustenance, represented by the exposed outer white band; and (2) the green mountains of Bougainville, depicted by the radial green triangles. The field of black between the kapkap and upe symbolizes the black skin of the Boungainvilleans. Overall, the elegant design of the flag adopts an ethnosymbolist approach that utilizes symbols that resonate across the island.[14] Indeed, according to Anthony Regan, the dark skin color of Bougainvilleans (in relation to the other ethnic groups of PNG) is the principle marker of the pan-Bougainvillean identity that developed in the latter twentieth century.[15]

Like the West Papuans, the people of Bougainville are a diverse lot and the development of their secessionist drive and sense of national consciousness was assisted by various factors. One was a sense of ethnic difference from the mainland that was often symbolized by skin color. It is not uncommon for the Bougainvilleans to refer to the people of PNG as the *retskins* (redskins)[16] and, in return, to be called by a name that plays on their black complexion, such as *Bilong Suspen* (referring to the residue in the bottom of a sauce pan).[17] In his gripping memoir of the Bougainville Civil War, Yauka Aluambo Liria (an intelligence officer in the PNG Defence Force, PNGDF) recalls many instances of racist language and symbolism, such as when his friend declared that the conflict had been started by those "brainless black bastards" and that they should be killed.[18] Similarly, in his own personal story—part manifesto and part memoir—the Bougainvillean guerrilla leader and future president of the Autonomous Region of Bougainville, James Tanis, recalled the racial tension he encountered when he was sent as a teenager to attend the Sogeri National High School outside Port Moresby in PNG.[19]

These ethnoracial perceptions, which pre-dated PNG independence and contributed to the tension, may have lain dormant or diminished with time had it not been for another factor, the catalyst as it were: the Panguna mine. Copper (and gold) ore was discovered in the central highlands of Bougainville in the 1960s. Subsequently, Bougainville Copper Limited (BCL), whose chief investor was Conzinc Riotinto of Australia, was created after striking a deal with PNG to construct an open-cut mine. By the standards of its time, BCL actually possessed a fairly developed sense of corporate social responsibility and agreed to terms quite favorable to the PNG government, which received about 20 percent of the profits.[20] As a result, the mine became a substantial financial asset for PNG after it began operations in 1972 and would eventually account for 60 percent of the country's export earnings and 16 percent of its revenues.[21] The problem, however, is that the terms were rather miserly with respect to the local landowners. They received about 1 percent of the profits but bore the costs of the social disruption and environmental damage to their land. The open-cut design of the mine created a vast hole in the earth that was more than a kilometer wide.[22] The runoff from the mine spoiled local waterways, and the influx of non-Bougainvillean workers created social tensions.

These conditions gradually ratcheted up the pressure that would end in secessionism. On one hand, Bougainvilleans, especially those landowners from the region near to the mine, grew increasingly dissatisfied with the state of affairs. On the other hand, the mine was a vital revenue source for the government. When incidents did occur—such as when small-scale violence took place between locals and workers from the mainland—the government would increase its police presence and/or send in the riot squads. In his diary on the conflict, Liria expressed sympathy for the Bougainvilleans in regard to their treatment by the PNG state.[23] In his recollections of this period, Tanis passionately described the sense of outrage at the degradation of the land and abuses by the government.[24] Of course, when the secessionist struggle did finally take off, the PNG government worried about not only the potential loss of revenue but also the precedent-setting problems that all diverse, multinational states face when challenged by a breakaway region.[25]

Although the tactical behavior of an independence movement is structured by the setting, it takes individuals to put everything in motion. While moderate voices played a role in defusing the crisis of 1975–1976, and would do so again from 1997 onward, the roughly ten-year conflict that began in 1988 followed the rise of Francis Ona. From the highland region near Panguna and initially trained as a Catholic priest, Ona had for a time worked as a surveyor for BCL. After becoming disillusioned with the mining process and unfair treatment of the locals, he joined with a cousin to form the Bougainville Revolutionary Army (BRA). The BRA began with small acts of sabotage that gradually drew the police and PNGDF into spiraling acts of violence. After nearly two years of conflict, Ona and his followers declared independence on May 17, 1990.[26]

Ona was an inspiring yet controversial figure. His challenge to the state and his outlaw status brought followers to him, especially when the state responded in a heavy-handed manner. He became the acknowledged supreme leader of the movement, and photographs from the time show him speaking to his troops while clad in his daily uniform that included a Japanese officer's sword from World War II.[27] He was, however, criticized for his remoteness and inability to connect with civilians[28] and was regarded by his peers as immoderate and uncompromising.[29] He refused to negotiate with the PNG government and remained a holdout from the peace process up until his own death in 2005.

One advantage of a lightning rod leader like Ona is their ability to bring capable personnel under their banner. One such person was Sam Kauona, a Bougainvillean and former officer in the PNGDF who went AWOL when his cousin was killed in the conflict.[30] Trained as an ammunitions technical officer, Kauona played an invaluable role in shaping BRA tactics. He was the architect behind the BRA command structure, which broke the force into subunits[31] that were divided by region.[32] Kauona was the second-in-command and at times the de facto military leader.

Another BRA leader was James Tanis, a younger lieutenant who gradually rose through the ranks. When the war broke out he was a university student in Port Moresby on a scholarship supplied by the mining corporation. It was on an academic break working at the mine in 1988 that he was tipped off by someone that the mining complex where he was working and living was going to be burned down that night. He vacated that evening to avoid the fire, an act that would later raise the suspicions of the authorities who then arrested him. Upon his release he found that his options were limited: The BCL wondered if he was connected to the BRA, and the BRA worried about his loyalties to the BCL. He then gravitated toward the BRA both because he believed in the cause and because he needed to prove his loyalty to Bougainville.

The conflict ran from 1988 to 1997 and can be divided into two periods. The first period started with the cycle of violence that began around the mine but escalated when the government launched Operation Footloose in early 1990. A failure in most ways, this first effort succeeded mostly in galvanizing the secessionist cause. As with the other independence movements covered in this book, the secessionists lacked unity.[33] Buka and the north and east coasts of the main island had a longer history of colonial contact, were more educated, and saw greater advantages to remaining a part of PNG.[34] In contrast, the central highlands along with Buin and the southern region were more inclined to break away. But the PNGDF was unable to exploit these divisions, and, on the contrary, drove many locals toward the secessionist cause by engaging in counterproductive behavior.[35] Liria's campaign diary provides an interesting account of this time. Written by a proud professional soldier who believes in his country and is opposed to secession, the diary catalogues the dangers of counterinsurgency.[36] The deployment force was too small, insufficiently trained, and weak in morale.[37] Their reliance on heavy weapons was too blunt and terrifying an instrument. Their willingness to beat prisoners and burn villages sowed bitterness.[38] Essentially, they lost the fight to win the hearts and minds of the local population. Realizing the failure, the government pulled the forces out in mid-1990.

The withdrawal of the governmental forces created a problem for the secessionists because it effectively removed the glue that held them together.[39] According to Tanis:

> In 1990 the government forces and administration withdrew. There was a painful lesson waiting for us. That is, it is one thing for a guerrilla army to win a territory but governing a territory after winning it is another thing. There was fighting among the leadership, not so much because of the power struggle but largely because of differing views on the next steps to take. We faced this problem because we came from all walks of life and had different backgrounds, united more by external forces than internal interaction within ourselves.[40]

The result was a fracturing between groups and the development of resistance to the BRA and to Ona's leadership. The biggest point of resistance was the

Bougainville Resistance Force (BRF), a group that was not opposed to independence per se, but rather BRA-led independence.

The second period began in late 1990 when the PNGDF returned in an attempt to exploit the new divisions and retake the territory. For the next seven years the conflict had two primary cleavages, between the BRA and the PNGDF and between the BRA and the BRF, which drew support from the PNGDF.[41] But it was ultimately a stalemate. The government succeeded in recapturing some 40 percent of the island, including Buka, but they could not defeat the BRA. Moreover, the consequences for the Bougainvilleans were catastrophic. Although battle-related deaths never exceeded the 1,000 per-year threshold (see table 7.1), it is estimated that as much as 20,000 people died (some 10 percent of the population), and many more were dislocated.[42] There were atrocities and extrajudicial killings, not just by the PNGDF, whose commanders often operated independently and fought private wars,[43] but also by Bougainvilleans against one another.[44] Much of this violence followed a Kalyvasian logic of score settling and local feuds,[45] and there are numerous heart-wrenching tales of kin-on-kin murder and betrayal. In 2013, I interviewed an educator in Buka who said that his sister had been murdered during the conflict by a man that he had known from his village. In his recounting, Tanis tells a story about how men under his command killed his brother-in-law while on patrol.[46] He claimed that one of the problems during this time was that there was a new kind of authority, one armed with weapons, and that the traditional lines of authority had broken down.

The final stage of the conflict took an interesting and unusual turn. Julius Chan had been elected PNG prime minister in 1995, and he initially worked hard to negotiate a settlement with the BRA. However, neither side was yet willing to moderate its views. As Chan grew frustrated in his ability to end the conflict diplomatically or militarily, he took a gamble that would ultimately bring down his government. He secretly hired Sandline International, a private security firm, to

TABLE 7.1. Conflict data for Bougainville, 1975–2016

YEAR	INTENSITY LEVEL[a]
1990	1
1992	1
1993	1
1994	1
1995	1
1996	1

Source: Uppsala Conflict Data Program.
Note: Years with fewer than twenty-five battle deaths are omitted.
[a]1 = 25–999 battle-related deaths; 2 = 1000+ battle-related deaths[47]

train the PNG special forces, gather intelligence, and conduct offensive operations that would defeat the BRA.[48] Some $36 million was paid to Sandline without official PNG parliamentary support and without the full knowledge of the PNGDF. When news of the affair was leaked, the Chan government came under intense criticism and the army leadership revolted. In the scandal that followed, Chan was pressured internally and externally (by Australia in particular) to resign.

The peace process that began in 1997 and ended in 2001 had many factors. First, war weariness had set in and it had become clear to both sides that victory would be costly and hard to achieve.[49] Second, the international community played an increasingly important role in pushing for an agreement. Reports of casualties and human rights abuse had gradually altered the position of key states like Australia from strong support for PNG to a stress on a diplomatic solution. In the early years of the conflict Australia has supplied the PNGDF with Iroquois combat helicopters and other material, but had pulled its support in the face of mounting criticism regarding Australia's role in the conflict.[50] Indeed, Peter Singer argues that Julius Chan went to Sandline partly because Australia was limiting its military supplies on account of the human rights record of the PNGDF.[51] The Sandline scandal merely focused international and domestic attention on the need to reach a diplomatic solution.

Regan argues that several additional factors helped advance the peace process.[52] One was the gradual strengthening of moderate voices on both sides. Another was the "light intervention" of the international community, including several peace monitoring groups that were sponsored by the United Nations, New Zealand, and other regional actors. This light intervention worked partly because it was requested by both sides in the conflict. Finally, Regan and others contend that the peace process was assisted by a strong culture of reconciliation in Melanesian society.[53]

The peace agreement that was signed in 2001 was momentous not only because it ended the violence but also because it opened a potential pathway for Bougainvillean independence. In short, the agreement stipulated: (1) autonomy for Bougainville, constitutionally entrenched as part of the Autonomous Region of Bougainville; (2) withdrawal of the PNGDF from Bougainville and weapons removal; (3) a nonbinding referendum on independence sometime between 2015 and 2020.[54]

There is an interesting debate, particularly among Australian academics, regarding the strengths and weaknesses of the 2001 Bougainville peace agreement.[55] It delves into important topics like how to implement a peace agreement, how to make it endure, and the importance and design of referenda. The last issue is relevant here because it pertains to the referendum on Bougainville's independence. The 2001 agreement utilized the concept of a deferred and nonbinding referendum; deferred because it pushed the date of the referendum to a time fourteen to nineteen years out; nonbinding because the PNG state is not legally bound to honor the result. The advantage of this type of referendum was that it could get both parties to agree—that is, there was a bargaining space—and that it gave both sides time to heal and hopefully determine their political relationship in an amicable manner. The disadvantage was that it may have only postponed the inevitable secession of Bougainville, and not put in place the necessary structure that would enable PNG to win over a majority of the Bougainvillean voters. Indeed, voices within the PNG state have increasingly questioned the wisdom of investing resources in Bougainville since it was likely to go independent anyway.[56]

A negotiated referendum can structure expectations and shape outcomes. It is actually quite rare for this type of referendum to be legally binding. Even the 2014 Scottish referendum was not legally binding—it was, however, perceived to be politically binding given the participation of the British government.[57] The PNG government was aware of this commitment when the agreement was signed and signaled that it was a one-off offer and not something that any other group in PNG could obtain.[58]

The referendum was held in late 2019 in an orderly and highly monitored fashion. When the ballots were counted, 98.3 percent had voted for independence, a clear victory for the secessionist cause. It is now up to the PNG parliament to negotiate a solution with Bougainville, a process that is currently being worked out. The gate is open and the Bougainvillean nation stands on the threshold.

Strategy and Tactics

By what strategy and set of tactics did the Bougainvillean secessionists achieve this outcome? At the strategic level, they did the same thing that all of the other groups covered in this book have done. They made a go at the home state and tried to get it to remove the home-state veto. Simultaneously, they did an end run and brought the international community into the game to apply pressure on PNG. They may not have the achieved their goal in the same way, or in the same time frame, as some of the leaders like Francis Ona had wanted. In fact, independence may elude them for a number of reasons—for example, PNG may still refuse to permit independence—but taking the long view, the strategy appears to have worked in their case.

It is in the domain of tactics that Bougainville differs from the other case studies. To achieve their end, the secessionists successfully used violence and drew attention to their cause by showcasing human rights grievances. Much of this has to do with the setting. Unlike Northern Cyprus, Bougainville was (and remains) integrated with the larger state. As such, it was in a position to put direct pressure on the state. As an unfortunate, or in some ways fortunate, consequence of that integrated and overlapping sovereignty, friction followed, conflict arose, and human rights abuses occurred. Perhaps things would have been different had the region been part of a more robust democracy and had the tactic of electoral capture been a more attractive tool. Here, I have to engage in some conjecture because PNG is typically regarded as a democracy, albeit a weak one and borderline case.[59] Research suggests that secessionist energy is more likely to find institutional expression in highly democratic societies.[60] Perhaps that would have occurred with Bougainville. Ultimately, the structural conditions in Bougainville fit the combative strategic type.

The key difference between West Papua and Bougainville was the ability of the latter to challenge the state. One could point to a number of reasons for this. Indonesia has thirty-one times the population of PNG (266,794,980 to 8,418,346),[61] and an active army over 200 times the size of PNG's (395,500 to 1,900).[62] Although West Papua does possess a larger population than Bougainville, it represents a comparatively smaller portion of the overall Indonesian population (1.6 percent) than the Bougainvilleans do in PNG (2.9 percent).[63] Indonesia is a bigger and more powerful state in both absolute and relative terms. Perhaps more importantly, Indonesia's military had combat experience from the independence conflict with the Dutch, and with regional civil wars in East Timor, Aceh, and others. In contrast, the PNGDF was arguably a less experienced military, the Bougainville episode being its biggest conflict. In his diary, Liria was critical of the PNGDF and felt that some of the deployments were meant to simply give units the chance to "experience the Bougainville operational lifestyle."[64] One of my Bougainvillean interviews was with a man who was in Buka during the mid-1990s, and he claimed that there was an element of theater to the PNGDF deployment. Some aspiring politicians joined the force and made sure they were seen, but never engaged.[65] He recalled the absurd image of a patrol boat returning to Buka one night while blaring the Doors song *The End*. The entire deployment was rich in atmosphere.

But what about the insurgents themselves; how did they compare? A key factor in a secessionist struggle is external support. It is difficult for a rebel group to challenge the state unless it has an external benefactor, particularly one that supplies arms and training. My interviewees cited this as a shortcoming of the West Papuan movement—there was no external patron beyond some members of the Melanesian Spearhead Group, like Vanuatu, who provided mostly rhetorical support. A similar situation existed for Bougainville. The closest thing to an external patron was the Solomon Islands, the neighboring state just to the south (see figure 7.1). The Solomon Islands government was sympathetic to Bougainville and was willing to look the other way as activists and external members of the movement ran medical supplies up the island chain and through the PNGDF blockade,[66] a pattern that led to some naval incursions into Solomon waters by PNGDF ships.[67] In his interview with me, Moses Havini said that there were always ships running the blockade from the Solomons and that he went back on two occasions.[68] However, Bougainville did not receive outright military support. Unlike Northern Cyprus, there was no Turkish protector willing to intervene. There was no Russian patron or Cold War superpower willing to provide material and equal the odds. In that sense, the BRA was on its own.

However, the BRA had at least one important starting advantage relative to the Free Papua Movement: access to weaponry that had been left behind from World War II. When I asked Tanis how they were able to challenge a military force that possessed modern weaponry, he said they were able to salvage considerable material from the old US base at Torokina.[69] Much of the material was quite durable, and, in any case, some of the BRA personnel like him had an engineering background and could refurbish the weapons. The weapons were light enough to be transported through the forest on foot, and yet powerful enough to attack enemy positions and aircraft. This weaponry essentially provided a foundation with which the guerrillas could conduct hit-and-run tactics on the PNGDF and, gradually, seize newer and more modern weapons from their opponents.[70] It is estimated that the BRA, consisting of roughly 2,000 troops depending on the period, possessed around 500 automatic weapons and as many as 3,000 reconditioned World War II weapons.[71] Photographs and descriptions of the Bougainvillean and West Papuan combat capabilities illustrate the contrast. One photograph shows BRA fighters posing next to a restored US World War II bomber turret gun (a heavy-caliber machine-gun) with ammunition belts.[72] Another photo shows them holding a restored Japanese cannon (also from the war). Similar photos and descriptions from West Papuan show the guerrillas holding spears, bows and arrows, and a pair of prized Mauser bolt-action rifles.[73]

I do not want to overstate this weapons-based argument, because there are numerous factors that determine the fighting ability of an insurgent group. Leadership and chance are also important. But the outcome speaks for itself. The BRA was able to fight the PNGDF to a hurting stalemate.[74] In relative terms, they were a strong combative movement, partly because they faced a relatively weak state and partly because of local conditions. Although methods of nonviolent civil resistance can be tremendously useful, violent tactics can be effective under certain conditions.

However, violent insurgency on its own is unlikely to work unless the group can successfully communicate to the international community. This was a problem in the early days of conflict because Bougainville was blockaded, the media had limited access, and PNG had the support of key regional actors like Australia. Liria wrote that the BRA was successful from the beginning in all aspect of strategy save one: gathering international support. He writes: "Despite numerous desperate attempts, no practical international support was forthcoming, even after the withdraw of our troops [in 1990]. That failure alone was to remain the BRA's single biggest setback."[75]

The fact that the secessionists gradually overcame this failure largely comes down to the work of one man, Moses Havini, their representative and diplomat to the world and the founder of the Sydney-based Bougainville Freedom Movement. Havini was born in Buka, educated at the University of Papua New Guinea, and had served in various governmental posts prior to the war.[76] His wife, Marilyn Havini, was an Australian citizen, and as a result they were evacuated from Arawa in 1990 and relocated in Sydney along with their four children. Havini told me in a personal interview that he was contacted several months later by the BRA and was asked by their leadership to serve as their external diplomat. When Havini said that he needed more time to make that decision, they replied that they had no time. They were calling him on a phone line that was temporarily rigged by a supporter in Rabaul, and that the line would be cut and communication would be severed. Havini accepted the task and began to build a diplomatic wing from scratch.[77]

Havini's efforts to put Bougainville on the international agenda provide a fascinating window into rebel diplomacy. He gathered around him a support group of volunteers, mostly Australian activists who were interested in the cause. They collected donations with which they could purchase media material and fly Havini to different locations for speaking and networking engagements. Some of his travel took him to Geneva, where he would lobby the United Nations. During that time he befriended and learned from Xanana Gusmão, the East Timorese independence leader, as they pitched their respective causes to the international community.[78] In the beginning he sought to dress his cause in the language of decolonization, like Gusmão, but he failed to get traction here because Bougainville was perceived to have a weaker case than East Timor.[79]

Eventually, Havini directed his energy at showcasing human rights abuses in Bougainville at the hands of the PNGDF. He said that he would use every opportunity he could to get on the media and use incendiary language. One of his favorite expressions was: "This is Australia's Vietnam!" The message was simply that Australia supported PNG, had an old colonial relationship with it, and was complicit in the atrocities that PNG was now committing in Bougainville.[80] Havini was a charismatic figure, and inspired numerous activists and journalists to take up the cause. Still, he struggled to get the world to pay attention.

A breakthrough came when his team smuggled two boxes of disposable cameras into Bougainville. This was the idea of one of his volunteers, an American expat in Sydney, who pointed out that they needed photographs of the conflict and donated the cameras. The instructions were to take pictures and send the cameras back to Sydney. Havini said that only one camera ever came back, but it contained photographs of children who had been killed when a church was shelled by the PNGDF. He took the photographs to the media and cited that moment as a turning point in Australian public opinion regarding the conflict and Australia's role in it.

Tactics of compellence and normative appeal have different causal pathways. The BRA used violent methods to impose costs on the PNG government for not negotiating. They created a hurting stalemate. Meanwhile, Havini and his Bougainville Freedom Movement targeted preferences. They changed preferences on the issue and brought into the game previously neutral or indifferent parties. In doing so, they went around the home state and brought added pressure to bear.[81] The eventual outcome was a peace agreement and the promise of an independence referendum.

There is, of course, a danger of reading too much strategic thinking into this behavior. The independence effort was always a divided group with shifting alliances, sometimes working at cross-purposes. After all, Ona never agreed to the peace and remained in the field until his death in 2005. Moreover, Havini worked rather independently of the BRA efforts in Bougainville, and they hardly represented a unified command structure. Like the other movements, we can see the usual obstacles to sound strategy: they are playing a game where the rules are imperfectly defined, actors have multiple goals, and the secessionists are divided. Interestingly, while all parties agreed that the Bougainvillean secessionists were divided, there is some disagreement as to whether this was a bad thing. Many analysts argue that the division undermined the group's effectiveness,[82] but sometimes division can provide bargaining leverage. Both Kauona and Tanis claimed that Ona's refusal to negotiate and come to the bargaining table ultimately helped them negotiate a better deal from the PNG government, who feared that their interlocutors would flock back to Ona if they were not satisfied with the terms.[83]

One of the disquieting questions regarding secession is whether violence works.[84] Is violence a useful tactic for winning independence, and is it more efficacious than nonviolent or institutional methods? Perhaps the case of Bougainville provides a tentative "yes" to that question, given that the civil war ultimately led to a peace agreement that could yield full independence in the near future. Indeed, in light of the recent referendum in late 2019, Bougainville may become the next nation to join the sovereignty club. But the answer to that question comes with caveats. First, if it does come, independence was paid for at a terrible price—up to 20,000 killed and a shattered society. Second, what is the reference group for comparison? Secessionist movements face different tactical settings, and it would be an exaggeration to say that the Bougainvilleans chose violence when the Catalans have not, because the menu of options was different in each case. Had the Bougainvilleans possessed the same institutional options as the Catalans, perhaps they would already have won their independence without the bloodshed and would now be a full UN member. My research with Louis Wasser concluded that violence is not a more useful tactic once you control for the type of movement,[85] for set against the potential success of Bougainville are a myriad of violent failures like Biafra, Mindanao, and Ambazonia. The potential and perceived utility of violence is an issue that I return to in chapter 12.

8

NEW CALEDONIA
The Melanesian Tricolor

> **Our celebrations are like the work of the needle used to bind the straw at the top of the house so that all the strands come together to form a single roof, as all our words come together to form a single Word.**
>
> —Jean-Marie Tjibaou

New Caledonia is a fascinating case.[1] It is located on the opposite side of the Earth from Paris, at the far edge of the French administrative state, a legacy of empire. It is truly antipodean. Its largely, but not exclusively, indigenous-driven independence movement bears many of the characteristics of the other movements featured in this book. Its tactics of compellence have included nonviolent civil resistance, the use of violence, and electoral capture. These choices have been shaped by its relationship to the state, and, as I discuss below, we can discern a decades-long trajectory from the use of extrainstitutional to institutional methods as French democracy gradually enfranchised the indigenous group, the Kanaks,[2] and gave them political voice. It is on the normative front that New Caledonia differs most from the other movements in this study, for, unlike them, it is classified as a non-self-governing territory and therefore eligible for independence via the path of decolonization.

Given its status, one would think that New Caledonia would be bound for independent statehood. It is on the decolonization list, a distinction that still privileges a small set of nations worldwide, essentially a ticket into the sovereignty club. Moreover, via the Nouméa Accord, New Caledonia was granted a referendum on independence, which took place on November 4, 2018, and two potential follow-on referenda should the "No" vote win the first time around. Relative to the Catalans, who strive to win a referendum from Spain, or the West Papuans, who endeavor to get on the decolonization list and to get a referendum, the people of New Caledonia are fortunate. And yet independence may remain elusive for the simple reason that the Kanaks, the colonized group, are no longer a majority in

New Caledonia, and may not be able to convince enough voters to choose separation. There is a tension in this case between the principle of decolonization and
the democratic principle that each citizen should have a vote and that the majority prevail. Both sides of the independence issue will have to reckon with this tension in the years to come.

Background

New Caledonia is a set of islands in the southwest Pacific Ocean roughly halfway
between Fiji and Australia. The total land area consists of 18,575 square kilometers,
and the population as of 2014 was 268,767.[3] There is a main island, Grand Terre,
which accounts for nearly 90 percent of the landmass, and a series of smaller islands including the Loyalty Islands off the east coast (See figure 8.1). The original
inhabitants of the islands are Melanesian, and it is estimated that their ancestors
first came some 3,000 years ago. Like West Papua and Bougainville, the indigenous Melanesian population spoke a myriad of languages prior to European contact. Currently, there are twenty-nine or thirty Austronesian languages spoken
across the islands.[4] There is no record of a unified government prior to French
colonization. As with Bougainville, the name New Caledonia was bequeathed by
Europeans. In this case the islands were named by the explorer James Cook,
who sighted Grand Terre in 1774 and felt that it reminded him of Scotland
(Caledonia).[5]

The relationship between France and New Caledonia began during the reign
of Emperor Napoleon III. The islands were subdued militarily in 1853 and formally annexed in 1864.[6] Outwardly, the rationale for seizing the islands was the
so-called civilizing mission, or *mission civilisatrice*,[7] but of course the French had
clear geostrategic motives for gaining a foothold in Oceania. Indeed, until 1884
the governor of New Caledonia was also the commander of the French naval forces
in the Pacific.[8] A crucial aspect of the early relationship—one with immense
downstream consequences—was the fact that New Caledonia was a penal colony,
from 1864 to 1894. In some ways, New Caledonia is the French Australia because
in both cases a European settler population was built upon the penal colony. Some
convicts returned to the metropole when their sentence was complete, but many
stayed. They, along with the related nonconvict population of prison guards, military personnel, doctors, administrators, and so on, created an anchor population that gradually drew other voluntary settlers from Europe. Roughly a third
of contemporary New Caledonians have European ancestry—they are often referred to as Caldoches[9]—and many of them are descended from these early convicts and settlers. The seeds for the contemporary ethnic division in contemporary

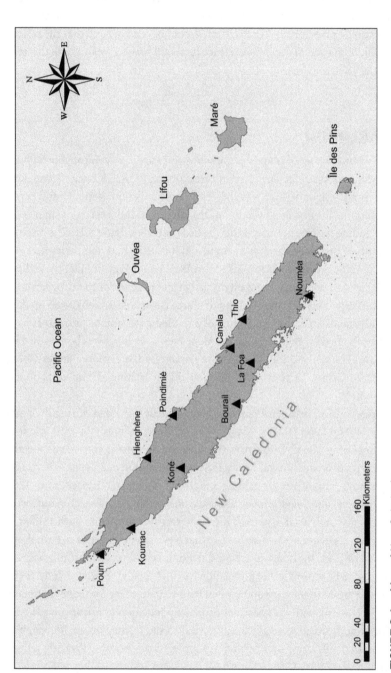

FIGURE 8.1. Map of New Caledonia

New Caledonia were in many ways sown during this time. But unlike Australia, where the European settlers migrated in numbers so great as to relegate the aboriginal groups to a small minority, the French settlers in New Caledonia never outnumbered the Kanaks, and presently represent a smaller voting bloc.

The names of ethnic groups can have curious origins and the Kanaks are no exception. *Kanaka* is a Hawaiian word for "person" that was spread throughout Oceania in the 1800s as part of the developing maritime and plantation pidgin vocabulary.[10] The French modified the term to *canaque* and applied it to the Melanesians in New Caledonia. Apparently, the term often carried a pejorative undertone during the first century of French domination. However, it was revalued as Kanak during the Kanak Awakening of the 1970s, and it is now regarded with pride as a unifying ethnic category for Melanesians of what are in fact diverse tribal and linguistic lineages in New Caledonia. The pejorative name and even the language of the oppressor have been co-opted by the oppressed.

Oppression is a strong word but it is nevertheless an apt description for at least the first 100 years of French control. French colonists began to settle on the west coast of Grand Terre in the 1850s, beginning a process whereby the Europeans gradually absorbed more arable land. Then, in 1887, the native regulations, or *Code de l'indigénat*, were codified.[11] This was a system of administration used throughout the French Empire. In New Caledonia, it placed limits on Kanak movement across the islands, and set curfews and conditions of forced labor. This was an apartheid-type system that lasted into the mid-twentieth century. Jean-Marie Tjibaou, the Kanaks' charismatic leader in the 1970s and 1980s, stated that he was inspired to seek independence by "the stories of taking people for work and of working in road gangs—a bit like forced labour. The gendarmes regularly took a certain number of men each month from the tribe to go and work for the settlers, and there was a guard with a baton and a gun to make the people work."[12] It was not until 1953 that French citizenship was extended to the Kanak population, 100 years after forced annexation.

Three long-running themes were in place by the 1870s.[13] First, European settlers were beginning to displace the Kanaks and create friction. Second, nickel had been discovered in the territory and the French began to appreciate the potential mineral wealth. It is estimated that New Caledonia holds as much as 25 percent of the world's nickel reserves, and the mineral represents about 90 percent of the region's total export value. Third, the forced accession of the islands and subsequent treatment of the original inhabitants led to a series of revolts that would eventually feed the Kanak national narrative.[14] Of these, the biggest was the 1878 revolt that apparently resulted in over 1,000 deaths (mostly Kanak).[15] Another revolt took place in 1917, resulting in over 200 deaths—one of the killed was Tjibaou's grandmother.[16]

World War II served, not unusually, as an inflection point in the political trajectory of New Caledonia.[17] Although the territory was not subject to a Japanese occupation, France had been defeated by Germany in 1940 and the New Caledonian government was forced to choose between Vichy France and the Free French government. It chose the latter and, in doing so, became immediately dependent on the Anglo-American powers for protection. During the war, Nouméa served for a time as the headquarters of the US Army and Navy in the South Pacific, and the thousands of US service men and women temporarily doubled the population. As in Jayapura, West Papua, which also served as a US base after its liberation from the Japanese, the presence of African American soldiers in uniform, in positions of responsibility, apparently the equal of the white soldiers, boosted the determination of the Melanesians to seek a new relationship with their overlords after the war.[18]

It was in the aftermath of World War II as the principle of decolonization spread through the international system that the Kanaks became enfranchised, found political voice, and began to forge a nation. For a brief moment New Caledonia was on the UN List of Non-Self-Governing Territories. However, in 1947 France was able to get the territory removed from the list through an administrative change that converted the colony to an overseas territory. In doing so, it blurred the distinction between internal and external territories, and argued successfully that New Caledonia was no longer a colony.[19] This worked for a time, but the Kanaks had been on the UN list and they certainly qualified for decolonization given the standard application of *uti possidetis juris*. Therefore, as we will see, France could not completely foreclose this route to independence. Of perhaps greater importance was that by extending suffrage and educational opportunities to the Kanaks—by acting as a responsible government—France created the conditions for the development of an independence movement.

The Development of Secessionism

It is fitting that the Kanak independence flag would have a tricolor design (see figure 8.2). It is the chief vexillological image of the mother state, France, and a commonly used template throughout the Francosphere. It is also a symbol of revolution and republicanism. *Le Tricolore* was adopted at key moments in French history, beginning with the French Revolution.[20] The irony is that the Kanaks have effectively co-opted the underlying significance of the French design and turned it back upon their colonial master. The flag features three horizontal bands: blue represents the sky and the ocean that surrounds New Caledonia; red symbolizes the Kanak blood that has been spilled in the long struggle for independence; green

FIGURE 8.2.   The independence flag of New Caledonia

signifies the land and life of the people. Superimposed on the tricolor design, left of center, is a golden circle with an intricate black design inscribed inside of it. Here, gold represents the sun and source of life. The black image inside the circle represents a common totem placed upon traditional Kanak dwellings: a *flèche faitière*, a type of arrow, thrust through several tutut shells. Although I have not uncovered information about its creator, the flag was apparently adopted at the first congress of the Kanak and Socialist National Liberation Front (Front de Libération Nationale Kanak et Socialiste, FLNKS) in 1984.

It is important to note that while the independence effort in New Caledonia has been Kanak-driven, it is not exclusively Kanak. Other ethnic groups have supported the independence drive at various points, including immigrants from France, elements of the white settler community, Wallisians (immigrants from Wallis Island), among others. In one interview with high-ranking officials, I was told that there is a general historical arc in the mass appeal of independence.[21] From the 1950s into the 1970s, the movement included substantial numbers of "European" New Caledonians, many of whom were drawn to the cause by its message of socialist liberation. From the late 1970s to the 1990s, the movement became more ethnically focused, especially during the violent events of the 1980s. However, after the Nouméa Accord of 1998 the independence movement attempted to broaden its appeal and present a pan-ethnic message as a means of forming a winning coalition in advance of the 2018 referendum and the potential referenda to follow. That seventy-year arc from broad to narrow and back to broad again traces the development of the movement.

The first period from the 1950s through the 1970s was dominated by the Caledonian Union (Union Calédonienne, UC). This was a broad multiethnic coalition that included white settlers, Kanaks, laborers, and avowed socialists who were all opposed to French centralism and the "old clientelist oligarchy."[22] Their motto was "Two colors, one people," and their leader in the early days was Maurice Lenormand, an immigrant from France. The UC began as an autonomist party that sought greater rights from France and reacted negatively to the increased centralization (Gaullism) that occurred with the advent of the Fifth Republic in 1958. It fit the mold of a decolonization movement whereby the inhabitants of the colony gradually came to resent the colonial power structure and push for separation. Over time, the leaders of the UC became increasingly secessionist. But there was a problem: If they went for full independence, what sort of nation would they be? Would they follow a Western-derived "civic" model, or emphasize their indigenous identity?[23] This question has troubled the independence effort ever since.

A new period began with the cultural movement known as the Kanak Awakening. One cause of the awakening was the fact that France had enfranchised the Kanaks and now sent promising students to France for study. An early Kanak leader was Nidoïsh Naisseline, the son of a high chief from Mare, who had gone to France in the 1960s to study sociology at the Sorbonne. Like other Kanaks, he was exposed to, and could quote, the writings of Jean-Paul Sartre, Frantz Fanon, and Mao Zedong, among others. Moreover, he had participated in the student rebellions of 1968, and brought these ideas back to New Caledonia. Upon their return Naisseline and others formed an activist/revolutionary group called the Foulards Rouge (Red Scarves). They would meet in small groups to discuss politics, write political pamphlets, and paint political graffiti around Nouméa.[24] Their activities led to numerous arrests that mostly gave publicity to their political agenda. Maurice Chaniel, a prison guard who got to know them, reflected that "We had sent lambs to France, they sent us back Che Guevaras."[25]

It was during this time that the Kanaks arguably found their greatest leader, and certainly the person most associated with the Kanak Awakening. Jean-Marie Tjibaou was from the east coast of Grand Terre. He had also studied in Lyon and at the Sorbonne. Like many other future secessionists in New Caledonia, Bougainville, and West Papua, he had also trained as a priest. But he had left the ministry because he felt that the institutions of the Catholic Church were insufficient for supporting Kanak liberation.[26] In her memoir from the 1980s, the Australian journalist Helen Fraser reflects that Tjibaou was an extraordinary leader—canny, charismatic, warm, funny, even good with children—and that he always gave the impression that everything was moving in the direction he intended.[27] When I interviewed the Kanak political leader Sylvain Pabouty in his Nouméa office on May 11, 2018, I noticed that he had a picture of Tjibaou featured prominently above his desk. Tjibaou was the chief architect of the 1975 Melanesian 2000 Festival, a cultural festival to celebrate Kanak arts and culture. Nations need their cultural museums and the Kanaks were given a marvelous one in 1998 when the Jean-Marie Tjibaou Cultural Center was opened on the outskirts of Nouméa.[28] This stirring museum, designed by Renzo Piano, is a testament to Tjibaou's vision, even though he did not live long enough to see it.

Perhaps it was inevitable that the Kanak Awakening would create a rift within the large tent of the UC. The articulation of the Kanak identity was not the same thing as the New Caledonian identity, itself still in a nascent stage, and many non-Kanaks grew estranged. This problem was less acute in numerous other regions around the globe experiencing decolonization because the indigenous groups were in the majority and the colonists were few. The Anglo-settler states of Australia, Canada, and New Zealand are an exception, as had been the United States much earlier, but in those cases the settler population was large, dominant, and possessed with sufficient cultural gravity to develop their unique national identity. But the white and other non-Kanak New Caledonians were caught between a distant metropole that protected them and a rising indigenous nation that too often saw them as the "other." There are some parallels with the white minorities of South Africa and Rhodesia, but those populations existed in substantial numbers and possessed a firmer sense of local identity. In her memoir, Fraser relates an interesting comment from a "fifth-generation" Caldoche who said that "his fellow Caldoches would only really become New Caledonians and people of the South Pacific when they learned not to be ashamed of their convict past."[29] Fraser noted that the Caldoches did not demonstrate the kind of pride in their convict ancestry that she saw in her native Tasmania, and inferred that they had not yet developed a sense of self apart from the metropole.

The developing Kanak national consciousness combined with a radicalization in some wings of the independence front to alienate non-Kanaks and increase ethnic polarization.[30] By 1977 the UC had adopted a nationalist platform, now largely under the leadership of Tjibaou. Meanwhile, more overtly militant groups like Parti de libération kanak (Palika) arose and began to argue for the merits of using violence to gain independence.[31] It was in this climate of increasing ethnic polarization that the right-wing loyalist party Rally for Caledonia in the Republic (Rassemblement pour une Calédonie dans la République, RPCR) was founded. The party was grounded in the traditional white settler community (the Caldoches), it had absorbed defectors from the UC, and it had its own dynamic leader in a man named Jacques Lafleur.

The secessionist movement was in full bloom by 1980. Independence leaders had won 35 percent of the vote in 1979,[32] polarization was feeding the nationalist narrative, and, we will see, the various wings of the movement were beginning to show tactical diversity. The Kanaks also believed that France was deliberately encouraging migration to New Caledonia from France and other territorial regions as a way to decrease the Kanak vote share. In 1984, most of the Kanak independence groups merged to form the FLNKS, the overarching pro-independence alliance that would dominate secessionist politics for the next twenty years, if not longer. The Kanak tricolor was first flown in the early days of the FLNKS.[33]

The 1980s represent a kind of peak in the development of New Caledonian secession. They were a time of conflict, of violence, referred to as *les événements* (the Events, the Troubles). To be sure, violence was the not only method used. As I discuss in the next section, the independence effort pursued its aims in a somewhat diffuse manner using violence, nonviolence, and electoral capture. But an escalating cycle of violence between the secessionists and the loyalists on the far right caught the public attention. Demonstrations by one side often invited a counterdemonstration, and some of these led to violent altercations, such as the brawl at the Place de Cocotiers in July 1982.[34] By late 1984, Kanak secessionists were creating sporadic road blocks around the island as a form of civil disobedience, and on occasion they seized farms belonging to settlers. These acts served to strengthen the extreme wings on both sides. A particularly violent act, known as the Hienghène Massacre, took place in December of that year when ten FLNKS members were ambushed and killed by settler militia. Two of the dead were Tjibaou's own brothers.

The tensions of the 1980s culminated with a series of signal events. First, the Kanaks were able to get New Caledonia put back on the UN List of Non-Self-Governing Territories on December 2, 1986. This was a substantial victory for the independence leaders as it increased the pressure on France to negotiate. For its part, the French government vacillated between a desire to accommodate and a more conservative tendency to crack down on the Kanak disobedients. Indeed, some in the metropole called for a strong stance against the independence forces, and the Gaullist Charles Pasqua stated that "The defense of Bastia (Corsica) begins in Nouméa."[35]

Second, these tensions culminated in the bloodiest episode of the Troubles, the Ouvéa Massacre—an event that is chronicled in the 2011 film *Rebellion*. In order "to force France to negotiate" Kanak commandos killed four gendarmes in Ouvéa and took another twenty-seven hostage on April 22, 1988.[36] Two weeks later, French special forces made an assault on the cave where the hostages were held and nineteen people were killed (seventeen Kanak commandos and two French soldiers). Although the Kanak secessionists had initiated the crisis, France was subsequently criticized for overreacting and allegations continue to this day that many of the Kanaks were captured and then executed. In the popular imagination many people hold this story to be true. During my interviews in Nouméa, several people cited these executions as part of the historical narrative of the Troubles.

The Ouvéa Massacre focused attention on the escalating crisis in the islands and paved the way for two further developments. The deaths had alerted both sides to the dangers of further escalation and raised the specter of colonial war for France. The immediate result was the Matignon Accords, signed on June 26, 1988, between Tjibaou and Lafleur. They were designed to arrest the hostilities and buy time for the peace process by granting amnesty to those involved in the Ouvéa hostage crisis, and by setting in place a ten-year period of consensus building that would end with a referendum on independence.[37] The Matignon Accords were a sensible, rather centrist solution that nevertheless alienated the extremists on both sides of the issue. One result was yet another infamous chapter in the events of the 1980s, the murder of Tjibaou and his colleague Yeiwene Yeiwene by a Kanak radical named Djubelly Wea on May 4, 1989, at a memorial on Ouvéa for the massacre the year before.[38] Like Mahatma Gandhi, Tjibaou was martyred for his moderation.

The Matignon Accords along with the memory of the bloody events of the 1980s led ten years later to the Nouméa Accord. Although the Matignon Accords had called for an independence referendum, the prospect was abandoned during the 1990s by the independence leaders who saw that they lacked the support to win the vote.[39] In return, Kanak leaders like Roch Wamytan and Sylvain Pabouty were able to negotiate a highly unusual agreement for a separatist region, certainly one that is unique within the French territorial system. The preamble to the Nouméa Accord states that "This territory [Grand Terre] . . . was not empty" when the French claimed it in 1853. Yet, France "did not establish legally formalized relations with the indigenous population." This is effectively a statement of inherent sovereignty, one that implies that France has illegally occupied the territory. The French government's concession on this point, signed by Prime Minister Lionel Jospin (as well as by the FLNKS and RPCR), was a substantial victory for the independence side as it underlined their colonial status and legacy. It is this sort of recognition that indigenous legal movements such as the Murrawarri Republic hope to gain.

The Nouméa Accord includes a set of noteworthy stipulations.[40] These include the establishment of a new congress in New Caledonia and an "irreversible transfer of administrative powers from Paris to local authorities and the new Congress." The aim of this ratchet-like mechanism was to prevent the kind of power transfer reversals that had occurred in the past. The accord also stipulated a new constitutional status of "shared sovereignty" for New Caledonia.[41] Finally, the accord called for a "further 15–20 year transition before a referendum on self-determination for New Caledonia, possibly leading to the 'emancipation' of the territory."

The years since 1998 have constituted the third phase of the independence movement. The Nouméa Accord has defined this period by shaping the space for political contestation. It was ratified by 72 percent of the population and was considered a substantial gain by Kanak leaders like Wamytan.[42] The independence movement has been almost fully institutionalized, and has competed through the electoral system to see powers devolved to New Caledonia. And critically, as the independence referenda have drawn near, the independence leaders have attempted to broaden their message in hopes of capturing a majority. As James Crawford notes, the Nouméa Accord has implied a "special, perhaps privileged position for that group [the Kanaks] in deciding the future disposition of the territory," but it also made clear that the participation of the other non-Kanak populations is essential.[43] The referenda on independence are to be decided by a majority vote.

Strategy and Tactics

Decolonial movements are in many ways a composite of the other types. They exist in diverse settings, from democratic societies (French Polynesia) to less institutionalized domains (Western Sahara), where conflict is more common, to situations of de facto statehood (Somaliland). As such, they exhibit a wide range of tactics. What unites them is their historical relationship with the central government and their resulting ability to argue that they should qualify for decolonization. At the strategic level they are the same as all other movements. But at the tactical level they have an extra card up their sleeve. When playing the sovereignty game, the New Caledonian secessionists have shown substantial tactical diversity that has evolved over time and only recently come to focus almost exclusively on institutional methods and the message of a multiethnic identity. Their chief normative appeal has focused on the principle of decolonization. In many ways this is a secessionist success story. It took several decades, but the independence leaders compelled the French state to negotiate. How did they do this?

At various points the independence movement deployed all three forms of compellence tactics. The use of nonviolent civil resistance methods became increasingly common in the 1960s and 1970s as groups like the Foulards Rouge and Palika began to advocate for forms of peaceful contestation with the state. These groups arose as part of the Kanak Awakening, and the practitioners were well versed in revolutionary theory. In the early days they held clandestine meetings and set out to raise political awareness by spreading political pamphlets and through the use of graffiti.[44] For their disobedience they were arrested numerous times, but this was part of their agenda for winning over the population. The prison guard Maurice Chaniel wrote, "For the first time, I felt a kind of shame in doing my job [incarcerating the dissidents]."[45] Palika formed committees in each tribe across the islands, adopted a Leninist worldview, and aimed for structural change and the reclaiming of stolen lands by using peaceful forms of political action.[46] Like other independence organizations, Palika competed electorally, but it saw elections not as an end in itself—the system was structurally rigged against the Kanaks—but rather as a means of raising national consciousness. Groupe 1878, a Palika offshoot, organized marches and sit-ins as a way to focus attention on land issues on Grand Terre.[47] By the time the FLNKS had formed in 1984, the repertoires of contention had expanded to include hunger strikes, road blocks, and the intentional shutdown of public services.

For secessionist movements there is a moment when violence is put on the menu of options. Some groups like the contemporary Catalan secessionists have not crossed this threshold, perhaps because of their confidence in institutional options, the relatively high standard of living, or the fact that most Catalans have no personal memory of violence against the state. But for the West Papuans, violence against the Indonesian state was always there. What are the factors that put violence on the menu? The case of New Caledonia provides a cautionary tale because that line was crossed in the 1980s and for a time violence was used.

As secessionism developed it was not long before some of the independence organizations began to divide over the issue of using violence.[48] For example, in 1984 the Naisseline-led Kanak Socialist Liberation (Libération Kanak Socialiste, LKS) party distanced itself from other independence parties that advocated violence.[49] The LKS felt that peaceful options had not yet been exhausted; the rest went on to form the FLNKS. The gradual use of violence by the FLNKS created further divisions as some were repulsed by it, while others saw it as the only way forward. It was during this time that young Kanaks were sent to Libya to be trained in terrorist tactics. This was actively publicized by the FLNKS for prestige and coercive purposes, as Yeiwene made clear: "You will soon have a glimpse of their training in Tripoli. Because from now on they will know how to explode bombs and make Molotov cocktails. . . . That's why we have taken care to explain to the militants that there will perhaps soon be deaths."[50] Similarly, the various committees of the FLNKS began to circulate copies of Gillo Pontecorvo's movie *The Battle of Algiers* in order to study the successful tactics of the Algerians.[51]

Various reasons were given for why violence was adopted. Eloi Machoro was one of the chief tacticians of the independence movement, an intimidating personality and perceived man of action. When asked about how the violence began, he said that it had started long ago by the colonizers.[52] Machoro was killed by the gendarmes during a cycle of violence in early 1985. Many cited the increasing frustrations of failed promises from France that drove them to use violent methods.[53] But clearly the escalating cycle of action and reaction developed a causal power and gradually shifted preferences. One leader, Alphonse Dianou, had preached Gandhian nonviolence until he experienced police beatings.[54]

Collectively, these acts of violence had utility because they focused attention on the issue of New Caledonian independence. The attacks combined with the roadblocks and other forms of civil resistance to create a crisis across the island. In fact, a kind of split sovereignty emerged as the FLNKS took control (for a time) of some of the east-coast towns like Canala and Thio, converting them into secessionist strongholds.[55] Given the small population, it is unlikely that the secessionists could have prosecuted a full civil war against a committed France, but it is not clear that the Kanak leaders thought they could or even had to. The violence was mostly intermilitia—the Hienghène Massacre was carried out by armed settlers—or against the gendarmes who often acted in a somewhat neutral manner. In general, the French government was wary of appearing to act in a heavy-handed manner.[56] That is why the strident reaction to the Ouvéa hostage crisis shocked the Kanaks and the rest of New Caledonia, if not much of France, and ultimately help set the stage for negotiations. In the end, the French government was limited not in its capabilities but in its willingness to respond with sufficient force to crush the secessionists. The domestic and international perception of the situation mattered.

A major reason that the Kanaks were able to get France to negotiate was their success in internationalizing the issue. They prevailed on the normative front, pitching the decolonization argument, and brought international pressure to bear on France. In multiple interviews I was told that this was always a major pillar of the independence strategy.[57] Although France argued that New Caledonia was an internal matter, and succeeded in doing so for roughly thirty years, the FLNKS was able to change international opinion by the mid-1980s. In part, the map of the world in 1986 was different from 1947, the year France successfully removed New Caledonia from the decolonization list. The number of sovereign states had more than doubled, and a great many of the entrants had been born from decolonization. These newly decolonized states saw in New Caledonia a far-flung colony controlled by a powerful European state. Even the Anglo-Saxon states of Australia and New Zealand questioned French motives in denying independence to New Caledonia. I was told in an interview that Bob Hawke's government of Australia supported the Kanak cause because decolonization was still a highly visible cause in the 1980s.[58] Of course, French popularity in Oceania was quite poor at the time on account of its commitment to nuclear testing in Polynesia, and, relatedly, its infamous bombing of the Greenpeace ship the *Rainbow Warrior* in Auckland harbor on July 10, 1985.

Despite the blocking efforts of France, the FLNKS was able to mount an end run. They cited UNGA Resolution 2621, which forbade member states from permitting (if not encouraging) the influx of settlers to change local population balances, and accused France of doing just that.[59] They enlisted the help of local Melanesian states and a sympathetic nonaligned movement to build international support. Then, on December 2, 1986, the UNGA voted eighty-nine to twenty-four (with thirty-four abstentions and eleven absences) to put New Caledonia back on the List of Non-Self-Governing Territories, stating that "New Caledonia had an inalienable right . . . to self-determination and independence" and further condemning France's policy of using migration to suppress self-determination.[60] France had fought hard to defeat the UNGA vote, pressuring former colonies and dialoguing with NATO allies—as well as criticizing Australia for meddling[61]— but it lost the argument internationally.

Although France initially tried to mitigate the UNGA vote, the Kanaks had won a moral victory. Importantly, the international support did not produce substantial material aid in the form of weaponry or military assistance. Tjibaou made this point when he said: "For the moment, we have this diplomatic support, but where material support is concerned, we have nothing."[62] There was the Libya connection; indeed, the FLNKS justified their relationship with Colonel Qaddafi by saying that states like Australia gave only moral support.[63] And interestingly, that connection was partly worked out through contacts with the independence effort in Aceh (see chapter 6).[64] But this assistance was marginal in the end. Of greater importance was the rhetorical value in getting on the decolonization list because this changed preferences on the matter and brought greater international scrutiny. Ultimately, it helped clear the way for the Matignon Accords in the wake of the Ouvéa Massacre, and ten years on, it set the stage for the Nouméa Accord.

The New Caledonian secessionists have engaged in tactics of electoral capture for decades. They gained 35 percent of the vote in 1979. Since that time various parties from FLNKS to Palika have run for office and developed constituencies. An interesting feature of the 1980s is that secessionist political parties competed electorally while also engaging in tactics of both nonviolence and violent resistance. This is unusual given the tension between the use of violent and institutional methods.[65] Perhaps in this case both approaches could be adopted for a short time because, like the Troubles in Northern Ireland, the violence was low-level, democratic institutions were robust, and the state had the military capability to suppress the movement if necessary. It is, however, clear that the Matignon negotiations and, subsequently, the Nouméa Accord created a peace by intensifying institutional competition. An independence referendum was now on the table, and both sides had strong incentives to win over the population.

The Nouméa Accord further institutionalized the secessionist effort and, in doing so, altered the tactical setting. I stated previously that New Caledonia represents in many ways a success story where secession is concerned. That is only party true. The Kanaks were able to get back on the decolonization list and be given several chances at choosing independence via a referendum. This is a victory that remains out of reach for most independence movements. And yet independence may remain elusive here for the simple reason that the secessionists may not be able to win a referendum. As various analysts have observed, by the time the Kanaks had the constitutional pathway to sovereignty, they no longer had the numbers.[66] David Chappell refers to this as the "double legitimacy" issue, referring to the rights of indigenous Kanak and those who came after.[67] The rights of both parties are recognized in the Nouméa Accord. In cases of decolonization such as this, voters are usually given three options: integration with the home state, associated statehood, and independence. Although these categories can be chopped into finer slices, the choice between them has largely shaped the political debate since 1998.[68] There is much to be said for institutionalizing an independence process. It changes the tactical setting and renders violent conflict less likely. As one high-level interviewee said of New Caledonia, institutionalization creates lock-in for the politicians on both sides; they have a personal stake in the process and they all know each other.

Since the 1990s, if not before, a major strategic aim for the Kanak secessionists has been to build a winning coalition. As the Kanaks represent less than half the population of the island, they need to broaden their message to appeal to elements of the traditional settler population and the other recent immigrant groups. They need to pitch a multiethnic identity, a truly New Caledonian identity. Otherwise, by focusing on indigenous rights and Kanak identity, they risk alienating non-Kanaks, who rightly question their role in a postindependence Kanak nationalist state.

The challenge in pitching this broader message is to offer something better than the opposition. One of the most prominent contemporary leaders of the anti-opposition side is Phillipe Gomès, an Algerian-born Pied-Noir who immigrated to New Caledonia in 1974 at the age of fifteen. Gomès is a centrist, the founder of the political party Caledonia Together (Calédonie Ensemble), currently the strongest party in New Caledonian politics. In a personal interview, Gomès predicted that the "No" campaign would win the 2018 referendum by taking 70 percent of the vote.[69] He stated that although the FLNKS was right in the 1980s—that is, they were on the right side of history—they lost their way after the Nouméa Accord devolved power and the Kanaks became fully enfranchised. In a critique that I have heard in reference to both Scottish and Catalan independence, he said that the independence side cannot provide a compelling argument for why independence would make New Caledonia better off. That is, how will the big issues of currency, justice, law and order, defense, and foreign relations be managed? Various interviews confirmed this problem: independence represents uncertainty for those who are not committed to Kanak nationalism, and the independence side has thus far failed to reduce the uncertainty. At a 2018 talk, Daniel Goa, the president of Union Caledonia, stated that the anti-independence side has been successful at drawing people away from the question of "dignity" to the question of the "balance sheet"— that is, getting voters to focus on the finances and functionality of an independent New Caledonia instead of the moral question of decolonization.[70]

In May 2018, President Emmanuel Macron visited New Caledonia on a regional tour that included a visit to Australia. In a smart and carefully orchestrated manner he discussed the upcoming referendum, and said that it was not for him to tell people how to vote, but he hoped that New Caledonians would decide to remain with France. In a move that might have backfired, he participated in the thirty-year commemoration of the Ouvéa Massacre. Despite warnings that he should not attend, he reached out to potential spoilers and Kanak leaders to ensure that he followed all local protocols. Essentially, he appealed to the hearts and minds of the New Caledonians—the Kanaks, the settlers, and the immigrants— rather than resort to scare tactics. In all my interviews I was told that Macron showed a deft hand and that his skilled diplomacy was an effective countersecession strategy.

The pro-independence side also expected the "No" vote to win the 2018 referendum. Indeed, in my interviews I could not find anyone who thought the "Yes" vote would win. The independence leader Sylvain Pabouty, founder of the political party Southern Unity Dynamic (Dynamik Unitaire Sud), has been involved since the 1990s.[71] He stated in an interview that is important that the independence side win at least 30 percent of the vote as that would help sustain the effort and maintain momentum. He echoed the comments of others when saying that the independence side, especially the FLNKS, needs to build a more coherent argument for why independence is best for a majority of the population. For his part, he felt that Kanak side needed to redouble its efforts toward seeing the Nouméa Accord implemented and that power be fully devolved.

Although the secessionists lost the 2018 referendum, they did better than expected. The results showed that 43.6 percent of the voters chose independence, with 56.4 percent opposed. Although this was a decisive win for the "No" vote, it was much closer than any of my interviewees predicted, or any of the pre-referendum polls forecast. This suggests that the independence effort is alive and well.

And yet the future of the New Caledonian independence movement is unclear. As a fully institutionalized movement it will struggle to win as long as it fails to capture the middle and constitute a majority. Perhaps with time that will happen. Gomès has argued for a unique and emerging New Caledonian identity that combines universal values, Christianity, and Kanak culture.[72] Another interviewee said that young educated Kanaks are less wedded to the independence effort, particularly when they have studied overseas, thus reversing the pattern from the 1960s to the 1980s in which young Kanaks would return radicalized after their time in France. As long as this middle holds, independence will remain out of reach, unless the middle gradually comes to identify with a broader understanding of New Caledonian independence.

That said, there is always the danger of the secessionist movement becoming more violent and less institutionalized.[73] In my interviews it was stressed that the Kanaks cannot be made to feel ashamed if they lose the referendum. I was told that there is still a simmering level of anger on both wings of the issue, and that there is a high level of gun ownership on the islands.[74] Concerns remain over mining rights,[75] and there is still a substantial class disparity—described to me as the "Squats and the Yachts"—that often falls along ethnic lines. One prominent interviewee said that if the independence side loses all three referenda, it will be forced to conclude that the Nouméa Accord has failed to meet the goal of decolonization and will have to consider alternative methods.

The principle of decolonization has created one of the surest pathways into the sovereignty club. It has been so successful in answering the question of "Who counts?," at putting a wedge between those who count and those who do not, that many regard it as a phenomenon altogether different from secession. But that distinction is imperfect because there are borderline cases, and, as the example of New Caledonia shows, several decolonial movements endure. Although the independence effort has stuck to a consistent normative appeal focusing on decolonization, it has shown remarkable tactical diversity where compellence is concerned. Here, we can see how different methods were used at different points in time, sometimes simultaneously. We can grasp the pressure that their use put on the state. We can comprehend how institutional access, and the gaining of political voice, gradually pushed back against the perceived need and desire to use violence. Finally, we can also appreciate how the erosion of institutional access can increase the temptation to take up arms.

NORTHERN CYPRUS
The Red Banner Reversed

Question asked when I crossed the Ledra Palace Checkpoint:
"Are you going to the Occupied Territory?"

The last case study focuses on Northern Cyprus[1]—formally known as the Turkish Republic of Northern Cyprus (TRNC)[2]—a breakaway region that encompasses one third of the island of Cyprus in the eastern reaches of the Mediterranean Sea. Its tactical setting is different from the other case studies for a rather straightforward reason: it is sundered from the home state, the Republic of Cyprus, by a UN-backed buffer zone known colloquially as the Green Line. As a result, there is no overlapping sovereignty between the secessionist region and the rest of the country. The secessionists cannot engage in the compellence tactics of electoral capture, insurgency, and civil resistance. These levers are unavailable to them. Instead, they focus on defense, deterrence, and the keeping of the territory they possess. Meanwhile, their primary normative appeal has stressed earned sovereignty—that is, demonstrating to the world that they are an empirical state that has earned sovereign recognition.

All of the case studies in the book represent a kind of cautionary tale—of democratic deadlock, suppression, violence, and so on. The story of Northern Cyprus shows what happens when a breakaway region is converted into a de facto state. It is a fitting case study to end with because in temporal terms a secessionist movement can be viewed as a series of moments or images. In some ways the situation in Northern Cyprus represents a moment *after* the moments we saw with Catalonia, West Papua, and the others. That is because the Northern Cypriots are no longer engaging with the state in direct terms via the ballot, the demonstration, or the gun. The conflict here is calcified, frozen, and externalized.[3] De facto movements are the most externalized of the secessionist kinds, involving intricate diplomatic relations and geopolitical complexity. Such conflicts can endure for long periods because of the status quo bias that sets in and the inability of the relevant parties to make a change.

Background

Cyprus is a large island tucked into the corner of the eastern Mediterranean (see figure 9.1). When visiting, I was told that the mountains of Turkey are visible on a clear day, though there are some 75 kilometers of water between the island and the mainland. It is the third largest island in the Mediterranean, covering 9,251 square kilometers. It has a rich history and has seen numerous empires come and go, from the Romans to the Ottomans to the British.

According to a 1960 census, the inhabitants of the island were divided into a number of cultural groups.[4] The largest were the Greek Cypriots, accounting for 78 percent (441,568) of the island's population, who possessed a history on the island stretching back to classical times. The second largest group were the Turkish Cypriots, comprising 18 percent (103,822) of the population, a group that came over during the Ottoman period and had been there for several centuries. The remainder of the population was made up of several smaller groups, including: (1) Maronites (~6,000), inhabitants of Cyprus for over 1,000 years; (2) Armenians (~4,000), a population that came during the Ottoman period; and (3) Latins (~500), descendants of Venetian settlers. Other cultural groups migrated to Cyprus after 1960—as I discuss below, Northern Cyprus now holds a substantial population of mainland Turks—but these were the identifiable ethnic groups at the birth of the Cypriot state in 1960.

Like West Papua, Bougainville, and Abkhazia, Northern Cyprus is a case of recursive secession. That is, it is effectively an attempt to secede from a sovereign state that had only recently become a sovereign state. The state in question is the Republic of Cyprus, which became officially independent of the United Kingdom on August 16, 1960.[5] The British took informal control of the island from the Ottomans in 1878, formally annexed it in 1914, and made it into a crown colony in 1925. The geopolitical climate changed after World War II and the British gradually warmed to the idea of permitting Cypriot independence.[6] The chief problem in doing so was managing the simmering ethnic tensions on the island. This is a challenge with secession broadly speaking; the fragmenting and creation of a new political unit alters the demographic distribution and power balance in the new state, empowering some and inspiring others to seek their own, even smaller, political unit.

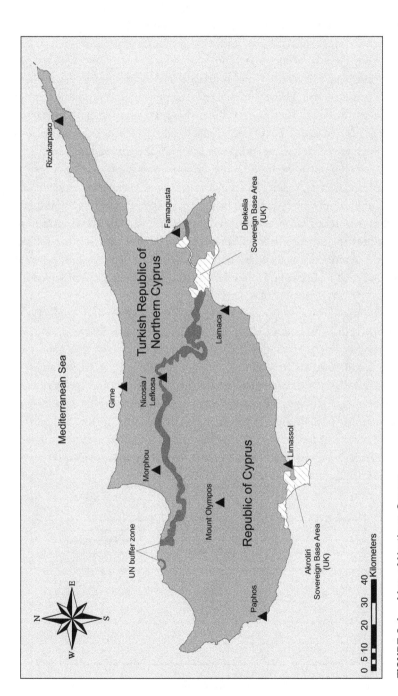

FIGURE 9.1. Map of Northern Cyprus

In *Bitter Lemons*, the British author Lawrence Durrell offers a nostalgic and heartbreaking account of the rise of ethnic tensions on Cyprus during the 1950s.[7] The Greek Cypriots and Turkish Cypriots were not geographically divided like they are now. There were intermixed communities across the island, with the two populations living side by side. Intermarriage was uncommon, but peaceful coexistence was the norm. I leave it to others to investigate the roots of the Cypriot conflict and provide a full explanation, but certainly the prospect of independence played a part. For decades many Greek Cypriots advocated for *enosis*, that is, unification with Greece following independence from the United Kingdom.[8] This effort picked up momentum in 1955 with the formation of Ethniki Organosis Kyprion Agonos (EOKA), a guerrilla group pressing for Cypriot independence and eventual unification with Greece, led by Georgios Grivas, a Cypriot-born retired colonel of the Greek army.[9] The pursuit of *enosis* drove a wedge between the two communities because the Turkish Cypriots feared for their position as a minority group in a more distinctly Greek nationalist culture.[10] The resulting tensions created cycles of recrimination and ethnic identity hardening, and provided the material for Durrell's sorrowful account.[11]

The half-decade until 1960 was characterized by increasing ethnic conflict, and a British-led but multinational effort to create a peaceful new sovereign state. As table 9.1 shows, most of the conflict occurred during this period. EOKA targeted the British and Turkish Cypriots, and were retaliated against by British authorities and Turkish Cypriot combatant groups like Volkan and the Turkish Resistance Movement.[12] In this scenario, the British found themselves in a position of trying to protect both themselves and the minority Turkish Cypriots, a point that would later serve as fodder for the argument that they possessed an anti-Greek and pro-Turkish bias. By the autumn of 1956, the British had some 30,000 troops on the island attempting to defeat EOKA.[13]

TABLE 9.1.   Conflict data for Northern Cyprus, 1945–2016

YEAR	INTENSITY LEVEL[a]
1955*	1
1956*	1
1957*	1
1958*	1
1959*	1
1974	2

Source: Uppsala Conflict Data Program.
Note: Years with fewer than twenty-five battle deaths are omitted.
[a]1 = 25–999 battle-related deaths; 2 = 1000+ battle-related deaths
*Period of British rule[14]

Chief obstacles to creating the state were the relatively weak sense of Cypriot national identity and the fact that the ethnic cleavage on the island was really just a small part of the larger fault line between the Greek and Turkish national blocs. It is true that some Cypriots have felt and do feel more Cypriot than Greek or Turkish,[15] but large portions of these communities felt, at least in the early days, more Greek or Turkish than Cypriot.[16] These compound identities combined with the geopolitical setting to create a delicate situation. Both sides of the conflict had a patron (Greece and Turkey) that was willing to intervene and both patrons were valuable members of NATO. From the beginning the Cypriot conflict was unusually externalized, involving diplomatic relations between the British, Greeks, and Turks, among others, and the emerging leadership on the island. It was during this time that the two Cypriot communities found their respective leaders in Archbishop Makarios III, for the Greek side, and Rauf Denktash, for the Turkish side. Both men were charismatic, cunning negotiators and committed to their causes.

The result of this bargaining was the 1960 Cypriot constitution that came into effect with the state's independence. Observers called Cyprus an "international state" because of the granting of rights to the United Kingdom, Greece, and Turkey, and because it inculcated the sense that the two communities had mother nations.[17] The constitution prohibited both unification (with Greece or Turkey) and internal secession,[18] an attempt at striking a balance between the competing demands of *enosis* and *taksim* (partition). Another aspect of the constitution was the addition of three treaties with the British, Greek, and Turkish governments.[19] The Treaty of Guarantee gave these states explicit right to intervene in the case of unrest on the island. The Treaty of Alliance allowed for the stationing of 950 Greek soldiers and 650 Turkish in Cyprus. Finally, the Treaty of Establishment permitted the United Kingdom to retain two Sovereign Base Areas that it still holds nearly sixty years on (see figure 9.1). As we will see, these treaties have had important downstream consequences.

The Development of Secessionism

The flag of Northern Cyprus is modeled rather consciously on the Turkish flag, *al Sancak* (the Red Banner). The Turkish flag is quite old, and its central image is the white crescent and star set on a red field. This was essentially the Ottoman flag, formally adopted by the Republic of Turkey on June 5, 1936. The origins of the imagery are lost to legend, not unlike the *Senyera* of Catalonia, but a popular tale attributes it to the founder of the Ottoman House, Osman I (1299–1324). However, one vexillological text traces its origins to Byzantine times.[20] In any case, *al Sancak* is an iconic image of the Turkish nation.

It is therefore noteworthy that the Northern Cypriots have chosen a flag that is the reverse of *al Sancak*, depicting a red crescent and star on a white field, with the addition of two horizontal red stripes, one on the top and one on the bottom (see figure 9.2). Its design was the result of a competition, and it was formally adopted (Law No. 15) by the TRNC on March 7, 1984.[21] Although I did not discover an agreed-upon meaning behind the two horizontal stripes in my research, one interviewee stated they symbolized the mother nation of Turkey (top stripe) and the Turkish Cypriots (bottom stripe) going forward together into eternity.[22] Another interviewee said that he did not know the meaning behind the stripes, and speculated that they may have been added to increase the perception of difference from *al Sancak*.[23] Whatever the case, the use of the crescent and star is clearly meant to celebrate the Turkish identity of Northern Cyprus. It serves as a potent symbol to the Greek Cypriots that the Turkish Cypriots are part of an old, powerful, and proximate nation. A visitor to the divided capital of Nicosia (its Greek name; Lefkosa in Turkish) is confronted with an arresting image when they look north. There, set on the southern face of the Kyrenia (Pentadaktylos) mountains are both flags: *al Sancak* and its reverse, the flag of Northern Cyprus. Each flags covers about 50 acres of the mountain slope, they are observable at night, and, apparently, they are visible from space.[24] Written beneath *al Sancak* in Turkish, for all to see, is the Kemalist motto: "How happy is the one who calls himself a Turk!"[25]

The Northern Cypriot flag was not officially adopted until 1984, twenty-four years after the birth of the Cypriot state. What happened during that time to push

FIGURE 9.2. The independence flag of Northern Cyprus

the Northern Cypriots toward demanding full independence? The main part of the explanation for this development was the constitutional breakdown and related crisis of the 1960s and early 1970s. Hardliners on both sides created problems for the power-sharing agreement. According to the constitution, the council of ministers was to consist of seven members of the Greek Cypriot community and three Turkish Cypriots.[26] That 70:30 ratio became the standard in the distribution of power, except for the military, which was 60:40. The Greek Cypriots felt that this ratio overrepresented the Turkish voice in the government—it did if one compared the population numbers. However, the Turkish side felt that it was necessary to protect their community's interests. It did not help that Makarios, now the country's first president, continued to talk openly about *enosis*, a concept that was anathema to the Turkish Cypriot community. Eventually, in late 1963, Makarios proposed thirteen amendments to the constitution that were meant to create more favorable terms for the Greek community. The amendments were rejected by the Turkish government in Ankara, an action that infuriated much of the Greek Cypriot community. It was not long before small acts of violence escalated into renewed internecine conflict.

The 1963–1964 winter in Cyprus, or Black Christmas as it has been called, was a time of unrest. In his account of this period, Aytug Plumer, a former TRNC minister, describes the fear that gripped the Turkish Cypriots.[27] They were outnumbered and vulnerable to attacks from EOKA, and the protective British forces of the late 1950s were gone. Plumer argues that the bitter memory of that period shaped all subsequent negotiations between the two communities because the Turkish Cypriots would always require a strong security guarantee.[28] After much negotiation between the key external powers, the UN Security Council passed Resolution 186, authorizing the United Nations Force in Cyprus (UNFICYP) on March 4, 1964. On March 27, the force was deployed on Cyprus with 6,369 troops of various countries.[29] The UNFICYP is still operational to this day, though the numbers have decreased, and it currently patrols the Green Line.

Although the UNFICYP was established in 1964, it would be another ten years before the Green Line was established. In the early years of its deployment, the UNFICYP worked to stop the violence. During this time the two communities were still distributed across the island in a mixed fashion. Various attempts were made by the local leaders and international agents to negotiate a working peace. At one point, Dean Acheson, former US secretary of state, led an American effort to find a solution, but it failed along with the other attempts. By 1967 the violence had begun to subside, but a dangerous split developed in the Greek Cypriot community between Makarios, who was moving toward a more moderate position, and the newly formed EOKA-B, a strong pro-union splinter group that had the backing of the Greek government.[30] As tensions mounted, the EOKA-B attempted to assassinate Makarios several times and eventually staged a coup on July 15, 1974. The new president was Nicos Sampson, a former EOKA gunman and supporter of *enosis*.

De facto states almost always have a strong supporter that can even the odds and create conditions of symmetry between the minority group and the state.[31] On July 20, 1974, Turkey invoked the Right of Guarantee and intervened militarily. The Turkish prime minister, Bulent Ecevit, consulted the British government prior to the intervention, but decided to act when he perceived that the British were unable or unwilling to intervene.[32] Consisting of some 40,000 soldiers with air support, the Turkish military achieved local superiority. The ensuing conflict resulted in several thousand casualties (see table 9.1) and took place in two stages. In the initial stage, the Turkish army secured a small area and attempted to negotiate a political settlement. When that faltered, a second stage began as the Turkish forces fanned out and seized the entire northern third of the island. The first stage had been to secure the peace, the second was to secure sufficient territory to change the facts on the ground. A period of ethnic unmixing occurred in the wake of the intervention.[33] Some 160,000 Greek Cypriots (one-third of the Greek community) abandoned their homes in the north to seek refuge in the south. Likewise, roughly 40,000 Turkish Cypriots moved from the south to the north. As we will see, the memory and bitterness of this internal population transfer and refugee crisis serves as a continuing obstacle to negotiation.

The Turkish Cypriots were now in a much stronger position from which to bargain. They were protected by the Turkish army, the two populations were now divided, and the boundary of the two communities was forming along what became known as the Green Line. But they still aimed for a highly decentralized, if not confederal, bicommunal relationship. In February of 1975, they declared the Turkish Federated State of North Cyprus, and it was hoped that the concept of this new territorial entity would assist them in the bargaining process. However, more deadlock followed as Makarios (back in power) and Denktash failed to find a middle ground. After another eight years of failed negotiations involving multiple parties, including the UN, Northern Cyprus declared independence on November 15, 1983.[34] Although Denktash had been considering the move for many months—the catalyst was evidently the passing of a UN resolution condemning armed occupations.[35] Northern Cyprus (the TRNC) had unilaterally declared its intentions of becoming a sovereign state.

Strategy and Tactics

Experts on Cyprus (and the Cypriots themselves) will often say that the Cyprus problem is unique or sui generis, that it is unlike any other independence movement. I have found that all independence efforts are discussed in this way, and it is partly true; there are local factors that contextualize every conflict. But at the high strategic level, they are all the same. The chief obstacle to their ambitions is the home state, in this case the Republic of Cyprus. The home state is a member of the sovereignty club and it has substantial advantages over its opponent. To become a recognized sovereign state, Northern Cyprus has to get the home state to remove the veto and enlist the international community in its project.

It is at the tactical level that one can differentiate Northern Cyprus from other movements, but even here we can see that their tactics conform to type. Like other de facto state movements, the tactics of the Northern Cypriots are characterized by an inability to compel the home state using violence, nonviolence, and electoral capture. Instead, they have to settle for defense and deterrence—that is, dissuading the home state from trying to retake the territory. Northern Cyprus has been strikingly successful in this regard since 1974. The key to that success, of course, has been the Turkish army, which can defend the Green Line and deter the Greek Cypriot forces from trying to reclaim the north. That power balance along with the corollary diplomatic relations (discussed below) have lent the conflict an unusual degree of immovability.

The division between the two sides is in many ways frozen in time. The Green Line is an oddly drawn and at times jagged belt of territory that includes built structures that are effectively lost to both sides. For example, the large seaside district of Varosha has remained abandoned for over forty years, and its crumbling buildings are visible from the southern sections of Famagusta. Similarly, the old Nicosia International Airport has sat idle in the buffer zone all these years, with large passenger planes sitting on the tarmac. The two capitals, Nicosia and Lefkosa, are merely two halves of the ancient walled city that is now bisected by the Green Line. However, that line is not simply a wall or a neat 100-meter strip of land separated by barbed wire. Rather, there are old houses and buildings inside the zone, and at times the sides of these buildings constitute the wall. Exploring the small alleys on either side of the line can be a surreal experience, something out of a science fiction novel, and for a child growing up in those neighborhoods it must have felt like the world mysteriously terminated at the end of the block.

The fixed nature of the Green Line and separation of the two populations have removed the ability of the Northern Cypriots to compel the Greek side to negotiate. In my interviews and conversations on both sides of the line I would ask how long the status quo could continue. The common answer was that it could endure indefinitely, because the Greek Cypriots had no interest in compromising and they could not be forced to negotiate. The normal levers of compellence are unavailable here. This is the downside of achieving de facto statehood: it is a kind of perpetual liminal state stuck between reintegration, which the separatist side does not want, and full statehood, which the home state cannot be forced to permit. Nevertheless, the Northern Cypriots have achieved a security that those with memories of the conflict will not easily give up, and the Republic of Cyprus is dissuaded from attempting to use force.

For Northern Cyprus the real game has taken place on the diplomatic front through engagement with the Republic of Cyprus and the international community. The leadership tried from the beginning to cast the image of Northern Cyprus as an empirical state, a sovereign body that should be recognized. Perhaps more than anyone else, Denktash worked to build a legal and semantic conception of statehood. Trained as a lawyer in the United Kingdom, he approached the problem by trying to adjust the terms that were used.[36] He studiously avoided terms like "minority" and apparently introduced new terms like "sovereignly" to describe the Turkish Cypriots.[37] The objective was clear: to present the Turkish Cypriots as a sovereign polity that should be equal in status to the Greek Cypriots.

Overall, progress for Northern Cyprus has been frustratingly slow. Although it was expected that the international community would come to acknowledge the "facts on the ground,"[38] acquiring recognition, even by degrees, has been an uphill battle. Small gains have been made and some observers have suggested that there is a kind of creeping legitimization. The TRNC has achieved observer status in a number of organizations, including the Organization of Islamic Cooperation and the Economic Cooperation Organization. Another interesting example is its membership in the CONIFA, a FIFA-like organization for stateless nations, and in June 2017 it hosted the European Cup. The TRNC has opened up de facto embassies in a number of cities such as London, Washington, DC, and Brussels.[39] Importantly, international support for Northern Cyprus has generally increased at moments when the Republic of Cyprus was seen as recalcitrant. One prominent example was the failed Annan Plan, high-level negotiations opened in 2004 that pushed for a Swiss-model solution based on a bizonal, bicommunal federal republic.[40] The plan had substantial international support but ran afoul of the usual concerns on both sides of the Green Line that had scuppered so many past proposals. However, in this case, a clear majority of the Turkish Cypriots voted for the plan, and it was the Greek Cypriot electorate who rejected it.[41] In the wake of the failed referendum, the UN general secretary and several prominent foreign leaders called for an end to Northern Cyprus's isolation.[42]

Nevertheless, the chief obstacle to change remains the home state veto. As Tahsin Ertuğruloğlu, the former TRNC foreign minister, said: "They [the Republic of Cyprus] are a member of the club, we are not."[43] Ertuğruloğlu spent years dialoguing with other former ministers, and ran the TRNC embassy in London for five years, but he was frustrated in his efforts to gain recognition. One foreign minister of a sovereign state told him that they (Northern Cypriots) were "seen as a secessionist ethnic minority," and therefore illegal. Although he worked to change their image and promote the alternative language of a sovereign polity, Ertuğruloğlu felt that the "international community considers them to be outlaws even if they haven't committed a crime."

For its part the Republic of Cyprus has been unusually successful in isolating Northern Cyprus.[44] Just as Denktash and the TRNC leadership has attempted to cultivate an image of statehood by using the appropriate language and building the relevant state structures, the Cypriot leaders have tried to delegitimize them when referring to the "so-called Ercan Airport" or "so-called Eastern Mediterranean University."[45] Language is important for framing the debate, and one can see this in the way that Greek Cypriots refer to the north not as the TRNC but as the Occupied Territory. There is some variation in how home states respond to de facto state movements. Moldova has cautiously engaged with Transnistria, even if it withholds recognition. Somalia denies Somaliland, but in a passive way on account of the state's limited capabilities. Cyprus, however, actively denies Northern Cyprus and has attempted to isolate it from the international community. According to James Ker-Lindsay, Cyprus's countersecession strategy is built on four pillars: (1) maintaining an unambiguous claim to the territory; (2) relentlessly working to prevent any degree of recognition of the TRNC; (3) stopping any form of informal legitimization; and (4) pursuing legal avenues for challenging the continuing existence of Northern Cyprus.[46]

Cyprus's project of isolating the north has been greatly assisted by the initial international reaction to the 1983 unilateral declaration of independence.[47] Three days after the declaration on November 18, 1983, the UN Security Council passed Resolution 541, which "deplored the declaration of the Turkish Cypriot authorities of the purported secession of the part of the Republic of Cyprus and called upon all States not to recognize any Cypriot State other than the Republic of Cyprus."[48] This was an unusually strident reaction from the international community, an act of collective nonrecognition that was similar in form to the nonrecognition of Manchuria, Rhodesia, Namibia, and the Bantustans.[49] Whereas most independence efforts are outwardly deemed a domestic affair, the movement in Northern Cyprus had been formally condemned. It is as though the club of sovereign states had decided to preempt the potential applicant by saying that they were not worthy by their very nature. Only one state dared to lean into the wind and recognize Northern Cyprus: its patron, the Republic of Turkey.[50]

The failure of the Annan Plan is merely one chapter in a series of diplomatic defeats. I have heard various metaphors used to describe the Cyprus problem— it is the diplomats' graveyard, it is a padlock without a key. Commentators point to various moments over the last forty years where a negotiation might have been reached. Chief among them is perhaps the moment in the early 1990s when Cyprus was admitted to the EU, an occasion on which many felt the EU squandered its ability to force a solution as a precondition for admittance.[51] A major part of the underlying problem is simply that the two sides define the problem differently. As I was told in a number of interviews, the Greek Cypriots focus on the 1974 Turkish invasion and subsequent illegal occupation and the Turkish Cypriots stress the 1963–1964 sectarian conflict and related feeling of vulnerability. One side resents the Turkish presence and the other requires it to ameliorate the deeper security problem.

Secessionist dynamics are often the product of the recession of empire. In an interview, Ertuğruloğlu pointed to a map of the eastern Mediterranean and said that Cyprus was one of the last islands to resist Hellenization.[52] Nearly all of the others had been absorbed into the Hellenic world that had expanded as the Ottoman Empire declined. In the wake of that decline were pockets of Turks who became increasingly vulnerable to Greek nationalism. Such anxieties fed the drive for *taksim* in the 1950s, and the corollary protest against *enosis*, and are still present in the cultural narrative of Northern Cyprus. For example, the Dervish Pasha Mansion is an historical museum in Lefkosa that was once the home of a Turkish Cypriot newspaper publisher in the late 1800s. A plaque at the entrance clearly states the reason why Pasha went into publishing: to fight British colonialism, to stand against *enosis* and the spread of Hellenism, and to be a voice for the Turks in a time of Ottoman decline.

For their part, the Greek Cypriots are largely focused on challenging the illegal Turkish occupation. Much of this has involved legal cases against Turkey— what has been called "lawfare"—and, indeed, in some cases they have been victorious.[53] In 1996, the European Court of Human Rights found in favor of Titina Loizadou, a Greek Cypriot from the north coast of Cyprus who claimed that the Turkish military had effectively denied her right to private property when she lost her home during the 1974 invasion. This was an unusual and watershed decision given the implication that Turkey could be held legally and financially responsible for the loss of land and possessions of the Greek Cypriots who fled south.[54] More generally, there are monuments to the occupation across the island, from the still visible crumbling structures within the buffer zone to the fact that nearly all of the maps in the south refer to land north of the Green Line as the

"Turkish Occupied Territory." Just south of the Ledra Palace checkpoint in Nicosia is a replica of the Kyrenia town hall, as the Greek Cypriots knew it before they fled the northern city. It is a museum of sorts, and a reminder of what was lost.

These competing narratives of invasion (by the Turks) and existential vulnerability (from the Greek Cypriots) reduce, and perhaps eliminate, the bargaining space. Although negotiations have long focused on a federal solution, polls consistently show that a federation is not the preferred solution for either side.[55] The Greek Cypriots prefer a unitary state where minority rights are given to the Turkish Cypriots. In contrast, the Turkish side prefers a confederation, which generally implies a political arrangement even more decentralized than a federation, one in which the units (not the center) have residual rights and the ability to opt in or out as they wish. From the perspective of political order, confederation is an interesting and somewhat unusual choice for a breakaway region. It is an arrangement that hovers on the line between a highly decentralized state and a collection of independent states that have come together to pool certain competencies. However, I was told in my interviews that it presupposes as the building blocks sovereign states, which can enter or exit the arrangement as they wish, and that it follows from Denktash's view that Northern Cyprus needs to be conceived first as a sovereignty that is free to negotiate on equal terms.[56]

In my interviews and conversations in Cyprus, I regularly asked what happens in the long run? To my surprise, I was always greeted with a shrug of the shoulders, a look of resignation, and some comment about how the status quo will continue. One would think that as the memory of the conflict recedes and as life on both sides of the line goes on an agreement could be reached. But none of my interviewees thought this was the case for, in fact, the narrative on each side endures. Polls show that younger Greek Cypriots are less keen on reintegration than the older generation.[57] Most of them were born after the conflict, have no memory of the north, and have never crossed the Green Line, despite the fact that is has been open since 2003. Education in the south stresses the narrative of Turkish occupation. Meanwhile, the demography of Northern Cyprus has gradually changed with the immigration of mainland Turks to the island. Less secular than the Turkish Cypriots, the settlers possess a deeper affinity to Turkey and possess little desire to unify with a Greek-speaking south they do not know. Professor Ahmet Sözen refers to this demographic change as the Hatay-ization of Northern Cyprus—a reference to the mainland region of Hatay that came under Turkish control in 1939 and was gradually assimilated.[58] Overall, public sentiment in Northern Cyprus has trended away from a federal solution.[59]

A commonly given explanation for why the status quo will continue is that there is no change factor. To be sure, the Turkish Cypriots have incentives to make a change. Being a member of the sovereignty club has its benefits.[60] International rules regarding shipping and air traffic make it illegal for Northern Cyprus to open up to direct traffic.[61] Indeed, to fly into the north's Ercan airport usually requires a stopover in Turkey. Northern Cyprus cannot access formal financial aid, and its profits are often boycotted unless routed first through Turkey.[62] The TRNC has done its best to advance the economy given these constraints—it has done particularly well in creating institutions of higher education that cater to foreign students[63]—but isolation has come at a cost. The problem is that the Republic of Cyprus prefers the status quo to any outcome that Northern Cyprus will agree on. It holds the home-state veto, it can continue to block the diplomatic efforts of the north, and it cannot be easily compelled. When I asked Tahsin Ertuğruloğlu how change might come, he shrugged and replied: "perhaps through a major change some day in the international community that would force Greek Cyprus to remove the block or else recognize the north."[64]

The case of Northern Cyprus provides an illustration of how some independence movements are forced to play the sovereignty game. In some ways the Northern Cypriots are a success story. They have won their autonomy, their freedom, and their security. That is no small thing for those who remember the Black Christmas of 1963. And for some secessionist movements, such as West Papua or Tibet, that outcome would indeed be a victory. Nevertheless, the victory is incomplete, as the Northern Cypriots know, because they are caught in a twilight state between reintegration and full statehood. Severed from the home state, they have lost many of the levers of compellence that are available to other kinds of movements, for better and for worse, and are relegated to a status of de facto statehood with no end in sight. They may have become fully sovereign had they made their run in earlier times—they seem to pass the Canning Test and meet the Montevideo Convention criteria[65]—and they may yet earn their recognition as the international community changes its views. But for the moment, they provide a cautionary tale of where secessionist ambition can lead.

A MACROANALYSIS OF
SECESSIONIST TACTICS

This chapter begins the transition from the case studies to the final sections of the book in which I zoom out to view the dynamics of secession from a wide angle. Here, I conduct a quantitative, macroanalytic analysis of secessionist tactics over the post-1945 period by studying the behavior of 136 movements at the time they became active. Much will be lost at this level of analysis, such as the history and local conditions for any given movement, but there is also much that is gained in a somewhat horizontal sense. That is, I can group these movements by kind and then examine the correlation between their expected tactics, according to my theory, and the actual tactics they have adopted. I can see if the results and underlying patterns that were revealed in the case studies can be extended to a broader, large-N format.

My theoretical framework yields a number of testable implications. If the theory is correct, we should expect to see: (1) democratized movements that compete electorally and appeal to the freedom to choose; (2) indigenous legal movements that also aim for electoral capture but showcase their inherent sovereignty in their normative appeals; (3) weak combative movements that engage in nonviolent civil resistance and showcase human rights abuses; (4) strong combative movements that adopt violent forms of compellence and appeal to norms regarding human rights abuse; (5) decolonial movements that adopt different tactics of compellence depending on context and appeal to norms related to decolonization; and (6) de facto state movements that engage in dissuasion (not compellence) and the normative appeal to earned sovereignty. All of these hypotheses were supported in the case studies. The goal in this chapter is to examine whether they extend beyond the examples of Catalonia, the Murrawarri Republic, West Papua, Bougainville, New Caledonia, and Northern Cyprus. Are they generalizable, and to what extent can we predict the tactics of a secessionist movement by looking at its setting?

The remainder of the chapter proceeds as follows. I first describe the data on secessionist movements, and I explain how they were sorted into the six secessionist kinds. I then elaborate the data used for the dependent variables: compellence and normative appeal. Finally, I conduct a quantitative analysis in two sections that are organized around the two dependent variables.

Data

The analysis in this chapter utilizes a dataset on secessionist movements, their compellence tactics, and their tactics of normative appeal. The data on secessionist movements are updated from my 2016 book *Age of Secession: The International and Domestic Determinants of State Birth*;[1] the data on compellence tactics are drawn from my 2019 article with the *Journal of Conflict Resolution*, co-authored with Louis Wasser;[2] the data on normative tactics were created for this project. The combined dataset is displayed in the appendix.

Secessionist Movements

A secessionist movement is a nation that actively seeks to obtain independence from the larger state. As I discussed in chapter 2, secession(ism) is a contested topic that is hard to pin down conceptually. The dataset used to create the 200-year trend in secessionism (see figure 2.1) relies on a broad understanding of the concept, one that includes the violent and illegal cases, as well as the instances of decolonization. That broad understanding was useful for the study it was created for in my 2016 book. However, for my purposes here it is necessary to pare down in two important ways. First, I exclude all of the cases prior to 1945 because the strategic playing field for secessionists was different in earlier periods. The rules and practices related to recognition were different and, as a result, the strategy of secession was different. As I argued in chapter 2, the years since the end of World War II constitute a particular era in the longer story of secession, one defined largely by the normative collision between self-determination and territorial integrity and the resulting constitutive regime. To be sure, that regime has evolved over the decades, but these are incremental shifts in relation to the larger system-level shifts that delimit the different eras. My focus in this book is the sovereignty game since the mid-twentieth century.

The second way in which I pared down the larger set of secessionist movements was to remove cases where the strategic playing field is substantially different. In my article with Wasser, we argued that not all secessionist movements face the same challenges.[3] The classic cases of decolonization—such as Nigeria and Cameroon—had different incentive structures because their imperial metropoles were pressured to release them and could do so without worrying that the contagion of secession would spread to their home territories. Similarly, classic binary cases like Slovakia operated in a different strategic environment because the central government in Prague could permit its independence without the usual concerns over precedent setting that other governments face.[4]

The end result is a set of 136 secessionist movements between 1946 and 2011. These are movements that lasted at least one week, included at least 100 people, laid claim to a territory not smaller than 100 square kilometers, possessed a flag, and declared independence.[5] The size criteria exclude micro movements like the Principality of Hutt River and the Principality of Snake Hill. Although I discuss these movements at points throughout the book, I exclude them from the analysis for two reasons: (1) to my knowledge, there is no comprehensive dataset on all of these micro movements; (2) they face different strategic realities because of their size and because they are sometimes (though not always) farcical efforts and money-making gimmicks. Most readers will accept that they are different in kind from Scotland and belong in a different study.

The most important and consequential criterion is the requirement that a declaration of independence be made. This criterion is meant to signal intent.[6] In ideal terms, it should differentiate between those minority nations and ethnic groups who seek some sort of symbolic recognition and/or regional autonomy versus the ones that aim for full sovereign independence. The first set is quite large and hard to delimit, consisting of the Navajo, the Manx, and the Gallegos, to name a few. The second set is smaller, a subset of the first set, and consists of those groups who have crossed the line and become fully secessionist. Operationally, I define that line as the moment when: (1) a declaration of independence is made; (2) a secessionist conflict begins and a declaration follows later; or (3) secessionists begin nonviolent political action and a declaration follows later. A movement ends when: (1) the group formally renounces its independence claim; (2) an agreement is struck granting independence or some other concession short of independence, or (3) five years pass without secessionist activity.

As always, these operational criteria have important consequences for the resulting data structure. In general, they provide indicators for when a movement begins and ends. For some movements, like the Latvians in 1991, this is an accurate result because the movement mobilized that year in reaction to events in the Soviet Union, and Latvia seceded not long after. But some movements, like the Nagas, have existed for long periods and adapted their tactics over time to a changing tactical setting. And other movements, like the Catalans and the Iraqi Kurds, have had different incarnations over time because they have stopped and then restarted. In truth, these minority nations do not disappear, they just cease to be overtly secessionist for a period. The data structure does not capture all secessionist activity; it captures noticeable moments, or tremors.

A different problem is that some movements are excluded from the dataset because they have not yet declared independence, even though they are clearly engaging in secessionist activity. As we saw in the case study chapters, declaring independence is itself a strategic act.[7] In terms of data collection, this matters less for past movements because I can pin their start date to when secessionist activity began, knowing that a declaration followed later. But some contemporary movements like Greenland and French Polynesia fall into this category of movements that are secessionist but undeclared. Of these liminal cases, the most prominent is New Caledonia, a movement that is actively pursuing sovereign statehood politically and through sanctioned referenda, but has not yet declared independence. Had this study been done ten years from now, some of these movements would likely count using the stated criteria. Nevertheless, this does not constitute a methodological problem. The primary definition in the book, what served as the basis for the case studies, is that a secessionist movement is a self-identified nation inside a sovereign state that seeks to separate and form a new recognized sovereign state. The operational criteria for the dataset attempt to identify instances of that phenomenon.

Carrying out the analysis required that I sort the 136 movements into the six secessionist kinds: democratized, indigenous legal, weak combative, strong combative, decolonial, and de facto. As I described in chapter 3, these are conceived as clusters of characteristics and the actual cases may not fit them perfectly. Nevertheless, broad patterns should emerge. Crucially, the movements were not sorted because of their chosen tactics—a move that would result in circular reasoning—but for reasons pertaining to their local conditions. I use the conditions to predict the tactics.

Figure 10.1 depicts the decision tree with which I used the presence or absence of conditions to sort the movements. I began by identifying the de facto state movements, arguing that their disconnected relationship with the home state prevented them from engaging in standard compellence tactics. As listed in the appendix, I counted seven as de facto state movements: Abkhazia (1991 onward); Gagauzia (1991–1995), Artsakh/Nagorno Karabakh (1991 onward), Somaliland (1991 onward), South Ossetia (1991 onward), Transnistria (1991 onward), and Northern Cyprus (1974 onward), the only one whose beginning did not coincide with the end of the Cold War. To construct this list I took a conservative position

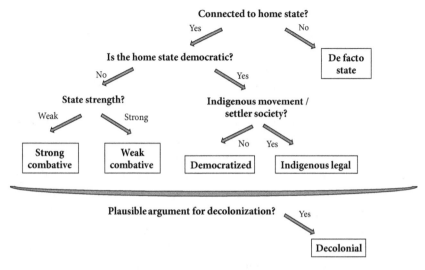

FIGURE 10.1. Decision tree for sorting tactical kinds

on the work of Nina Caspersen, Adrian Florea, and Scott Pegg, arguing that many of their de facto states should not count according to my terms because they were in the midst of a civil war (Chechnya) or still integrated politically (Iraqi Kurdistan) with the larger state.[8] This resulted in the exclusion of some borderline cases, like Tamil Eelam, but in my conception a de facto state movement is completely severed from the larger state and has endured as such. Such cases are rare, for as Zachariah Mampilly recounts, even the residents of Tamil Eelam continued to receive public benefits from the Sri Lankan state during the years of conflict—the two were never completely sundered.[9]

The next decision point in the sorting pertained to their institutional setting. A total of forty-four movements counted as high institutional, meaning that the larger state possessed sound democratic institutions. To qualify, the larger state had to meet at least two of the following conditions: (1) be coded as a democracy by Boix, Miller, and Rosato;[10] (2) be coded as 6 or higher on the Polity2 score by the Polity IV Project, a commonly used threshold for democracy; (3) be coded as 5 or higher on the ID score in the Polyarchy Dataset, also the chosen threshold for democracy. The purpose behind this triangular coding was to take a conservative position and filter the borderline cases that may have counted in one dataset but not the others. Of these forty-four movements, only three counted as indigenous legal on account of their status in settler societies: (1) Hawaii since 1994; (2) Lakotah since 2007; and (3) the Maori since 1975. Note that the dataset for secessionist tactics ends in 2011, and thus excludes movements like the Murrawarri Republic that declared independence in 2013.

Combative movements account for eighty-one cases (59 percent of the total). These are identified by the fact that they are integrated with the larger state, located in weak or nondemocracies, and are unable to make a persuasive appeal to decolonization. The difference between weak and strong types is their strength relative to the state, which ultimately influences their tactics of choice. I coded twenty-nine of the movements as weak and fifty-two as strong based on the CINC score of the state given in the Correlates of War (COW) National Material Capabilities index.[11] Here I simply used the average CINC score (.032) of the home states in the secession data to divide the set. Strong states possessed weak movements in relative terms; weak states possess strong movements, relatively. Although this is an imperfect proxy given that it does not factor in the actual strength of the movement—there are no data to my knowledge that provide a CINC-like score for secessionist movements—the strength of the larger state should be a good predictor of the balance between the two parties. Nevertheless, I do run a robustness check in the analysis that combines the two sets to study the relationship between tactics and the strength of the state.

The final tactical kind is the decolonial movement. As figure 10.1 illustrates, the defining feature here is not the degree of integration with the state, whether that state is democratic or particularly strong, but how the independence-seeking nation is viewed in relation to decolonization. I counted five movements as decolonial: Somaliland (1960), Southern Cameroon (1960), Western Sahara (1963), West Papua (1963), and East Timor (1975). This is a conservative rendering. Western Sahara is an easy choice because it is on the UN list of Non-Self-Governing Territories, the only territory currently on that list that has mounted a formal secessionist movement.[12] To include the remaining four territories, I looked at their administrative status at the moment of independence for the larger state that they became part of.[13] Somaliland, or British Somaliland as it was called, was separate and independent in 1960 when it was joined to the Italian Somaliland.[14] Southern Cameroon (or British Cameroon) was attached to French Cameroon (Cameroon) at the moment of independence in 1960.[15] Finally, both West Papua and East Timor were separate administrative units of different countries at the time of accession by Indonesia in 1963 and 1975, respectively. Importantly, all four of these territories were once on the UN list of Non-Self-Governing Territories but removed for reasons that remain controversial.[16] Overall, all five territories were first-order administrative units in their own right, and therefore can make a compelling argument for eligibility for decolonization.[17]

To be sure, other secessionist movements have attempted to place their cause under the banner of decolonization. Bougainville's administrative origins are different from Papua New Guinea—a point made by the secessionist leaders in their argument for independence[18]—but it has nevertheless been a part of the larger territory since 1899. Similarly, the Anyi have argued that they had separate territorial rights under the French, and therefore should have qualified for decolonization separate from the Ivory Coast.[19] Such arguments are directed at not only the usual set of European colonial masters, as this quote regarding Ache shows:

> The Achenese will not obey the republic [Indonesia]. We must free Aceh from the republic. They have promised many things, but the people do not get them. We don't want to live under colonialism.[20]

Empire is in the eye of the beholder and the accusation of colonialism is all too common. But whatever their merits in general, these arguments have less valence where the application of *uti possidetis juris* is concerned.

Tactics of Compellence

Secessionist movements need to make a change. They need the international community to recognize them as sovereign states, and one way of doing that is to make it costly to ignore them. Secessionist movements can deploy their assets to incur costs on the home state and/or international community by not complying with their demands. To study compellence tactics, I used new data on secessionist methods created by Wasser and myself.[21] We modeled three tactics in which the movements pursue independence via: (1) institutional means (e.g., electoral capture, referenda); (2) civil resistance and nonviolent extra-institutional means (e.g., protests, sit-ins, strikes); (3) violent extra-institutional means (e.g., insurgency, terrorism, armed rebellion). These tactics represent different values of the dependent variable (compellence), and can be examined in relation to the kind of movement. Note that many movements used combinations of these different tactics; only 26 (19 percent) used only one tactic. Table 10.1 shows the frequency

TABLE 10.1. Combination and frequency of compellence tactics

COMBINATION	FREQUENCY
Institutional	9
Institutional + civil resistance	20
Institutional + violence	9
Institutional + civil resistance + violence	28
Civil resistance	8
Violence	9
Civil resistance + violence	53
N	136

and combination of selected tactics. The appendix provides a complete list of each movement and their chosen tactics.

Tactics of Normative Appeal

Normative appeal is analytically distinct from compellence because the intention is to change preferences, not incur costs. Here, secessionist movements pitch their cause in a manner that resonates with the perceived pathways to independence that were discussed in chapter 2. Normative appeal is aimed at hearts and minds. It can change the position of key actors, provide justification for behavior, and bring into the game previously uninvolved parties who can then apply pressure on the home state.

To study normative appeal, I created new data on the rhetoric used by secessionist groups around the time they became active.[22] Using Factiva and ProQuest, I performed a content analysis of the direct quotations of movement leaders, supporters, participants, and third-party observers. Results were produced by searching on the name of the movement *and* one of the following terms: secession, secede, independence, sovereignty, autonomy, or separatism. For the high-profile and more commonly discussed movements, the number of cited articles was capped at thirty (a large but not too large number), all randomly selected. For the movements with thirty or fewer results, all articles were used.

To conduct the content analysis I searched on terms that lexically captured the meaning behind the different normative appeals. For example, to identify utterances that conveyed the concept of earned sovereignty I searched for "de facto," combinations of "equal" with "status" or a synonym, or a string that denoted the upgrading or formalization of status. Table 10.2 lists the different search terms

TABLE 10.2. Normative appeal search terms

NORMATIVE APPEAL	SEARCH TERMS
Earned sovereignty	De facto; equal + (status, footing, representation, partnership); (formalize, upgrade, convert, conversion, promotion) + Status
Decolonization	Coloni (for derivatives like decolonization, colonialism]; occupation; occupied; liberat (for derivatives like liberation, liberate)
Freedom to choose	Choose; choice; chosen; determine; decide; decision; democracy; democratic; right to decide (choose) + destiny (or fate or future)
Inherent sovereignty	Inva (for derivatives like invaded, invade); *terra nullius*; sovereignty + (never ceded, never relinquished, never eliminated); inherent sovereignty; original sovereignty
Human rights	Genocide; ethnic cleansing; human rights; oppression; repression; suppression; massacre

(and strings) that were used for each normative appeal. In some cases, root words like "coloni" or "liberat" were used.

In summary, the analysis utilizes a dataset of 136 secessionist movements between 1946 and 2011. Each movement is sorted into one of the six secessionist kinds based on structural conditions inside the state and in its relation to the movement. Is the breakaway region regarded as a de facto state in the prominent datasets? Is the home state a democracy? Is it an indigenous movement in a settler state? What is the strength of the home state? Does the independence movement have a reasonable claim for meeting the conditions for decolonization? Next, I identified the compellence tactics for each movement and the normative appeals they made. I now turn to a study of the relationship between the setting and the tactics that were used.

Analysis

The examination of secessionist tactics is organized into two parts. The first focuses on tactics of compellence. The second centers on tactics of normative appeal. Each constitutes a dependent variable.

Compellence

To test my argument, I begin by exploring the relationship between secessionist kinds and their tactics of compellence. In accordance with my theory, I expect: (1) that movements in democratic settings (i.e., democratized and indigenous legal) will favor institutional tactics; (2) that weak combative movements will prefer tactics of nonviolent civil resistance; and (3) that strong combative movements will be more likely to choose violent methods.

Two caveats are required. First, I predict that decolonial movements will choose compellence tactics that vary with their setting (see table 3.1). It turns out that all five of the decolonial movements under examination qualified as strong combative types because of the low CINC scores of their home state, and I therefore placed them in that group. Second, the de facto type is an outlier because these movements are sundered from the home state and therefore lack the ability to engage in compellent acts. As a result, they are removed from the analysis in this section. The remaining movements are all connected to the home state in a way that makes compellence possible. Rather than a kind of split sovereignty in which the two sides are separated by a defended boundary, these movements experience forms of dual and overlapping sovereignty—they are part of the larger state in an empirical sense.

I tested my argument in two ways. First, I looked at the simple relationship between kind and tactic. As stated, I anticipate that secessionist movements in highly institutionalized settings—that is, both the democratized and indigenous legal movements—are more likely to adopt tactics that use the institutional process. An analysis of the data displayed in the appendix reveals that a total of forty-four movements took place in democracies, and twenty-six (59 percent) of these used institutional methods. In comparison, only thirty-seven (43 percent) of the remaining eighty-six movements used institutional methods. The difference between the two averages is statistically significant.[23] I next looked at combative movements. I hypothesize that strong combative movements are more likely to use violence than weak combative movements. Overall, fifty-one (91 percent) of the fifty-seven strong combative movements used violent methods, while only twelve (41 percent) of the twenty-nine weak movements did so. In statistical terms, these averages are significantly different.[24] Finally, weak combative movements were more likely to use civil resistance methods than violence. All told, nineteen (66 percent) of the twenty-nine weak combative movements used civil resistance, whereas only twelve (41 percent) of the twenty-nine movements adopted violence. Again, the difference between these averages is statistically significant.[25] Overall, these findings are consistent with my expectations.

Second, I tested these relationships in a unified manner using logistic regressions. Here, I put aside the sorting of secessionist kinds and focused exclusively on the type of regime (democracy, nondemocracy) and overall strength (CINC score) of the home state, modelled as independent variables in the analysis. I used two control variables: (1) the number of peaceful secessions from the same state over the previous five years; and (2) the ethnic distinctiveness of the aspiring nation.[26] Violence, nonviolent civil resistance, and institutional tactics were used as dependent variables in three separate regressions. This format represents a different way to test the hypotheses.

The results are listed in table 10.3. Democracy is negatively and significantly related to the use of violence, and positively and significantly related to the use of institutional methods. A secessionist movement is 23 percent more likely to use institutional methods when the larger state is a democracy. Meanwhile, there is a highly significant relationship between the strength of the state and the choice of secessionist tactics. Strong movements—that is, where the state is weak—are far more likely to use violence. In addition, secessionist movements in strong states are also more likely to use institutional means. One of the factors driving this finding is that strong states are quite often democracies, and therefore in a better position to provide institutional options. Interestingly, the use of nonviolent civil resistance methods does not correlate strongly with either regime type or state strength.

TABLE 10.3. Logistic regressions of compellence tactics

	TACTIC / METHOD		
	VIOLENCE	CIVIL RESISTANCE	INSTITUTIONAL
Democracy	−.73* (.48)	.27 (.50)	.10** (.43)
% change	−15		23
CINC score	−23.63*** (5.41)	−.97 (5.19)	18*** (5.08)
% change	**−33%**		**38%**
Recent secessions	−.02 (.11)	.26 (.57)	1.32 (1.15)
% change			
EthnoDistinct	.21 (.30)	.00 (.31)	−.31 (.28)
% change			
Constant	1.95*** (.41)	1.27*** (.35)	−.80** (.32)
N	127	127	127
Wald Chi²	(4) 24.97	(4) 1.32	(4) 23.44
Probability > Chi²	0	0.86	0
Pseudo R²	0.16	0.01	0.13
Log likelihood	−64.14	−63.72	−76.3

Note: Marginal change calculated by moving the democracy variable from 0 to 1 while holding the other variables at their mean. The marginal change for CINC is calculated by moving the value from 1 SD (.044) below the mean (.03) to 1 SD above while holding democracy at its mode (0) and the other variables at their mean.
*p<.10; **p<.05; ***p<.01

Overall, these results are broadly consistent with my theory. Secessionist movements in highly institutionalized settings are more likely to compete electorally, and less likely to use violence. As noted in the case studies, there is kind of tension between these two tactics, and the institutional structure of the state shapes the outcome. Secessionist movements in weak states are more likely to utilize violence, particularly when democratic options are unavailable. Finally, nonviolent methods of civil resistance are harder to predict—they appear to be used in diverse settings (democratic and nondemocratic, strong and weak states). However, as discussed above, weak movements are different from strong movements in two crucial ways that support my argument; they are more likely to use nonviolent civil resistance methods and less likely to adopt violent tactics.

Normative Appeal

The content analysis of the rhetorical arguments made by all of the secessionist movements produced results that were largely consistent with my central argument. The analysis returned a total of 3,479 articles, an average of twenty-six per

TABLE 10.4.   Distribution of normative appeals by secessionist kind

	SECESSIONIST KIND	EARNED SOVEREIGNTY	DECOLONIZATION	FREEDOM TO CHOOSE	INHERENT SOVEREIGNTY	HUMAN RIGHTS	TOTAL
1	De facto	52 (76%)	5 (7%)	4 (6%)	1 (1%)	6 (9%)	68
2	Decolonial	10 (13%)	34 (45%)	10 (13%)	7 (9%)	14 (19%)	75
3	Democratized	33 (12%)	82 (29%)	125 (45%)	12 (4%)	28 (10%)	280
4	Indigenous legal	0 (0%)	13 (32%)	4 (10%)	20 (49%)	4 (10%)	41
5	Combative (all)	48 (11%)	81 (18%)	113 (25%)	13 (3%)	190 (43%)	445
	Total	143 (16%)	215 (24%)	256 (28%)	53 (6%)	242 (27%)	909

movement, and within this set the search terms came up 909 times. As table 10.4 illustrates, there is a strong correlation between the kinds of movement and the predicted normative appeal, signified in the table in each case by a shaded cell. Note that the weak and strong combative types are collapsed into one category because it is predicted that both will stress human rights in their normative appeals.

The appeal to earned sovereignty was the primary normative appeal for de facto movements. The argument that the movement in question has earned its status and should be upgraded or recognized came up in fifty-two of the sixty-eight utterances, 76 percent of the total. The remaining secessionist kinds used that language far less commonly. Indeed, the average rate of use between de facto movements and decolonial movements—the second most likely type to appeal to that norm—passes a difference of means test.[27] This striking result is depicted in figure 10.2 by the soaring black percentile column on the far left.

The language of decolonization came up frequently in the content analysis, accounting for nearly a quarter of the results. As predicted, this was the argument of choice for decolonial movements—it was returned in 34 of the 75 (45 percent) utterances. These movements appealed to decolonization more than any other norm and, as figure 10.2 illustrates, this was a rate of use that was more than double that of their next most commonly used argument (human rights). They also appealed to the norm more than any other secessionist kind. With the exception of indigenous legal movements, the next most likely group to appeal to the norm, the average rate of use by decolonial movements was significantly different from all other kinds.[28]

As theorized, democratized movements commonly appealed to the freedom to choose their political fate. This appeal came up in 125 of a total of 280 utterances (45 percent). Democratized movements were statistically more likely to use this argument than any other argument.[29] In addition, democratized movements invoked the freedom to choose more commonly than the other kind of movement. The next most likely group to use the argument was combative movements,

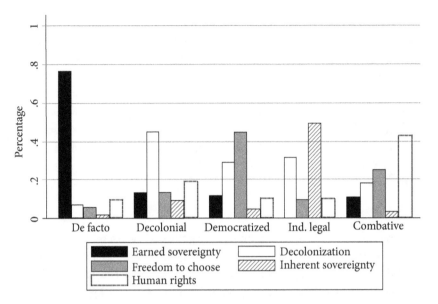

FIGURE 10.2.   Rate of normative appeal by secessionist kind

an interesting finding that I return to below. Importantly, the freedom to choose was the most frequently returned norm in the content analysis, coming up in 28 percent of the results.

The argument regarding inherent sovereignty was the least commonly used normative appeal, uttered in only 6 percent of the results. However, as expected, the indigenous legal movements were the ones who regularly used it. It appeared in nearly half of the articles that discussed secessionism in relation to Hawaii, the Lakotah, and the Maori. Interestingly, these groups were also likely to appeal to decolonization, though they did so less frequently. It is important to not overstate these findings given the small sample size. Nevertheless, it is clear that these groups use similar tactics when pitching their cause.

The analysis produced interesting and nuanced results for the combative movements. As predicted, combative movements appeal to human rights norms more than any other rhetorical argument.[30] The high percentile column on the far right of figure 10.2 depicts this outcome. In addition, combative movements were more than twice as likely to appeal to human rights as the next mostly likely kind, decolonial. That said, the combative group is larger and more heterogeneous than the other kinds and other normative appeals were frequently used. For example, the freedom to choose argument was used in 25 percent of the utterances. The appeal to decolonization was also common. Nevertheless, despite the relatively varied character of the combative movements, human rights were the most common theme in their rhetorical arguments.

Overall, the results largely confirm my hypotheses regarding normative argu-mentation. Secessionist movements tend to appeal to the norms we would ex-pect given their setting. These patterns are observable in figure 10.2 and are statistically significant. Notably, the appeal to the freedom to choose was the most commonly returned argument in the content analysis, accounting for 28 percent of the results. This makes sense because all groups can appeal to it, from the Ab-khazians to the Uighur to the Scots. In contrast, the other appeals are more case-specific; not all groups can persuasively appeal to decolonization or earned sovereignty. The setting shapes the appeal, but the freedom to choose covers all settings.

The preceding analysis tested a number of hypotheses in a macroanalytic format. These hypotheses, which were stated at the beginning of the chapter and devel-oped theoretically in chapter 3, are predictions about the tactics that different se-cessionist groups will use depending on their setting. All of the hypotheses found statistical support, meaning that, in the aggregate, secessionist behavior plays out as I have argued. There are exceptions, to be sure, and some movements will act in a manner that blends different kinds of movement. But as a kind of scatter-shot, the large-N analysis supports my argument.

11

THE CAUSES AND CONSEQUENCES OF BAD STRATEGY AND POOR TACTICS

Rebellions are built on hope.

—Jyn Erso, *Rogue One*

Judean People's Front! We're the People's Front of Judea!

—From *Monty Python's Life of Brian*

Some readers will ask whether I read too much strategic thinking into secessionist behavior.[1] After all, secessionists regularly make bad choices. This chapter is about those bad choices and the tactics that follow from them. I argue that there are different causes of bad strategy. These include incomplete information, wishful thinking, and mixed objectives. The product of these causes is a game where play is varied and where actors often make poor choices. The game is coherent enough to shape play but sufficiently vague to produce misaligned tactics. I outline these causes and their consequences and, in doing so, begin to set the stage for a more prescriptive discussion in the concluding chapter.

Incomplete Information

Until now I have described the strategic playing field as a clear and coherent space where secessionist movements know the rules and act accordingly. Indeed, I have used the metaphor of the "game" when referring to the subject matter as the sovereignty game. However, there are many ways in which it differs from other games that come to mind. It is not like chess, where the rules are clearly specified. It is perhaps closer to poker, with its emphasis on risk and bluffing, but even there the rules are bounded. A person sitting down to play Texas Hold'em can be confident that the rules of play are fixed and not subject to change. In contrast, the sovereignty game is shaped by an evolving set of formal and informal rules and practices. These rules and practices are not clearly specified or listed in a way that a practitioner could Google on the Internet, as they might if they prepared for a poker game. Moreover, the contours of the sovereignty game shapeshift over time and sometimes they do so in reaction to how the game is played. As a result, all players maneuver in a setting that is characterized by incomplete information.

One tragic example is the 1998 Biak Massacre in West Papua, also known as Bloody Biak. This occurred as part of, and perhaps ended, what was known as the Papuan Spring, a period of hope following the fall of President Suharto. In July of that year, West Papuans clamoring for independence gathered beneath the water tower in Biak City. They sang and they danced and they hoisted the Morning Star flag on the local water tower. Six days later the demonstrators were violently dispersed by the Indonesian military and more than 100 people were detained. According to reports, many of the detainees were beaten, raped, and murdered, and their mutilated bodies were dropped into the sea.[2] In the wake of the massacre, the independence leader Filep Karma stated that he had operated under the belief that if they raised the Morning Star flag on the water tower and kept if aloft for twenty-four hours, then the United Nations would recognize their independence.[3] When they kept it up for forty-eight hours, and recognition did not come, and the Indonesian authorities still cracked down violently, Karma concluded that "this theory is not true." This story illustrates the problem of incomplete information, for as Karma tells it, they mistakenly believed that international support and recognition would follow from a specific action—in this case, raising the flag for twenty-four hours.

Although the Biak example is somewhat extreme, and the beliefs that motivated the action appear naïve, it highlights a problem that all secessionist movements share. They do not know the reservation price for international support. In my interviews with Catalan *independistas*, I was always impressed with their faith in the willingness of the European Union to step in should the tensions escalate. There is surely a point at which a prominent leader like Angela Merkel would apply pressure on the Spanish government to negotiate with Catalan secessionists, but that point is unknown, perhaps even to Merkel. I attended a 2015 conference in Erbil where Kurdish leaders speculated on whether the successor to US president Barack Obama would abandon the One Iraq policy and open a path to the independence of Iraqi Kurdistan. In an interview, Rashid Nur, the Somaliland representative to the United States, stated that support of the African Union was critical, but that he and his associates could not specify the conditions under which the AU would give its support.[4] This information problem is amplified once we consider that international actors often have an incentive to not reveal their reservation price. By publicly stating the conditions under which Merkel would pressure Spanish prime minister Rajoy to negotiate with Catalonia, she would influence Catalan tactics. There is a potential moral hazard problem here, not to mention the fact that political leaders can damage their diplomatic relations.

There are numerous other ways in which secessionists simply have incomplete information. One striking similarity between the Scottish and New Caledonian independence referenda was the debate about whether each region would be better off as its own sovereign state. In both cases the pro-independence side made arguments about its economic assets, its natural resources, and its ability to join regional trading organizations as well as the international community.[5] For its part, the anti-independence side did its best to highlight the economic vulnerability of the potential state. Although both sides brought political and economic reports to bear in their arguments, it was very difficult to produce a reliable cost-benefit analysis. How would the new state arrange for debt repayment with the former central government? How would employee pensions be worked out? At what rate could the new state expect to join international organizations? This is not well-trodden ground and there are no clear answers to these questions. To choose an independent state is to choose an uncertain future and secessionists need to reduce that uncertainty just as the home state has reason to increase it. That uncertainty shapes preferences in legal referenda like Scotland's, particularly among older and/or less risk-tolerant voters. It matters even more when the referendum and larger independence bid is considered illegal. In preparation for the September 27, 2015, Catalan parliament elections, the pro-independence side stressed uncertainty reduction in its messaging to older voters.[6]

The fog that permeates the sovereignty game can also be legalistic. In the early days of their independence bid, the Bougainvilleans attempted to portray their cause as one of unfulfilled decolonization. After all, they had been colonized and their inclusion in Papua New Guinea was an artifact of European colonization. But they gradually learned that their cause did not fit the template for decolonization because they were not a colonial unit in 1975 and thus they gradually shifted their normative appeal to focus on human rights.[7] At a self-determination workshop in West Papua I was asked to explain the way in which colonial units were identified by applying the principle of *uti possidetis juris*. That somewhat confusing process came as news to almost all of the attendees. For the Murrawarri Republic, full independence will turn not only on how Australian law interprets their case but on how it may come to be interpreted in the future.

The point behind these illustrations is to argue that what may look like irrational, futile, or just plain dumb behavior can appear quite reasonable to the secessionists. Part of the reason for this discrepancy is the fact that secessionists play the game with incomplete information. This complicates their ability to assess their chances, particularly when we consider that key actors may not have an incentive to clarify their intentions.[8] As a result, many of the actions taken can, in retrospect, look foolish.

Wishful Thinking

The problem of incomplete information is exacerbated by a tendency that I have observed with all secessionist movements, that of wishful thinking. This is the tendency to overestimate the likelihood that your desired outcome—in this case, independence—will come true. It is a pattern of thinking that is found in all games.[9] Sports players will often overrate their chances and they will believe in themselves that they can beat the odds. In this case, wishful thinking may be useful because it is motivational. However, wishful thinking is a well-known and pernicious problem with betting games, and here it is almost always regarded as a bad way to play. With respect to the sovereignty game, wishful thinking is both good and bad, but it is usually present.

There are at least two reasons why wishful thinking is present in secessionist movements. The first follows from the problem of incomplete information. Secessionists often do not know the exact outcome of their actions. They have to hedge and this leads to inexact calculations of chance.[10] Although one might expect that secessionists would be just as likely to underestimate their chances, and thus balance out those who overestimate, there is a second cause of wishful thinking that shifts behavior in the direction of overestimation: the simple penchant for hope. During interviews with secessionists, I was always struck by the amount of hope and optimistic thinking in their behavior. I have come to conclude on a part-observational, part-conjectural basis that this is simply an intrinsic feature of secession. In the end, secession is a form of rebellion and rebellion is a risky enterprise. Without a measure of hope at the core of the rebellion, it is likely to fade away.

In my interviews, the tendency toward wishful thinking was most acute when I asked about the key friction point(s). At what point will the central government negotiate? What will it take to get the international community to pressure the central government? Many Catalans sincerely believed that it would be enough to simply demonstrate on the streets, show enthusiasm for the cause, and be good democratic citizens. As the journalist Josep Maria Martí Font put it, "Catalans can feel that they have the moral high ground, talking about democracy, about our rights and how badly we are treated by Madrid, but we don't have an army, we don't have a treasury and we don't have anything except wishful thinking."[11]

This tendency to overestimate the chances is just as common with secessionist leaders as it is with the rank and file. When I asked how the Kurds intended to win the consent of Baghdad, one senior official from the office of the prime minister, Kurdish regional government, stated that they are "laying the groundwork, preparing Baghdad psychologically" and that "much of the region will support them because they are Sunni."[12] I was similarly impressed with the sincerity and self-confidence of Albert Royo, the secretary-general of DIPLOCAT, when he said that Catalonia could force Spain to negotiate and that it had substantial support from its European allies.[13] To be clear, not all secessionists are guilty of wishful thinking; some are quite clear-eyed or even pessimistic. Plenty of pro-independence Catalans expressed concern about their poor chances, but nevertheless stuck with the cause because they believed in it. Moses Havini, Bougainville's diplomat-at-large, grew somewhat pessimistic in the early days of the civil war but carried on out of duty.[14]

Although I have no scientific measure of wishful thinking and am basing my argument partly on mere observation, I argue that it can be a good, and perhaps is a necessary, characteristic for secessionist movements. For me, an "aha!" moment on this issue came at a workshop in West Papua on the use of nonviolent civil resistance to achieve independence. The workshop was illegal, and the participants, especially the West Papuans, risked prosecution or worse by attending. Those who ran the workshop had training as community organizers and they went to great lengths to build a culture of camaraderie. This was high-risk activism.[15] There were numerous trust-building exercises that produced not only laughter but also confessions and tears. And there was a clear message of hope that their cause, while difficult and dangerous, could be achieved. In a private conversation one of the organizers told me that it was vital that the participants believed that success was possible. It may be that hope plays a bigger role in a movement such as West Papua, where participants risk their lives, relative to Catalonia or even Scotland, where violence and prosecution are absent or less common. But even Scottish secessionists expend time for the cause and risk the damaging of social relations. Moreover, they are unlikely to have the same push factors as a West Papuan secessionist who faces greater oppression and fewer opportunities. Hope plays an important role even in democratized settings.

The downside to wishful thinking is that it can lead to poor tactical choices. More than one pro-independence Catalan confided in me that they felt the secessionist leadership was moving too fast. Added time was needed to consolidate the gains and build support. Various reasons were given for the overly rushed pace, but one of them was an inflated belief that independence could be won so soon. In fact, some felt that the October 1, 2017, referendum was a bad tactical choice given that it gave the Spanish government a reason for invoking Article 155 and imposing direct role on Catalonia. As we saw in chapter 4, one of the reasons for holding the referendum was to force a collision with Madrid, create friction, and win international support. The Catalan leaders appear to have miscalculated here and wishful thinking may have played a part. Similarly, many argue that the Iraqi Kurds misplayed their hand when they held a referendum on September 25, 2017.[16] In an interview with *Al Jazeera*, Bayan Sami Abdul Rahman, the Kurdistan regional government (KRG) representative to the United States, stated that the "KRG did not expect the 'unsophisticated' reaction to the referendum by the US and Europe."[17] By coming out against the referendum, key players like the United States only emboldened the Iraqi state to punish the Kurds. They had hoped for a better response.

Mixed Objectives

One of the most common causes of bad strategy and poor tactics is the fact that players often have mixed objectives. This is actually a broad category of issues organized around a key aspect of secessionist behavioral strategy. Consider that each side in a game of chess has one player with one goal (to win). There is no division within the player, where factions have competing objectives vis-à-vis one another, and there is no alternative end goal, unless one values losing as equal to or greater than winning. In contrast, the sovereignty game is characterized by mixed objectives and this can lead to poor tactical choices where the attainment of independence is concerned.

It is important to remember that not all minority nations want independence. I identified sixty formal secessionist movements as of 2017, but the number of potential secessionist movements is far larger. Ernest Gellner estimated that there were 800 potential nationalisms in the world, a conservative calculation by his own admission.[18] Although the majority of these are currently dormant with respect to self-determination goals, many of them seek forms of autonomy that fall short of full independence. As Philip Roeder illustrates, secession campaigns are merely a subset of those groups who seek some form of increased local control.[19] I discussed in chapter 2 how many groups modify their demands over time, moving between satisfaction and wanting greater autonomy to wanting sovereign independence, and so on. The objectives are mixed and this influences tactical choices. If one wants only independence and is prepared to pay a high price for it, as some Catalan secessionists do, then confrontation and increased friction with the state are acceptable. But if one is prepared to settle for an autonomy arrangement and may even rate that outcome as equal to or better than independence, as other Catalans prefer, then it would be less desirable to create conflict with the state that may remain your home. Fred Hooper, the chair of the secessionists of the Murrawarri Republic, stated in an interview that they desire as much local control as they can get.[20] Although they "want the maximum," an independent state, a form of "domestic dependent sovereignty" would be second best. Knowing that they have to work with the state and may have to settle for an autonomy arrangement, Hooper said that it is vital that their methods be seen as respectful and legitimate.

Related to the problem of competing end goals is the tendency for division within an independence-seeking nation. There is a delightful scene in *Monty Python's Life of Brian* in which John Cleese's character tells an interested party that they are not the Judean People's Front, but rather the People's Front of Judea, the PFJ as he calls it, and that this is different from another group called the Judean Popular People's Front. In the banter that follows, one member of the PFJ gets tripped up on the name of their own group. I was reminded of this scene on several occasions when an actual secessionist, from Bougainville to West Papua to Catalonia, would describe the evolution of the different factions within their cause. Each secessionist movement consists of a constellation of actors who possess varying, sometimes conflicting objectives.

The are many reasons for this variation. Sometimes factions are rooted in competing clans or subregions of the potential breakaway region. For example, there is an old division among the Iraqi Kurds between the Kurdistan Democratic Party, which centers on the Barzani tribe and is headquartered in Erbil, and the Patriotic Union of Kurdistan, which is led by the Talabani family from Sulaymaniyah. That division weakened support on the run-up to the 2017 independence referendum because many Kurds from the area around Sulaymaniyah saw the bid as an initiative of the of Barzani tribe, especially its leader, Massoud Barzani.[21] Indeed, the perception of personal ambition can be a cause of division. Potential secessionists sometimes reported that they were turned off from the cause by the overly ambitious personas of people like Alex Salmond, Carles Puigdemont, and Rauf Denktash. Just as factions can form around the competing ambitions of different leaders, they can also form around competing methods. I was often told by Catalan secessionists that Esquerra and Popular Unity Candidacy (CUP) were more comfortable with confrontation with Madrid than their counterparts in Convergència. A regular source of factionalism is the question of violence. When Palika arose as a faction competing with the Caledonian Union, it was over the matter of whether violence should be used.[22]

Internal division (factionalism) complicates the strategic and tactical playing field. One official who worked on both the Aceh and West Papuan negotiations stated that there was a period around 2007 when the Indonesian government was willing to negotiate with the West Papuans.[23] However, the West Papuans missed an opportunity to open a dialogue and negotiate certain matters because they were too divided and the competent personnel were not in the right positions of power to seize the opportunity. Organizationally speaking, they were not set up in the right way to pursue strategically sensible actions. In contrast, the Acehnese were much more united in 2004 when they negotiated autonomy and their leadership was effective. I have heard similar stories with many other movements. Negotiations between Cyprus and Northern Cyprus might have progressed at certain points had it not been for the actions of Rauf Denktash.[24] In late 2015, the Catalan independence effort stalled as the pro-independence side fought over whether Artur Mas, the most prominent independence leader, would remain the Catalan president. In an interview, Quim Arrufat, a representative from the CUP, stated that his party was prepared to risk another election as a result of the investiture crisis rather than accept Mas as president.[25] For him and the leaders of CUP, Mas was too conservative and too compromised by scandal. In the end, CUP won what was effectively a game of chicken and Mas stepped down to make way for Carles Puigdemont.

There is a vibrant literature on the effects of factionalism within self-determination groups.[26] In a recent book, Roeder examined the strategic game played by different factions within a given minority nation.[27] He argues that secessionist leaders need to win over a decisive majority of their platform population and he analyzes why some groups prevail over others. Although I do not model them directly, these dynamics do contribute to the sovereignty game. For in truth, many secessionist leaders are playing a two-level game, one faced inward toward in-group competitors and one faced outward toward the state and the international community.[28] One result of the internal game is that it complicates the external game. It leads to greater variation in tactical outcomes and some of the choices may weaken the overall independence effort. In other words, when pursuing on objective in the internal game, an actor may choose a tactic that hinders the external game.

Importantly, the existence of division does not necessarily yield poor tactics. The Bougainvillean secessionists were heavily factionalized during their decade-long civil war with Papua New Guinea (PNG). This led to many problems, not to mention faction-on-faction violence. But, according to James Tanis, the division helped in other ways.[29] For example, the 2001 peace agreement was boycotted by one secessionist faction led by the military leader Francis Ona. In fact, Ona never agreed to the peace before he died in 2005. Tanis stated that Ona's recalcitrance helped during the peace process because it improved the bargaining position of the moderate secessionists. They were able to say to their PNG interlocutors that if they refused their terms, it would effectively strengthen Ona's position and that he would be far harder to negotiate with. Overall, division complicates the strategic playing field; it hinders secessionists in some cases but helps them in others.

Kathleen Cunningham provided a particularly detailed study of this topic.[30] She found that the number of factions within a self-determination group—that is, groups seeking increased forms of self-determination up to, but potentially falling short of, independence—has two important effects. First, accommodation is more likely when there are more factions because the state can negotiate with the moderates and marginalize the radicals. This is basically what happened in Bougainville. Second, the larger the number of factions, the more likely violence becomes as marginalized groups come into conflict with the state and the moderates. Although she finds that these general patterns play out in a large-N analysis, it should be noted that she is conceiving of self-determination groups as informal and uninstitutionalized parties that the state struggles to identify. Her assumption is a better fit for uninstitutionalized secessionist environments like Bougainville and West Papua than it is the democratized settings like Catalonia. Thus, with institutionalization comes clarity, an issue I return to in the next chapter.

Secessionists regularly make poor choices and play the sovereignty game imperfectly. Readers who are familiar with a given movement will likely point to a number of bad moves. One example that comes up frequently in conversations is the short-lived Republic of Serbian Krajina. Apparently, the Serb minority within Croatia had a good argument for why they deserved a state, or at least a relocation of borders, but their actions along with that of the greater Serb nation created acrimony in the region and in the court of international public opinion.[31] They did not pitch their cause correctly. Perhaps their leaders possessed incomplete information about the game. Perhaps they fell prey to wishful thinking or suffered the conflicting imperatives of mixed objectives. These are the usual causes of bad strategy and poor tactics. Can these causes be addressed? Are there other possibilities of the sovereignty game in which the negative consequences could be ameliorated? This is the subject of the concluding chapter.

12

THE FUTURE OF THE SOVEREIGNTY GAME

> **There is a fundamental disconnection between the advancement of Western liberal democratic values—acceptance of gay rights and multiracial and multiconfessional difference—and the conservative emphasis that the club of states places on sovereignty.**
>
> —Vicent Partal, founder and editor-in-chief of VilaWeb, interview, November 5, 2015

At the strategic level, all secessionist movements are the same. It is hard to see the truth of this statement if one looks only at the local conditions for a given movement. The electoral tactics of the Scottish nationalists seem a far cry from the violent turbulence of Mindanao, the remoteness of peripheral Myanmar, or the ambition of the Murrawarri. It is natural for us to focus our gaze on these local factors, because for the most part that is where the secessionist cause originates. It is born in that community and in its relationship with the home state, and its tactics are shaped by that setting. But all of these movements are united by the goal of joining the community of sovereign states. There is only one United Nations, one club, and one entrance into it.

A central theme of this book is about what I, following Robert Jackson, have called the sovereignty game.[1] This is the strategic game played between independence movements and sovereign states in accordance with the rules given by the international recognition regime. Although the rules of the game are imperfectly specified, and are subject to change, they are still fairly coherent. Those rules shape the behavior of secessionists and states alike, and yield an identifiable set of different kinds of movements where the outcomes are often violent and nearly always suboptimal. Although highly institutionalized, democratized settings tend to clarify and formalize secessionist dynamics and push secessionists away from the use of violence, destabilization and social polarization can follow if clear rules are not put in place to reach a resolution. Meanwhile, secessionist movements in less institutionalized environments will often resort to violent methods, particularly when opposed by a relatively weak state. That is, unless the movement is separated from the home state by a militarized line and has achieved a de facto but unrecognized statehood. Movements such as these are caught in a liminal space between full sovereignty and reintegration, and have little choice but to wait for a geopolitical shift that will make recognition possible.

In this chapter, I conclude the book by considering the future of the sovereignty game. In the long run, the game will change as the international system changes. My purpose is twofold: (1) to identify ways in which it might change; (2) to take a position on those changes and argue that some are better than others. Although I necessarily take a more speculative tone in my analysis—I am talking about the future—I ground my reasoning in the normative and strategic framework developed at the beginning of the book. Those chapters outlined how the international recognition regime, and resulting sovereignty game, has developed over time. The intervening chapters examined the consequences of that game in the contemporary international system. In this chapter, I return to the high-level theorizing of the early chapers and, mindful of the lessons learned from the empirical chapters, zoom way out to consider the future of the sovereignty game.

I argue that the primary way in which the game could change in the near to medium future is through a reconceptualization of the rules guiding recognition— that is, the international recognition regime. I identify different configurations of the regime that have existed and could exist, and I specify the implications with respect to domestic and international stability, the fitness of states, and the frequency of secession(ism). I then turn to a more prescriptive analysis for how the game might be improved. I argue, with caution, for the merits of a regime that emphasizes consent-based democratized secession, in which independence movements have formal institutional access but where the conditions for political exit are nevertheless hard to reach. The resulting benefits for the sovereignty game are that conflict would be reduced both within and between states.

Alternative Games

At the most general level the sovereignty game can be modified by changing the nature of the players, their incentives, or by changing the rules. I contend that change in the nature of the players is unlikely over the short to medium run. Although there is a long-running discourse about change in the international system regarding the primacy of states and the possible rise of alternative political forms, sovereign states remain the basic units in international affairs.[2] Sovereign states possess an international legal personality that gives them access to a range of benefits. They are members of the sovereignty club and they are the substance of international law. Given that there is a clear value in being a state, it is no surprise that many stateless nations would aspire to become one. All of this could of course change in the future if the state is replaced by a different political form or comes to inhabit an environment composed of multiple political forms, but there is no convincing sign of this happening anytime soon.

There is some latitude for change in the incentives for states, and for aspiring states in particular. I have argued that states have many reasons for controlling admission to the sovereignty club, including concerns over the viability of new states, the dilution of vote share in international organizations, and, most importantly, the issue of uncontrolled fragmentation. The international system is now fully enclosed and has been since the start of the twentieth century.[3] There is no unclaimed land to expand into, or *terra nullius* upon which new states can be established—that is, unless new land is created off-world or from the sea. Therefore, any new state represents a subtraction in territory from at least one existing state. This presents an existential problem for states, one that varies in intensity depending on the fissiparousness of the state in question, and its ability to downsize in a controlled manner.[4] That basic need to control secession and limit fragmentation will endure.

The incentive structure for aspiring states is more malleable. As I said in chapter 2, only a fraction of stateless nations become secessionist. Many that do form secessionist movements ultimately reduce their ambitions. Although there are real benefits to joining the club of states, there are countervailing reasons for not doing so, including the ethnonational attachment to the larger state and the economic costs of becoming independent. For example, a majority of Cook Islanders currently prefer to remain a territory of New Zealand, and not seek independence, because of the economic benefits that come from the relationship.[5] All of this prompts the question: How can the incentive structure for potential and actual secessionist movements be altered? The answer, in the short run at least, is not by changing the actors but by changing the rules.

Using Robert Gilpin's terminology, we are more likely to see systemic change (change in the governance of the system) rather than systems change (change in the nature of the actors).[6] The international recognition regime is the set of formal and informal rules and practices that determine who counts, that is, which nations can be admitted into the club of sovereign states. These are the rules that form the strategic playing field, and shape the tactical behavior of secessionist movements. Different sets of rules yield different games. What alternative games are possible?

In chapter 2, I presented a framework for understanding how the international recognition regime has evolved over the last several centuries. It is the product of power and developing international norms. Powerful lead states have influenced the regime, especially the United Kingdom and the United States, and there is an episodic character to the regime that tracks power transition and hegemonic change. The engine of normative change is the dialectic between sovereign and liberal norms. Sovereign norms emphasize the state, and rights accrue to the state. Liberal norms stress the individual, and rights accrue to the individual. There are many friction points between these traditions. For example, a particularly relevant one in world politics is the tension between human rights and the freedom of the state to govern its own affairs.

This framework helps to illuminate a rough periodization to the international recognition regime. The first period refers mostly to the expanding European-based system of the eighteenth century, culminating with the American and French revolutions. I refer to this as a consent-based regime because the recognition of an independence movement was supposed to be withheld unless the sovereign from which the region aimed to separate gave its consent. Here, states effectively colluded to limit admission to the sovereignty club. However, this emphasis on state consent was overturned in the 1800s with the rise of the norm of self-determination, a liberal norm that challenged the sovereign tradition. As Mikulas Fabry recounts, during this period self-determination was regarded as a negative right.[7] The international community was obliged not to interfere, and an aspiring nation was expected to gain independence by its own hand. Once that self-determination was made self-evident, thereby passing the Canning Test,[8] the international community could recognize the de facto state by affirming its membership in the club. This regime of de facto recognition was a departure from the earlier consent-based regime, and it dramatically altered the strategic playing field for secessionists because they no longer had to await the consent of their sovereign; instead, they could defeat it through revolution and expect to be recognized by the international community.

The post-1945 period represents yet another solution for determining who counts. Following Fabry, I refer to this as a constitutive regime because it requires that states take a more active role in differentiating those who deserve independence from those who do not.[9] It is the result of a double normative movement during the twentieth century. First, self-determination came to be regarded as a positive right whereby states were now expected to assist self-determination efforts even if they had not prevailed over their sovereign and passed the Canning Test. Second, the rise of the territorial integrity norm (also called the border fixity norm) stressed the inviolability of existing borders and made territorial conquest taboo.[10] Given the competing demands of maintaining borders and helping aspiring nations to change them, the international community has had to develop criteria for who counts—the criteria that shape the contemporary sovereignty game.

In summary, I have identified three different periods in the evolving international recognition regime. The first was the pre-1815 consent-based regime. The second period lasted from approximately 1815 until World War I, and it stressed de facto statehood. The third period is the contemporary regime, which began after 1945.[11] Each of these represents a kind of solution for how to respond to independence movements. Of course, plenty of diplomatic decisions have gone against the prescribed method for determining who counts during the period in question. For example, France was willing to support the American revolutionaries prior to their victory over the British. Later, it was the British and the Americans who argued that de facto states should be recognized, and they were often opposed by the more conservative continental powers. Likewise, with respect to secession in the contemporary period, Russia and China are typically more conservative when it comes to interfering in the sovereign affairs of another state. Nevertheless, each solution broadly fits the period in question. Furthermore, they are useful for contemplating future configurations of the recognition regime. Can other alternative, as yet unrealized, solutions be imagined?

The tension between sovereign and liberal norms provides a useful framework for considering alternative configurations for the recognition regime. One possibility is the strengthening of a remedial right to secession. Remedial rights theory, also called just cause theory, posits that groups have a right to secede because other rights have been violated.[12] In its most common form, a minority nation gains the right when the larger state has failed to uphold the social contract by not providing an acceptable level of order and security. The appeal of the right rises in relation to the predatory nature of the state. A second possibility is the consolidation of a primary right to secession. Primary right theory, or choice theory, holds that a self-identified nation should be able to determine its political fate and secede from the parent state via a democratic process.[13] Like the first possibility—the entrenchment of a remedial right—this future constitutes a modification and extension of the current constitutive recognition regime. Both would represent a victory for liberalism, and a swing of the pendulum away from the sovereign tradition.

Set against these possibilities is a move in the opposite direction toward the fortification of sovereignty. A likely possibility here is added support for the territorial integrity norm and a roll back of the application of self-determination, especially in its current interpretation as a positive right. This would be a return to recognition by consent, a conservative exclusion mechanism that would resemble the eighteenth century in some respects. The key difference would be the retention of the norm of territorial integrity and its prohibition on conquest. Such a system would reinforce the existing territorial grid and promote territorial stability, but it would come at the expense of liberal rights. In sum, this gives us six potential configurations for the recognition regime, three drawn from the past and present, and three that are theorized.

Comparative Statics of Different Games

Let us now engage in a comparative analysis of the advantages and disadvantages of the configurative design of the recognition regime. In doing so I will proceed from the assumption that the legal or normative framework of the regime shapes the behavior of the key actors, in this case the home states and secessionist movements. There will be exceptions to be sure. Powerful actors will often do what they want, and secessionists may make poor strategic and tactical decisions, but in the aggregate these different configurations of the regime shape the strategic playing field. They create alternative sovereignty games.

Table 12.1 displays the six configurations and their expected outcomes. These are recognition by consent, de facto recognition, constitutive recognition in the form that has existed since 1945, and in the form it could take if a remedial right or primary right to independence became entrenched, and, finally, a consent-based regime that also stresses the territorial integrity norm. Each configuration is the product of the relative balance between sovereign and liberal norms and their particular interpretations. Whereas the sovereign tradition is clearly dominant in the consent-based systems, the remedial and primary rights regimes represent periods of relative liberal dominance. Meanwhile, the de facto and constitutive regimes represent more balanced configurations.

What are the implications of each of these configurations for the sovereignty game? The consent-based regime of the pre-1815 era is unattractive for a number

TABLE 12.1.   Alternative sovereignty games

	CONSENT	DE FACTO	CONSTITUTIVE	REMEDIAL RIGHT	PRIMARY RIGHT	CONSENT + TERRITORIAL INTEGRITY
Sovereign or liberal dominant?	Sovereign	Mixed	Mixed	Liberal	Liberal	Sovereign
Frequency of secession	Rare	Rare / common	Common	Very common	Common / very common	Rare
Trend in number of states	Declining	Declining	Proliferation	Proliferation	Proliferation	Slow proliferation
General effects?	Minority exclusion	Oppression, revolution	International discord, varied secessionist tactics	International discord, suppression, provocation	Cooptation, fragmentation	Minority exclusion
Fitness of new states?	Indeterminate	Strong	Strong / weak	Strong / weak	Strong / moderately weak	Indeterminate

of reasons. Chief among them is arguably the acceptability of territorial conquest, that is, the absence of the territorial integrity norm. As history shows, this
generates volatility with respect to interstate conflict. Here, borders would be un-
stable not on account of pressures from within but because of pressures from
without. The existing club members could change borders through conquest, but
aspiring nations would struggle to join the club unless they could win the consent of their sovereign. Therefore, secession should be rare, and there would exist
a declining trend in the number of states since the rate of state death ought to
exceed the rate of state birth. Minority nations are more likely to be excluded in
this environment given the lack of liberal norms that oblige the international community to consider their interests. Finally, it is indeterminate whether states born
into such a system would be institutionally fit and functional polities; much would
turn on the interests and motives of their former central government when permitting secession. Ultimately, a sovereignty game of this sort would be quite one-
sided. It is an unlikely future given that it would require not only the rollback of
liberal norms but also an abandonment of the territorial integrity norm.

It is fascinating to speculate on a sovereignty game built upon de facto recognition. Here, governments have to take care to prevent the rise of secessionist
groups strong enough to challenge the state, defeat it, and thereby garner international recognition. Meanwhile, dissatisfied minority nations have strong incentives to challenge the state when they anticipate success. In comparison to a
consent-based regime, we should expect to see greater patterns of oppression and
revolution. Secession should be more common, though perhaps not as common
as it would be in a constitutive system. Importantly, in this system there is no emphasis on territorial integrity, and borders would be subject to change from both
internal and external forces. Conquest and the seizure of territory would be acceptable forms of behavior. If the pattern during the nineteenth century is any
indication, the number of states ought to decline.

One intriguing aspect of the de facto state system is its implications for the
institutional and socioeconomic fitness of the states that would emerge from it.
Fabry argued that a downside of the current constitutive regime is that it sometimes admits weak and unfit states that meet the criteria for admission and denies other nations like Northern Cyprus that are actually functional states.[14] In
contrast, the de facto regime has the advantage that while states may be born from
blood, they will tend to be strong since the unfit will usually be defeated by their
government. It is for this reason that Fabry argues for a return to regime based
on de facto recognition. Although there is some merit to his argument, it is important to recognize that minority exclusion and civil war would be common in the
resulting sovereignty game. Moreover, a practical obstacle to implementing these
rules is that they would have few supporters. Most liberal thinkers accustomed

to humanitarian intervention will reject the argument that third parties should remain neutral while civil wars rage, and supporters of sovereignty would surely deny the principle that internal nations can gain recognition by prevailing over the state. The age of de facto statehood was a unique moment in international life, following the articulation of a negative right to self-determination, but prior to the advancement of a positive right and the sovereign emphasis on territorial integrity.

Constitutive designs produce different effects and different games. The inculcation of a positive right to self-determination creates pressure for consensus that is hard to attain in a diverse international environment and interstate discord can result. This is one of the reasons why Fabry argues that the de facto regime is superior: it requires less consensus and therefore makes for clearer recognition criteria. We already know the effects of the contemporary sovereignty game; it is the subject of this book. There has been a proliferation of states, and considerable tactical variation in terms of how secessionists pursue independence. Finally, the fitness of states has also varied given the emphasis on assisting minority nations to achieve statehood.

What should we expect from a regime in which the positive right to self-determination was expanded to include a remedial right to independence? From a liberal perspective, this is attractive because it invalidates the protection given to sovereign states when they are guilty of human rights violations. Much like the Responsibility to Protect (R2P) doctrine, it would subordinate sovereignty to liberalism and hold states accountable for their actions.[15] In such a system, secession ought to be more common, all else being equal, and the proliferation of states would continue. Perhaps regions like West Papua and Bougainville would become independent under these conditions. However, the general effects would not be unproblematic, and there are several potential negative outcomes. First, there is likely to be international discord since not all states will agree to a remedial right, certainly not those who are guilty of human rights violations. Indeed, states may have incentive to suppress potential movements from becoming a problem in the first place. Second, there is a potential moral hazard problem given that secessionists would have an incentive to provoke the state into behaving badly. Although the potential for moral hazard exists in the current sovereignty game, it would be amplified in one where a remedial right has more traction. Third, in regard to state fitness, a remedial right could lead to the creation of states whose primary virtue, with respect to obtaining recognition, is that they were the site of conflict, human rights abuse, or perhaps genocide. Such developments often occur precisely where state structures are weak.

When taking all of these factors into consideration, it seems that the inculcation of a remedial right would be most beneficial in a system where it is not invoked. If it is consolidated to the point where all actors accept it, then none would question its application. But that level of acceptance and corresponding willingness to abide the outcome would seem to imply a more disciplined and benevolent system of state governments where the treatment of peoples is concerned. It is hard to imagine that a government that violates the human rights of an internal nation would casually accept that nation's remedial right to independence once a red line was crossed. Discord would follow. Therefore, a system that is sufficiently socialized to embrace a remedial right would be a good system indeed. In the ideal form where all states abide by the norm and behave accordingly it would never be invoked and it would not shape secessionist tactics. But as long as a sufficient portion of states in the system are resistant to the norm, the potential negative outcomes will hold.

The consolidation of a primary right to independence is equally thought-provoking.[16] Although the frequency of secession would increase and state proliferation would continue, the pace of these phenomena would depend on the stipulations regarding state exit. For example, if binding independence referenda are easy to obtain and the victory requirement is a simple majority, then secession ought to be quite frequent. But as the opponents to Catalan secessionism often argue, setting the bar low invites other problems pertaining to excessive fragmentation, instability, and recursive exit related to the minority-within-minority problem. In a system where primary rights are observed, we ought to see an increased attempt by states to coopt minority nations, perhaps giving them greater political voice.[17] The state fitness problem is arguably less salient here than with the extension of a remedial right given that the new state, on average, would be born via a democratic plebiscite rather than through a conflict and related violations of human rights.

As always, the promise of the primary right depends on application. It matters not only how easy it is to obtain a referendum but also how home states interpret the process. If the international community came to embrace the value of a primary right and central governments were willing to honor the norm under specified conditions, then the outcome would be similar in form to a consent-based system. That is, states would give their consent to independence under certain conditions, and third parties would not have to fulfill an obligation to assist the aspiring nation. Here, the sovereignty game would be predominantly a domestic institutional affair, and the concerns raised by Fabry regarding the challenges of a constitutive system would not hold. Invoking a primary right does not imply resistance on the part of the state, and a corresponding need for third party involvement, in the same way that invoking a remedial right does. If, however, third parties intervene in a domestic dispute and pressure the home state to provide a plebiscite in line with the principle of primary rights, then the dynamic is different. But one wonders whether this would truly happen in the absence of some additional motivating factor such as a human rights violation, in which case the core motivating norm is remedial in nature and less about primary rights. In the end, the success of the norm will depend on the extent to which it is accepted by participating states rather than something that is pushed upon them by a select group of states within the international community.

The final configuration is a consent-based system that resembles the pre-1815 regime but retains the territorial integrity norm. This would be a conservative pro-sovereign system, one where new states can be born only via consent and where borders cannot be moved by either internal or external actors unless the state approves. None of the secessionist movements examined in this book would achieve independence under these conditions unless consent was given. Essentially, it would be eighteenth-century Europe with a taboo on conquest. I have argued elsewhere that this would be a remarkably stable system.[18] Secession would be rare, and states would slowly proliferate where consent was given. This is actually a rather plausible future given the rise of China, India, and other states that are relatively pro-sovereign on the issue of secession. Its chief merit is that it stresses stability and relies on consent, thus avoiding the problems inherent in a constitutive system. Its chief weakness is the rollback of liberal values and the license it would likely give states to ignore and exclude minority nations. It would be a one-sided sovereignty game, but a stable one.

Improving the Game

In light of the preceding discussion and the analysis throughout the book, I now offer a proposal for improving the sovereignty game. An improved game would be one in which intrastate and interstate discord is reduced, where liberalism and the advancement of individual rights is valued, and where new states are born as functional and viable entities. Different analysts may stress different outcomes but most readers will see the value in these. Importantly, as discussed, not all of these outcomes will necessarily move in the same direction. A system based on de facto recognition may produce robust states but violence will be common. A consent-based system might reduce interstate discord but push against liberalism and potentially trample on minority rights. Nevertheless, I contend that my proposal will produce positive outcomes across all of these dimensions. I propose that states be encouraged to democratize secessionism and accept a primary right to independence for minority nations, and that such policies be implemented at the prerogative of states themselves and not by outside actors.

A chief merit of this solution is that it democratizes and institutionalizes the tactical playing field. As we saw in chapter 10, secessionists are more likely to use tactics of electoral capture and less likely to use violence when they have institutional options. Importantly, it is not just that the ballot is more attractive than the gun in democratized movements. For at some level, violence ceases to even be on the menu of options. In my interviews with Catalan secessionists, it was clear that the use of violence was out of the question, it was abhorrent. Democratized movements shape tactics not only via the logic of consequences, but also through the logic of appropriateness.[19]

A related merit of institutionalizing secessionism is that it reduces information problems, clarifies the actors, and improves the chances that bargains can be struck. This was a key theme in Kathleen Cunningham's analysis of the bargaining between states and self-determination movements. She argues that the uninstitutionalized nature of self-determination movements creates problems for state governments.[20] Who are the key actors representing the secessionist cause? What is the relationship between the factions? Who speaks for which group and how can the groups be differentiated? For states facing an uninstitutionalized movement like West Papua, this is indeed a problem, one that has led to frustration on the part of the government when it was looking to negotiate.[21] However, for states facing democratized movements like Catalonia, the problem is less acute because the factions are represented for the most part by formal political parties. Democratizing secessionist movements reduces uncertainty and the problem of imperfect information. According to Cunningham, this reduces the chance of conflict between the parties.

An additional merit of this proposal is that it can remain a consent-based practice. That is, it does not have to be a solution imposed upon states by the international community. Indeed, it directly involves the institutions of the state, it requires them. One of the strengths of the consent-based system is that it minimizes international discord by removing the practice whereby the international community goes around a home state to recognize an internal movement. Here, attention is focused on the institutional relationship between the home state and its internal movement. The international community may pressure the state to provide institutional options but that dynamic brings the state into the process. It requires the involvement of the state. This contrasts with the inculcation of a remedial right, which ostensibly goes around the state when recognizing its internal breakaway region.

There are several potential critiques to this proposal. First, some might argue that it is a simple rehash of primary rights theory, that it is not new. There is, after all, a long-running discourse on this topic in political theory.[22] Although there is no question that I am building on this work, I am adding two elements. I am bringing an empirical dimension to the discussion that is normally absent in these more theoretically driven arguments. My analysis in this book shows the benefits of institutionalization with respect to reducing uncertainty and violence. More-

over, I am augmenting the traditional primary rights argument with an emphasis on state consent. Bringing the home state into the process ought to reduce
domestic and international discord.

Second, as critics of primary rights theory will point out, my proposal will generate instability and conflict inside countries. That is, by making secessionist
parties legal and by institutionalizing the right to hold independence referenda,
you embolden and incentivize secessionists and amplify the potential for fragmentation. This critique is correct, but it can be ameliorated by setting the bar
high, a good bit higher than the simple majority that was required in the 2014
Scottish referendum. There are different solutions for how to set the bar.[23] One
is to require a second referendum if the "Yes" vote only narrowly wins the first. A
different solution is to require that the great majority of the electorate agrees ahead
of time to accept the outcome. In relation to Catalonia, the economist Germà Bel
argued that 51 percent is enough to carry the vote as long as at least 80 percent of
the population agrees to accept the outcome.[24] Another more constraining solution is to insist that the electorate of the entire country, not just the breakaway
region, have a say.[25] I do not know the ideal formulation for this but it should set
the bar high enough to avoid excessive and divisive fragmentation, but not so high
that it pushes secessionists to try other extra-institutional methods. One of the
problems with contemporary Catalan secessionism is that while independence
parties are legal, secession itself is considered unconstitutional.[26] The inculcation
of a primary right and the allowance of a referendum with well-designed victory
conditions should ameliorate much of the social tension, and potentially reduce
the attraction of independence for moderate voters.

A third problem is that not all countries are sufficiently democratic, institutionalized, or simply willing to provide these pathways to independence. It is true
that some nondemocratic states will be ill suited for this proposal. It will not work
in all countries. However, referenda can still be held in countries with only weak
democratic institutions. The solution is to hold them and make the conditions
for victory hard to reach. For their part, many democracies are often guilty of
putting up blocks to secession by placing bans on secessionist parties or through
eternity clauses that make constitutional changes unconstitutional.[27] According
to Rivka Weill, the danger of these obstacles is that they can lead frustrated secessionists to utilize extrainstitutional, often violent, methods. States should fight the
temptation to erect these institutional bulwarks to secession. My proposal proceeds from the position that democratized secession has benefits over alternative
forms—it commits the secessionists to a nonviolent, institutional path. Such paths
may create forms of partisanship and political contestation but, provided state
exit is difficult to achieve, they are outweighed by the extrainstitutional methods
and potential violence that can otherwise result.

Another potential critique is that secessionists will still choose violence because they believe that it works. This is what Tanisha Fazal calls the secessionist dilemma, the notion that the international community encourages secessionists to be nonviolent, even though violence pays.[28] Louis Wasser and I investigated this issue in a 2019 article and found that secessionists were no more likely to secure independence by using violence than other comparable movements who chose peaceful methods.[29] In fact, one striking finding in our study is that all successful independence efforts use institutional methods at some point in the process. From that we inferred that the formation of an institutional wing provides secessionists with the means to dialogue with the state and/or international community. It makes them legible. Furthermore, we cautioned in our study that violence is not simply on the menu of options for all movements. Rather, some movements are born or develop in the circumstances of conflict. For them, the use of violence is more familiar, more present, but it does not increase their chance of becoming independent. Of course, some secessionists may believe that violence works, and that belief could be quite consequential. Nevertheless, such beliefs are formed in the absence of a more institutionalized primary right to independence. Should that right be stressed, as I propose, the temptation to use violence would be weakened further.

Notably, this proposal says nothing about the importance of a remedial right. Although I am sympathetic to the underlying principle of a remedial right, I maintain that it is quite difficult to implement. In a system where only half of the states supported it, the other half would stand in opposition. Therefore, attempts at implementation could generate discord. It would be different in a system where the great majority of states supported the principle, but that does not accurately describe the contemporary system. The inculcation of a remedial right works best where it has substantial buy-in and is therefore needed less.

Like the international recognition regime, the sovereignty game is a work in progress. The recognition regime provides the rules for the game, and they evolve in relation to one another. Using the theoretical framework developed in chapter 2, I identified different configurations of the recognition regime and latterly different possibilities for the sovereignty game. Some of these games were merely facsimiles of the past which therefore seemed archaic. But the theorized games are possible given what we know about how the recognition regime changes over time. I have argued for the merits of democratizing and institutionalizing secession in a manner that is consent-based and where the possibility for state exit is hard to reach. While this will not perfect the sovereignty game, it should improve it.

Acknowledgments

This book is in many ways a sequel to my 2016 book *Age of Secession: The International and Domestic Determinants of State Birth*. Whereas that book examined how central governments (metropoles) respond to secessionist demands, this one is an investigation into what secessionist movements actually do to achieve their ends. It switches the perspective. But this time around I have attempted to remedy a weakness of the first book. As my friend and mentor Tanisha Fazal commented, there were very few people in *Age of Secession*. That book offered a highly structural account of the topic and rarely touched down to talk about the activity of actual people. This time I took a more journalistic approach involving fieldwork and interviews, along with other forms of qualitative and quantitative methods, to talk about what actual secessionists do. I aimed to get inside their heads to explore their strategy and tactics as part of the game they play to win their sovereignty.

Most of the work for this book was completed when I was a faculty member in the Department of Government and International Relations at the University of Sydney. An early conversation with Ben Goldsmith turned me on to the prospect of writing a book on secessionist strategy. Along the way I received terrific feedback and support from my colleagues there, including James Der Derian, Charlotte Epstein, Graeme Gill, Gorana Grgic Max Grömping, Eda Gunaydin, Justin Hastings, Martin Kear, James Loxton, Megan MacKenzie, Diarmuid Maguire, Ferran Martínez i Coma, Gil Merom, Susan Park, Sarah Phillips, Jamie Reilly, David Smith, Frank Smith, Rodney Smith, and Colin Wight. The final stages of the book were completed at Syracuse University. In April 2019 I held a book workshop that was attended by Kathleen Gallagher Cunningham and Tanisha Fazal as outside discussants, and by a number of colleagues from the political science department at Syracuse, including Lamis Abdelaaty, Matt Cleary, Dimitar Gueorguiev, Audie Klotz, Seth Jolly, Angely Martinez, Brian Taylor, and Simon Weschle. That workshop led to a number of vital changes in the book, and I am grateful to the participants.

This book could not have been completed without generous support from a number of organizations. Chief among them is the Australian Research Council (ARC), which gave me a Discovery Early Career Research Award (DECRA), 2015–2018. That support funded the majority of the fieldwork, research travel, and related teaching relief. I also acknowledge financial support from the Maxwell

School at Syracuse University, the Appleby-Mosher Research Fund, the University of Sydney, Yale University, and the Barcelona Institute for International Studies (IBEI).

Elements of this book were presented at various other events over the last six years and numerous people have made valuable suggestions and criticism. These include Boaz Atzili, Karlo Basta, Charles Butcher, Sarah Croco, Renée de Nevers, Mikulas Fabry, Pablo Guillen, Seva Gunitsky, Margaret Hermann, Jacint Jordana, Burak Kadercan, Yannis Karagiannis, Jason MacLeod, Bart Maddens, Diego Muro, Sasa Pavkovic, Scott Pegg, Peter Radan, Ignacio Sánchez-Cuenca, and Lee Seymour. My 2014–2015 fellowship at the Yale Program on Order, Conflict, and Violence was a seminal period in the development of this book, and I thank Stathis Kalyvas, Joshua Goodman, Martijn Vlaskamp, and Louis Wasser, among others. I thank the faculty at IBEI for hosting me for a semester in 2015, a period that was vital for my interviews on Catalonia. To that end, I thank the numerous interviewees around the world who took time to speak with me. I am also deeply obliged to Roger Haydon at Cornell University Press for taking a chance on me, and for the marvelous feedback from the two anonymous reviewers.

Finally, I thank Alison, Henry, and Beatrice for their companionship during this time. They often accompanied me on fieldwork, and were always a source of inspiration.

Appendix

TACTICS OF COMPELLENCE
AND NORMATIVE APPEAL

TABLE A.1.

KIND^A	HOME STATE	SECESSIONIST MOVEMENT	YEAR	COMPELLENCE TACTICS			TACTICS OF NORMATIVE APPEAL				
				INSTITUTIONAL	NONVIOLENT EXTRA-INSTITUTIONAL	VIOLENT EXTRA-INSTITUTIONAL	EARNED SOVEREIGNTY	FREEDOM TO CHOOSE	DECOLONISATION	INHERENT SOVEREIGNTY	HUMAN RIGHTS
1	Cyprus	Northern Cyprus	1983	0	1	1	23	0	0	1	0
1	Azerbaijan	Artsakh	1991	1	0	1	12	1	1	0	0
1	Moldova	Transnistria	1991	0	1	1	0	0	0	0	0
1	Moldova	Gagauzia	1991	0	1	1	2	1	0	0	1
1	Georgia	South Ossetia	1992	1	1	1	2	0	1	0	2
1	Georgia	Abkhazia	1994	1	1	1	9	1	0	0	1
1/2	Somalia	Somaliland	1991	0	1	1	4	1	3	0	2
2	Indonesia	West Papua	1975	0	1	1	1	3	4	0	0
2	Morocco	Western Sahara (Saharawis)	1976	0	1	1	0	3	11	4	1
2	Cameroon	Southern Cameroons	1999	0	1	1	5	2	10	0	4
2	Indonesia	East Timor	1999	1	1	1	0	1	6	3	7
3	Denmark	Faeroe Islands	1946	1	0	0	0	3	1	0	0
3	Italy	Giulians	1947	1	1	1	0	1	2	0	0
3	Israel	Palestinians I	1947	0	1	1	0	5	0	2	0
3	Burma	Shans	1958	0	1	1	0	0	0	0	0
3	Burma	Kachin II	1961	0	1	1	2	0	1	0	0
3	Canada	Quebec	1962	1	1	1	7	1	7	0	0
3	Uganda	Bankonjo I	1963	0	1	1	0	0	0	0	0
3	India	Meitei	1964	0	1	1	0	0	0	0	0
3	Italy	Sardinia	1965	0	1	0	0	0	0	0	0

3	Italy	South Tyrol	1965	1	0	0	2	0	0	1
3	India	Mizos	1966	1	1	0	0	0	0	0
3	UK	Northern Ireland	1968	1	1	0	3	1	0	0
3	France	Brittany	1970	1	0	2	0	6	0	0
3	Papua New Guinea	Bougainville II	1975	1	1	0	2	1	0	0
3	France	Basques	1975	1	1	0	3	2	0	1
3	France	Corsica	1978	1	1	0	2	8	0	0
3	India	Tripuras	1978	0	1	1	0	0	1	0
3	Sri Lanka	Tamils	1981	1	1	2	8	4	1	2
3	Turkey	Kurds II	1984	0	1	0	0	0	0	0
3	India	Boro/Bodo	1986	0	1	0	0	0	0	0
3	India	Sikhs II	1986	1	1	0	2	0	0	0
3	Israel	Palestinians II	1988	0	1	0	5	26	1	0
3	India	Assam	1989	0	1	0	0	2	0	1
3	India	Kashmir II	1989	1	1	1	9	2	2	3
3	Papua New Guinea	Bougainville II	1990	0	1	0	2	2	0	3
3	Philippines	Abu Sayyaf	1991	0	0	0	0	0	0	0
3	Bosnia	Serbs	1992	0	1	1	4	0	0	2
3	Bosnia	Croats	1992	0	1	2	2	0	2	0
3	Ukraine	Crimea	1992	1	0	2	7	0	1	0
3	UK	Scotland	1992	1	1	1	9	0	0	0
3	Russia	Tatars	1992	1	1	5	4	2	0	0
3	South Africa	Inkatha	1994	1	1	0	5	1	1	1
3	St. Kitts and Nevis	Nevis	1996	1	0	0	6	0	0	0

(continued)

TABLE A.1. (CONTINUED)

KIND^A	HOME STATE	SECESSIONIST MOVEMENT	YEAR	COMPELLENCE TACTICS			TACTICS OF NORMATIVE APPEAL				
				INSTITUTIONAL	NONVIOLENT EXTRA-INSTITUTIONAL	VIOLENT EXTRA-INSTITUTIONAL	EARNED SOVEREIGNTY	FREEDOM TO CHOOSE	DECOLONISATION	INHERENT SOVEREIGNTY	HUMAN RIGHTS
3	Italy	Padania	1996	1	1	0	0	4	7	0	1
3	France	Savoy	1997	1	1	0	0	1	0	0	0
3	Solomon Islands	Guadalcanal	1999	0	1	1	0	0	2	0	1
3	Spain	Basques III	2000	1	1	1	0	15	3	1	2
3	Italy	Sardinia	2002	1	1	0	0	0	0	0	0
3	Yugoslavia	Montenegro	2006	1	0	0	4	12	0	0	0
3	Comoros	Anjouan II	2007	0	1	0	0	2	0	0	0
3	Yugoslavia	Kosovo	2008	1	1	1	3	6	2	0	10
4	New Zealand	Maori	1975	0	1	0	0	0	0	0	0
4	USA	Hawaii	1994	1	1	0	0	4	11	14	3
4	USA	Lakotah	2007	1	1	0	0	0	2	6	1
5	China	Eastern Mongols	1946	0	1	1	1	0	1	0	0
5	India	Kashmir I	1947	1	0	1	0	8	0	0	1
5	India	Hyderabad	1948	1	0	1	2	0	0	2	0
5	India	Nagas	1948	1	1	0	0	1	0	0	0
5	China	Tibet II	1950	0	1	1	2	0	0	0	0
5	China	Hui	1953	0	1	1	0	0	0	0	0
5	China	Tibet III	1956	0	0	1	0	0	4	2	0
5	China	Tibet IV	1979	0	1	0	0	2	0	1	0
5	USSR	Ajars	1988	0	1	0	0	0	0	0	0
5	USSR	Abkhazia	1989	1	1	0	3	0	0	0	0

5	China	Uighurs	1990	0	1	1	0	0	1	0	1
5	USSR	South Ossetia	1990	1	1	1	1	0	0	0	3
5	USSR	Chechnya I	1991	1	1	1	1	0	0	0	0
5	USSR	Azeris	1991	1	0	0	0	2	6	2	4
5	USSR	Tajiks	1991	1	0	0	1	6	0	0	1
5	USSR	Khyrgiz	1991	1	0	0	0	2	1	0	0
5	USSR	Uzbeks	1991	1	0	0	0	3	3	0	0
5	USSR	Kazakhs	1991	1	1	0	0	1	1	0	0
5	USSR	Moldova	1991	1	1	0	1	5	3	0	1
5	USSR	Estonians II	1991	1	1	0	1	0	3	0	1
5	USSR	Latvians II	1991	1	1	0	3	3	6	0	1
5	USSR	Lithuanians III	1991	1	1	0	1	6	3	0	1
5	USSR	Ukrainians II	1991	1	1	0	1	13	0	0	1
5	USSR	Belarus	1991	1	1	0	0	1	0	0	1
5	USSR	Georgia	1991	1	1	0	1	0	6	4	5
5	USSR	Turkomen	1991	1	1	0	0	0	0	0	0
5	USSR	Armenia	1991	1	1	0	0	0	0	0	3
5	Russia	Dagestan	1999	0	0	1	0	1	0	0	0
5	Russia	Chechnya II	1999	1	0	1	6	1	1	0	3
6	Pakistan	Pashtuns	1947	1	1	0	0	3	0	0	4
6	Burma	Arakanese I	1948	0	1	1	0	0	0	0	1
6	Burma	Kachin I	1949	0	0	0	0	0	0	0	0
6	Burma	Karenni	1949	0	0	0	0	0	0	0	0
6	Burma	Karens	1949	0	1	1	1	0	0	0	0
6	Burma	Mons	1949	1	1	1	0	0	0	0	1
6	Indonesia	Atjeh I	1950	1	1	1	0	0	1	0	0
6	Indonesia	Ambonese	1950	1	1	1	0	2	0	1	0

(continued)

TABLE A.1. (CONTINUED)

KIND^A	HOME STATE	SECESSIONIST MOVEMENT	YEAR	COMPELLENCE TACTICS			TACTICS OF NORMATIVE APPEAL				
				INSTITUTIONAL	NONVIOLENT EXTRA-INSTITUTIONAL	VIOLENT EXTRA-INSTITUTIONAL	EARNED SOVEREIGNTY	FREEDOM TO CHOOSE	DECOLONISATION	INHERENT SOVEREIGNTY	HUMAN RIGHTS
6	Sudan	South Sudan I	1956	0	1	1	0	0	1	0	2
6	Pakistan	Baluch	1958	0	1	1	0	0	1	0	2
6	Indonesia	Sulawesi	1958	0	1	1	0	0	0	0	1
6	Democratic Republic of Congo	Stanleyville	1960	0	1	1	0	0	0	0	0
6	Democratic Republic of Congo	South Katanga	1960	1	1	1	3	1	1	0	0
6	Democratic Republic of Congo	South Kasai	1960	1	1	1	0	0	0	0	2
6	Ivory Coast	Anyi	1961	1	1	0	0	0	0	0	0
6	Ethiopia	Somali I	1963	0	0	1	0	0	8	0	2
6	Thailand	Malays	1963	0	1	1	0	0	1	0	0
6	Vietnam	Chams	1964	0	1	0	0	0	0	0	0
6	Nigeria	Edos	1967	0	0	1	0	0	0	0	1
6	Nigeria	Ibos	1967	0	1	1	0	2	2	0	22
6	Spain	Basques II	1968	0	1	1	0	0	2	1	7
6	Pakistan	East Pakistan	1971	1	1	1	0	1	5	0	12
6	Iraq	Kurds I	1972	0	0	1	1	1	0	0	3
6	Philippines	Mindanao	1972	0	1	1	0	0	2	0	7
6	Spain	Catalans III	1974	0	1	1	0	0	0	0	2

6	Angola	Cabinda	1975	0	1	1	0	1	4	0	0
6	Bangladesh	Chittagong	1975	0	1	1	0	0	0	0	0
6	Iran	Kurds II	1979	0	1	1	0	2	0	0	5
6	Burma	Arakanese II	1980	0	0	1	0	0	0	0	5
6	Iraq	Kurds II	1980	0	1	1	0	0	0	0	1
6	Senegal	Casamance	1982	0	1	1	0	0	0	0	0
6	Uganda	Bankonjo II	1986	0	1	1	0	0	0	0	0
6	Indonesia	Atjeh II	1988	0	1	1	0	0	4	0	20
6	Namibia	Basters (Rehoboth)	1990	0	1	0	0	0	0	0	2
6	Yugoslavia	Slovenia	1990	1	0	1	0	6	0	0	0
6	Ethiopia	Tigray II	1991	1	0	1	0	0	0	0	7
6	Yugoslavia	Croatia	1991	1	0	1	0	7	0	0	0
6	Yugoslavia	Macedonia	1991	1	1	0	4	1	0	0	0
6	Iraq	Kurds III	1991	0	1	1	2	4	0	0	13
6	Croatia	Serbs	1992	0	1	1	0	4	0	0	3
6	Yugoslavia	Bosnia	1992	1	1	1	0	2	0	0	1
6	Azerbaijan	Talysh	1993	0	1	1	0	0	0	0	0
6	Ethiopia	Eritrea	1993	1	1	1	4	9	2	0	1
6	Yemen	South Yemen I	1994	0	1	1	0	0	0	0	1
6	Ethiopia	Somali II	1994	1	1	1	0	2	4	0	0
6	Iraq	Kurds IV	1995	0	1	1	3	0	0	0	7
6	Comoros	Moheli	1997	0	1	0	0	0	0	0	0
6	Comoros	Anjouan I	1997	1	1	1	3	6	0	0	0
6	Namibia	Lozi	1998	0	1	1	0	1	0	0	3
6	Yemen	South Yemen	2007	0	1	1	0	3	4	0	4
6	Sudan	South Sudan II	2011	1	1	1	2	0	0	0	11
6	Burma	Kachin III	2011	0	1	1	1	0	0	0	10

a 1 = de facto; 2 = decolonial, 3 = democratized, 4 = indigenous legal, 5 = weak combative, 6 = strong combative.

Notes

1. MANY SECESSIONIST MOVEMENTS, ONE INTERNATIONAL SYSTEM

1. Fearon and Laitin (2003) estimate that 52 percent of the civil wars between 1945 and 1999 involved secessionism. Similarly, Sorens (2012, 3) claims that "since the 1980s, at least half of all ongoing civil wars in any given year have been secessionist."

2. Griffiths 2016a, 57.

3. Walter 2009, 3.

4. Chenoweth and Stephan 2011; Fazal and Griffiths 2014; Fazal 2018a.

5. Griffiths 2016a, 205.

6. I have appropriated the term "sovereignty game" from Jackson 1990, 34–35.

7. Schelling 1966, 71–73.

8. Horowitz 1985, 230. Similarly, in Griffiths 2016a, I identified the international and domestic factors that influenced the response of central governments to secessionist demands.

9. Gourevitch 1978.

10. Pegg 1998; Berg 2009; Caspersen 2012; Florea 2014; Visoka 2018.

11. Keating 2004; Swenden 2006; Van Houten 2007; Beland and Lecours 2010.

12. Toft 2002; Walter 2006; 2009; Meetser 2012; Kraus 2013–2014; Cunningham 2014; Bakke 2015; Seymour, Bakke, and Cunningham 2016; Butt 2017.

13. Osterud 1997; Pavkovic and Radan 2007; Roeder 2007; Sorens 2012; Erman 2013; Coggins 2014; Griffiths 2015; 2016; Cunningham and Sawyer 2017; Krause 2017.

14. In a recent contribution, Roeder 2018 examines how breakaway leaders propagate a successful nation-state project.

15. Tarrow 2011; Chenoweth and Stephan 2011; Schock 2013.

16. Fearon and Laitin 2003; Kalyvas 2006; Weinstein 2007; Sambanis and Schulhofer-Wohl 2009; Toft 2010; Kalyvas and Balcells 2010; Mampilly 2011; Stanton 2013; Staniland 2014; Balcells 2017; Matanock 2017.

17. Bob 2005; Mampilly 2011; Jo 2015; Huang 2016; Coggins 2017; Stewart 2018.

18. Ratner 1996; Bartos 1997; Grant 1999; Crawford 2006; Fabry 2010; Sterio 2013.

19. Countersecession strategy is an exciting and developing research area (Ker-Lindsay 2012; Butt 2017; Weill 2018; Relitz 2019; Griffiths and Muro 2020).

20. See Kalyvas 2006; Cunningham 2014; Seymour, Bakke, and Cunningham 2016; Balcells 2017; Krause 2017.

21. Roeder 2018.

22. Lieberman 2005.

23. I do not disclose the names of the interviewees unless I have been given explicit permission to do so.

24. Griffiths 2016a.

25. Griffiths and Wasser 2019.

26. When referring to secessionist regions/nations, I utilize their preferred title (e.g., Artsakh instead of Nagorno Karabakh). This reflects a focus on the secessionist movement and not an advocation of their cause.

27. As an example of the political sensitivities related to fieldwork, in a June 2019 trip to Artsakh I met with Ashot Ghoulian, speaker of the Artsakh National Assembly. In the

twitter feed that followed the announcement of our meeting by the Artsakh parliament, I was asked by one commenter if my interview signaled that I supported the ethnic cleansing of Azerbaijanis.

2. STATES, SECESSIONIST MOVEMENTS, AND THE INTERNATIONAL RECOGNITION REGIME

1. Weber 1964; James 1986; Tilly 1992; Elliott 1992; Spruyt 1994; Agnew 1994; Ferguson and Mansbach 1996; Ruggie 1998; Jackson 2007; Nexon 2009; Butcher and Griffiths 2017.

2. Jackson and Rosberg 1982.

3. Krasner 1999. Krasner also identified two additional dimensions of sovereignty: (1) interdependence sovereignty, the ability of the state to regulate what crosses its borders; and (2) Westphalian sovereignty, the actual and formal exclusion of outside actors in the domestic authority structures of the state.

4. Pegg 1998; Caspersen 2012; Florea 2014.

5. Anonymous 2002.

6. Data taken from Griffiths and Butcher 2013. To determine international recognition prior to the establishment of the UN in 1945, we required that sovereignty "is either uncontested or acknowledged by the relevant international actors" (756).

7. Buchanan 1997; Griffiths 2016a.

8. The number of states in the early 1800s is undercounted. In our International Systems(s) Dataset (ISD), we only included states in the list that had a population of least 100,000, a coding decision that excluded many small states (Griffiths and Butcher 2013).

9. Lake and O'Mahony 2004; Butcher and Griffiths 2015; Griffiths 2014; Griffiths 2016a.

10. This claim should be qualified. Although there was certainly a higher number of state-like polities around the world in the preceding centuries, there is some point far enough back in human history where the number would be less than fifty-one. That point is unknown and difficult to determine without the relevant data and ability to define and compare political systems over time and space. See Butcher and Griffiths 2017 for a discussion on this topic.

11. Griffiths 2016a.

12. See Fazal 2007 for an analysis of state death.

13. Gleditsch and Ward 1999; Bremer and Ghosn 2003; Fazal 2007; Griffiths and Butcher 2013.

14. Crawford 2006, 45–46.

15. Some latitude is given for states like Switzerland that chose for political reasons to maintain an observer status in the UN until 2002 rather than seek full membership.

16. Griffiths 2016a, 205.

17. To count, the movement must last at least one week, include at least 100 people, lay claim to a territory not smaller than 100 square kilometers, possess a flag, declare independence, and claim territory that is contiguous with the larger state (Griffiths 2016a, 205). See chapter 10 for further explanation.

18. Manela 2007; Ahram 2019.

19. Griffiths 2016a, 5.

20. Radan 2008, 18.

21. See Crawford 2006; Radan 2008; Griffiths 2016a.

22. Figure 2.2 is a stacked line graph that distinguishes colonial from noncolonial cases depending on whether the secessionist region is separated from the larger state by at least 100 miles of water or foreign territory. See Fazal and Griffiths 2014, 84, for a discussion.

23. Boutros-Ghali 1992, 9.

24. Gellner 1983, 44–45.

25. Laitin 1998.

26. For an essay on this topic, see Van Dyke 1977.

27. Roeder 2018, 24–25.

28. See Sorens 2012 and Cunningham 2014.

29. Grant 1999; Buzan and Little, 2000; Crawford 2006; Fabry 2010; Erman 2013; Agne et al. 2013; Coggins 2014.

30. They are what Thomas Grant (1999) calls the Great Debate.

31. Buchanan 1965.

32. Mueller 1989, 131.

33. Jackson 1990, 196.

34. Caspersen 2012, 42; Fazal and Griffiths 2014; Griffiths 2016a.

35. Interview with Rashid Nur, Somaliland's representative to the United States, April 1, 2011.

36. That is not to say that full sovereignty is always preferred. Dependencies such as the Cook Islands have thus far preferred to maintain their connection to New Zealand. Indeed, Rezvani (2014) argues persuasively that partial independence is sometimes better.

37. Bahcheli, Bartman, and Srebnik 2004.

38. Halperin, Scheffer, and Small, 1992.

39. Crawford 2006, 183.

40. In the late 1960s, the United States and the United Kingdom suggested that an associated status be created for microstates (Crawford 2006, 184–185). The status would include fewer financial obligations but possess no voting rights. The suggestion gathered little support among other UN member states.

41. Griffiths 2015; 2016a.

42. For a quick primer on joining the UN as a full member, see Keating 2008.

43. Ker-Lindsay 2012, 130.

44. Crawford 2006, 180.

45. Interview with UN representatives, July 6, 2017.

46. See http://snakehillprincipality.blogspot.com.au/ and also Matt Siegel, "The Royal Me: What's with Australia's Secession Obsession?," *The Atlantic*, April 2012.

47. When discussing norms, I adopt the following definition: norms are "standards of appropriate behavior for actors with a given identity" (Finnemore and Sikkink 1998).

48. Sandholtz and Stiles 2008.

49. Spruyt 1994; Bartelson 1995; Osiander 2001.

50. Manela 2007; Fabry 2010.

51. Jackson 1990; Osterud 1997; Sandholtz and Styles 2008.

52. Krasner 2013.

53. Fabry 2010.

54. Armitage 2007; Pavković 2020.

55. There is no automatic tension between sovereignty and self-determination. The tension arises when stateless nations seek independence and their state denies them.

56. Gellner 1983, 43–44.

57. Mayall 1990; Beran 1998; Buchanan 2003; Wellman 2005.

58. Crawford 2006, 388–389.

59. Fabry 2010, 10; Jackson 1990.

60. Fabry 2010, 12; Manela 2007; Ahram 2019.

61. Fabry 2010; Berlin 1969. Interestingly, Jackson 1990, 25–31, used the concept in a related but somewhat opposite sense. For Jackson, positive sovereignty refers to the classical notion of the state, one that is deemed responsible, capable, and free to act substantively in international politics. Negative sovereignty is Jackson's term for quasi-states born from decolonization that are legal entities but not necessarily substantive ones. Both

scholars apply Berlin's distinction to different actors (stateless nations and states) and, as a result, they produce different theoretical frameworks. However, the frameworks are related in both conceptual and temporal terms. The transition of self-determination from a negative to a positive right occurs around the time that sovereignty moves from a positive to a negative right (in the post-1945 period). One could argue that the inculcation of a positive right to self-determination would require a parallel acceptance of negative sovereignty since the fitness tests of classical statehood and presumption of capability became less important. Framed in this way, it is interesting to speculate whether the two concepts have to move in relation to one another (negative/positive to positive/negative).

62. The question of "Who counts?" is a reformulation of the question "Who are the people?" The difference is that the former query is typically given by outsiders, while the latter is usually made by the people themselves as they try to determine who counts among them. See McCurry 2010, 11–37, for an interesting account of the Confederate States of America.

63. Crawford 2006, 108, 115.
64. Atzili 2012, 1.
65. Zacher 2001.
66. Fazal 2007.
67. Fazal and Griffiths 2014; Griffiths 2016a.
68. Fabry 2010.
69. Crawford 2006, 384.
70. Crawford 2006, 342.
71. Crawford 2006, 75.
72. Sterio 2013, 11.
73. Jackson 1990; 1993; Shaw 1996; Ratner 1996; Bartos 1997; Crawford 2006; Fabry 2010; Sterio 2013; Griffiths 2015; 2016a.
74. Ratner 1996, 617.
75. Jackson 1993, 122.
76. Jackson 1990; 1993; Shaw 1996; Ratner 1996; Bartos 1997; Fabry 2010.
77. Bartos 1997, 75.
78. Osterud 1997; Sterio 2013.
79. Bartos 1997; Radan 2002.
80. Jackson 1990; 1993; Shaw 1996; Ratner 1996; Bartos 1997; Crawford 2006; Fabry 2010; Sterio 2013; Griffiths 2015; 2016a.
81. Ratner 1996; Bartos 1997.
82. Griffiths 2016.
83. Ministry of Foreign Affairs of the Republic of Kosovo.
84. Griffiths 2016b.
85. In an interview with a Kosovo representative to Washington, DC, on October 20, 2010, I was told that Russia has signaled it will veto a Kosovar application to the UN. Therefore, Kosovo has not applied.
86. Norman 1998; Buchanan 2004.
87. Sterio 2013, 20; Shaw 2014, 187.
88. Crawford 2006, 118–119; Shaw 2014, 186–187.
89. Condoleeza Rice, secretary of state, February 18, 2008, "U.S. Recognizes Kosovo as Independent State." https://2001-2009.state.gov/secretary/rm/2008/02/100973.htm.
90. Meetser 2012; ; Kartsonaki 2020.
91. Caspersen 2015, 395–397; Berg 2009. For an early conceptualization of earned sovereignty, see Williams and Heymann 2004; Williams and Jannotti Pecci 2004.
92. Berg and Pegg 2020; Oltramonti 2020.
93. Beran 1998; Wellman 2005

94. Lecours 2020.
95. Buchanan 1998; Pavković and Radan 2007.
96. Crawford 2006, 384.
97. Crawford 2006, 390.
98. Jackson 1990, 34–35.
99. Caspersen 2015, 393.

3. A THEORY OF SECESSIONIST STRATEGY AND TACTICAL VARIATION

1. Schelling 1966, 3–20.
2. Interview, December 4, 2015, with the political director of the Catalan election on September 27, 2015.
3. Interview with Moses Havini, February 6, 2013.
4. Interview with Bayan Sami Abdulrahman, May 25, 2017.
5. See UNPO.org.
6. On Independent Diplomat, see Ross 2007.
7. Huang 2016, 124. For similar findings see Bob 2005; Jo 2015.
8. Fazal 2018b.
9. Osterud 1997; Griffiths 2016a.
10. This dynamic is similar to the logic of the boomerang model (Keck and Sikkink 1998).
11. Fazal 2018b. See Basta 2020 on the role of economic elites.
12. At the first conference in May 2015, several participants suggested that a change in US policy could come with the next, post-Obama, administration, and even speculated as to whether frontrunners like Hilary Clinton and Jeb Bush would be likely to make a change. The second conference in May 2017, occurred early in the Trump administration and many now wondered whether Trump's willingness to overturn traditional policy positions would play to the Kurds' advantage.
13. The Greek myth of Pandora's box is used as a metaphor for the contagion problem of secession—i.e., recognizing only one group may open Pandora's box—and it is often mentioned in the literature on secession in Africa (Englebert and Hummel 2005) and elsewhere (Saideman 1998).
14. Interview with Rashid Nur, the Somaliland representative to the United States, April 1, 2011. In that interview, Nur stated that a 2005 African Union Fact-Finding Mission had determined that recognizing Somaliland "should not be linked to the notion of 'opening Pandora's Box.'"
15. See Mampilly 2011, 74 for a related discussion about how rebels use strategy and ideology to achieve their ends.
16. Lukes 1974.
17. Schelling 1966, 71–73. Also see Art 1980; Pape 2003; Stanton 2013.
18. Bob 2005; Huang 2016; Coggins 2017.
19. Utomo 2019.
20. Jim Beatson, "Moses Havini: Leader of Struggle for Bougainville's Autonomy," *Sydney Morning Herald*, May 15, 2015.
21. Author's interview with James Tanis, October 12, 2012.
22. Tarrow 2011, 40.
23. Pegg 1998; Berg 2009; Caspersen 2012; Florea 2014.
24. Keating 2004; Swenden 2006; Van Houten 2007; Beland and Lecours 2010.
25. Toft 2002; Walter 2006; 2009; Meetser 2012; Krause 2013–2014; Cunningham 2014; Bakke 2015; Seymour, Bakke, and Cunningham 2016; Butt 2017.
26. George and Bennett 2005; Collier and Gerring 2009.
27. Aksoy and Kocacık-Şenol 2020; Basta 2020; Lecours 2020; Maddens et al. 2020.
28. Buchanan 1998; Pavković and Radan 2007.

29. Interview with Fred Hooper, August 10, 2018.

30. See Kalyvas and Balcells 2010 for a discussion of relative strength and the technology of rebellion. Also see Fazal and Konaev 2019.

31. See for example Chenoweth and Stephan; 2011; Tarrow 2011; Schock 2013; MacLeod 2015,

32. Interview with ULMWP representative in West Papua.

33. Premdas 2004, 240.

34. The resolutions in 1960 were Resolution 1514, known as the Declaration on Granting Independence to Colonial Countries and Peoples, and its annex, Resolution 1541. The 1966 covenants were the Covenant on Economic, Social, and Cultural Rights, and the United Nations Covenant on Civil and Political Rights. See Sterio 2013, 11.

35. The legal right to independence for colonized peoples was awarded to first-order administrative units of overseas European empires via the principle of *uti possidetis juris* (as you possess) (Jackson 1990; Ratner 1996; Bartos 1997; Crawford 2006; Fabry 2010; Sterio 2013). However, this created some ambiguity because many colonies were combined and divided over time and the status of some remains debatable.

36. See Wood 2003, 121, and Kalyvas 2006, 88, for consequences of dual sovereignty in civil war.

37. A potential counterexample is the Confederate invasion of the North that culminated in the Battle of Gettysburg. In terms of grand strategy, this was an attempt to compel the North to negotiate.

38. Interview with Masis Mayillian, June 3, 2019.

39. Caspersen 2012, 47.

40. For more on the Canning Test, see chapter 2.

41. Interview with Ashot Ghoulian, June 3, 2019.

42. Interview with Polisario Front representative.

43. Pape 2003; Kalyvas and Balcells 2010; Chenoweth and Stephan 2011; Tarrow 2011; Sorens 2012; Schock 2013; Stanton 2013; Cunningham 2014; Jo 2015; MacLeod 2015; Huang 2016; Balcells 2017; Coggins 2017; Krause 2017; Fazal 2018b; Stewart 2018; Horowitz, Perkoski, and Potter 2018.

44. Ahram 2019.

45. For interesting essays on the independence effort in Iraqi Kurdistan, see Danilovich 2017; 2019.

46. See Barkey 2019 for an essay on the Kurdish Awakening.

47. "Kurdistan Will Hold Independence Referendum in 2017, Senior Official," *Rudaw*, April 2, 2017.

48. Schelling 1966; Art 1980.

49. Morgan Kaplan, "For Iraqi Kurds, Trump Brings Hope for Independence," *Foreign Affairs*, April 12, 2017.

50. For more on this developing research area, see Ker-Lindsay 2012; Butt 2017; Weill 2018; Relitz 2019; Griffiths and Muro 2020.

51. Berg and Pegg 2020.

52. Ker-Lindsay 2012, 77–79.

53. For more on preventing legitimization, see Ker-Lindsay 2015; Berg and Pegg 2018.

54. Author's interview, June 18, 2018.

55. "Sri Lankan High Commission Writes to CONIFA Objecting to Inclusion of Tamil Eelam in World Cup," *Tamil Guardian*, June 3, 2018.

56. Weill 2019; 2020.

57. I was told by several interviewees in New Caledonia, on both sides of the issue, that Macron had been effective in his appeal to common bonds with the Kanaks (interviews in May 2018).

58. On the Uighur see Vicky Xiuzhong Xu and Jamie Tarabay, "In Australia, Muslims Call for Pressure on China Over Camps," *New York Times*, April 13, 2019.
59. Rohrbach 2020.
60. Butt 2017; 2020.

4. CATALONIA

1. In an interview on October 16, 2015, Pedret cited Axel Honneth's work on recognition as an influence on his own thinking.
2. Also in attendance were representatives from the Democratic Convergence of Catalonia (CDC), the Republican Left of Catalonia (Esquerra Republicana de Catalunya, ERC, usually abbreviated to Esquerra), and the Initiative for Catalonia Greens and the United and Alternative Left (Iniciativa per Catalunya Verds–Esquerra Unida i Alternativa, ICV-EUiA).
3. See Minder 2017, 80–81.
4. There is a dialect of Catalan spoken in Alghero, a small city in the northwest of Sardinia. This is a legacy of Catalan maritime trade and expansion during the thirteenth and fourteenth centuries.
5. Generalit de Catalunya [n.d.].
6. The lands on both sides of the Pyrenees from the Atlantic to the Mediterranean became a frontier region in which Emperor Charlemagne created four militarized buffer zones: the March of Gascony, the March of Toulouse, the March of Gothia, and the Spanish March (Davies 2011, 162).
7. Davies 2011, 170–171.
8. Hibbert 1949.
9. Minder 2017, 110.
10. Mission statement taken from website: https://www.mhcat.cat/enmhc/about_the _museum/organisation_mision_and_building/mission_and_strategy.
11. Information plaque at exhibit 7F in the main collection (October 15, 2015), Museu d'Història de Catalunya.
12. Claims of prior statehood are common for independence movements. For example, the Somaliland government points out that it was independent from June 26 to July 1, 1960, before it joined with Somalia.
13. "The Catalan Question Continues to Divide," *The Economist*, July 26, 2018.
14. Davies 2011, 162–163, 224.
15. Minder 2017, 25–26.
16. Eaude 2007, 60.
17. Catalonia made two declarations of nationhood during this period. The first was on April 14, 1931, the second was on October 4, 1934 (Minahan 2002, 2122).
18. Author's interview with Pere Aragonès i Garcia, November 4, 2015.
19. Tremlett 2006.
20. Fishman 1990; Solozábal 1996.
21. Linz 1989, 260.
22. Agranoff 1996.
23. Elazar 1994.
24. Minder 2017, 113–114.
25. Muñoz and Tormos 2015.
26. Euade 2007, 33; Davies 2011, 224; Minder 2017, 181.
27. Brubaker 2004; Lluch 2010.
28. Crameri 2014, 37–40; Minder 2017, 248–250.
29. See Maddens et al. 2020 for a discussion of Esquerra's nationalist party narrative.
30. Perales-García 2013, 111.

31. Interview with Carme Forcadell, December 21, 2015.
32. Cardús 2013, 98.
33. Perales-García 2013, 106.
34. Burg 2015; Lineira and Cetra 2015.
35. Harris 2014.
36. See Tilly 1992; Downing 1993; Spruyt 1994.
37. Bel 2015.
38. Crameri 2014, 42–43.
39. Bel, an economist of infrastructure, points out that federal funding on infrastructure in Catalonia is not only underfunded, but it also promotes an inefficient radial design that places Madrid at the center of flight and rail connections (Bel 2011).
40. The greater fiscal autonomy in the Basque country dates to 1980, during the transition, when the Basques negotiated for the revival of the "foral rights" related to tax administration (Minder 2017, 234). In a move that is now generally viewed as a mistake, the Catalan leadership under Pujol declined to push for the same rights.
41. Forcadell 2013, 16.
42. Interview with Vicent Partal, November 5, 2015.
43. Minder 2017, 5, 14.
44. See Minder 2017, 215–216 for a discussion of the history of Catalan associationalism.
45. Interview with Liz Castro, September 4, 2015. She referenced Putnam 2000.
46. Interview with Vicent Partal, November 5, 2015. On the role of business elites in secessionist projects, see Basta 2020.
47. One might suspect that Scottish nationalists would possess a similarly impressive intelligentsia, but a colleague of mine who is an expert on both regions stated that there a tradition in Scotland that academics are meant to remain neutral. In contrast, academics in Catalonia (and Spain) tend to be more political.
48. http://www.wilson.cat/en/qui-som/manifest-dels-14-punts.html.
49. Here I refer to the 2014 White Paper: "The National Transition of Catalonia."
50. Griffiths, Alvarez, and Coma 2015.
51. Interview, December 4, 2015.
52. Interview, October 7, 2015.
53. Generalitat de Catalunya 2014. According to several sources I spoke to in 2015, there was a more secretive strategy document.
54. Generalitat de Catalunya 2014, 13.
55. Many of my interviewees who were involved in this process showed a clear conviction in the cause, and, as they discussed the legal and philosophical process of state building, I wondered if they saw themselves as a contemporary Catalan version of the American Founding Fathers.
56. Art 1980.
57. Generalitat de Catalunya 2014, 28–34.
58. See Griffiths, Guillen, and Martinez i Coma 2015 for a game theoretic analysis for how Catalonia could compel Spain to negotiate.
59. Interview with Albert Royo, November 20, 2015. For more on DIPLOCAT, see Minder 2017, 146.
60. Interview with Albert Royo, November 20, 2015.
61. Minder 2017, 140–141.
62. Interview, December 10, 2015.
63. Interview with Susan DiGiacomo, December 8, 2015.
64. Generalitat de Catalunya 2014, 6.
65. Generalitat de Catalunya 2014, 19.

66. Perales-García 2013, 111.

67. Interview with Jaume Lopez, December 15, 2015.

68. Interview with Quim Arrufat, December 21, 2015.

69. Minder 2017, 122–123.

70. See Raphael Minder, "Stakes Rise in Standoff Between Catalan Separatists and Spanish Government," *New York Times*, October 27, 2015; Ryan Griffiths, "How Spain's New Fault Lines Could Shape Catalan Secessionism," *Global Observatory*, December 4, 2015.

71. Interview with Albert Royo, October 4, 2017.

72. Although some have questioned their veracity, there are reports that Angela Merkel called Rajoy on the day of the referendum to express her concerns regarding violent police action. See for example, Jon Rogers, "Catalonia Referendum: Merkel Demands Answers from Rajoy over Police Actions," *The Express*, October 1, 2017; and Greg Russell, "Merkel Told Rajoy 'Europe Cannot Accept' Police Brutality during Independence Referendum," *The National*, June 15, 2018. At the least, the emphasis on the Merkel-Rajoy connection underlines the belief in the potential for outside intervention.

73. This followed a parliament vote of seventy to ten with fifty-five abstentions.

74. Forcadell 2013 14–15.

75. Author's interview with Carme Forcadell, December 21, 2015.

76. A violent Catalan pro-independence group named Terra Lliurre (Free Land) formed in 1978, and was responsible for the deaths (partly accidental) of several people (Minder 2017, 231).

77. De la Calle 2015.

78. Minder 2017, 192–194. For a similar appeal from former Spanish prime minister see: Felipe González, "A los Catalanes," *El Pais*, August 30, 2015.

79. Interview with Arenas, December 2, 2015.

5. MURRAWARRI

1. http://www.cityofsydney.nsw.gov.au/council/about-council/welcome-to-country.

2. This is not always the case. For example, the United States was born from colonies that developed as extensions of Great Britain.

3. http://kyliegibbon4.wixsite.com/murrawarri-republic/map.

4. When I visited the Murrawarri Republic I traveled along the Mitchell Highway that runs north from Bourke to Cunnamulla. Although this is the major sealed road in the region, there are gravel and dirt roads that branch off it.

5. Abbondanza (2018, 5–6) concludes that the true territorial size of the Murrawarri Republic is inflated. Using the geographic coordinates on the republic's website, he calculates an actual size of 22,170 square kilometers.

6. In earlier work (Griffiths 2016a), I argued that secessionist movements that lack an administrative region are less likely to be permitted independence because the metropole has no internal border nor administrative status to rely on. Where will the borders be drawn, and how can that part of the region be permitted independence in a way that avoids the precedent-setting problem? As such, the Murrawarri Republic faces poor odds of gaining independence unless it can, at the least, acquire an administrative status.

7. https://www.google.com/maps/d/viewer?mid=1OCi6ggujg-qfrgl9892fFzuZ064&ll=-29.62715312636437%2C146.42916100000002&z=9.

8. Interview with Fred Hooper, August 10, 2018.

9. http://www.muruwari.com.au/.

10. Minahan 2016, 5.

11. Interview with Hooper, June 27, 2018.

12. One million is the highest estimate I have seen given for the precolonial population; the lowest is 300,000 (Abbondanza 2018, 1).

13. Despite the promising name given by Captain James Cook a decade earlier, Botany Bay was considered too desolate and so the expedition shortly relocated to the more promising anchorage of Port Jackson (which includes Sydney Harbour), 12 kilometers to the north.

14. Minahan 2016, 5.

15. McGregor 2009.

16. See the Murrawarri Republic website: http://kyliegibbon4.wixsite.com/murrawarri -republic/flag.

17. Interview with Hooper, August 10, 2018.

18. See the Murrawarri Republic website: http://kyliegibbon4.wixsite.com/murrawarri -republic.

19. Paul Gregoire, "Always Independent: An Interview with Murrawarri Republic Chair Fred Hooper," *Nuclear Worrier*, April 23, 2017.

20. Crawford 2006, 258.

21. Shaw writes: "Occupation is a method of acquiring territory which belongs to no one (*terra nullius*) and which may be acquired by a state in certain situations. The occupation must be by a state and not by private individuals, it must be effective and it must be intended as a claim of sovereignty over the area." (Shaw 2014, 363).

22. There is some debate about the extent to which *terra nullius* was used. See for example Reynolds 1996 and Borch 2001. In the case of Australia, the British believed that they had acquired an original land (Reynolds 1996, 86).

23. Crawford 2006, 279.

24. Abbondanza 2018, 3. There had been a running debate about the nature of traditional Aboriginal society and whether it "had become what eighteenth-century European jurists called civil—as opposed to natural—society regulated by a system of laws which people generally obeyed and was, as a consequence, the bearer and wielder of sovereignty" (Reynolds 1996, xvi).

25. Crawford 2006, 278.

26. Brennan, Gunn, and Williams 2004, 313.

27. Reynolds 1996, 1.

28. Reynolds 1996, 12.

29. John Howard, "Reconciliation Documents," *Media Release*, May 11, 2000.

30. Gregoire, "Always Independent." Interestingly, the declaration was modeled on Israel's declaration of independence.

31. Interview with Hooper, June 27, 2018.

32. Gregoire, "Always Independent."

33. Hooper states in an interview that the decision to declare independence was influenced by the example of the Principality of Hutt River in Western Australia, a micronation that has existed for decades. See Gregoire, "Always Independent."

34. Abbondanza 2018, 6.

35. Taken from the Euahlayi Peoples Republic website: http://www.euahlayipeoplesrepublic .mobi/.

36. Taken from the Sovereign Union website: http://nationalunitygovernment.org /tags/wiradjuri-central-west-republic.

37. Wutzke 1998; Brennan, Gunn, and Williams 2004; see Abbondanza 2018;

38. Interview with Hooper, June 27, 2018. In a different interview on August 10, 2018, I asked how they would treat non-Murrawarri people in their new state. Hooper replied that the white Australians and non-Murrawarri aboriginals currently living on the territory would be given the right to be equal citizens and that the state would be inclusive, but that the president of the republic would have to be Murrawarri.

39. See the Murrawarri Republic website: http://kyliegibbon4.wixsite.com/murrawarri -republic.

40. Interview with Hooper, August 10, 2018.

41. Ian Lloyd Neubauer, "Australia's Aborigines Launch a Bold Legal Push for Independence," *Time*, May 30, 2013.

42. Gregoire, "Always Independent."

43. Interview with Hooper, August 10, 2018.

44. This is not unusual for Australia, for it generally takes a rather passive approach to declarations of independence from the likes of the Principality of Hutt River and the Principality of Snake Hill, two groups who claim to have stopped paying taxes.

45. Interview with Hooper, August 10, 2018.

46. Reynolds 1996, 3.

47. Brennan, Gunn, and Williams 2004, 317.

48. Neubauer, "Australia's Aborigines Launch a Bold Legal Push for Independence."

49. Anderson 2014.

50. Reynolds 1996, XVI.

51. Brennan, Gunn, and Williams 2004; Mansell 2016.

52. Brennan, Gunn, and Williams 2004, 201.

53. Hooper stated that a second-best outcome is some form of "domestic dependent sovereignty." Author's interview, August 10, 2018.

6. WEST PAPUA

1. The exchange at the head of the chapter is one I witnessed at a meeting in West Papua in 2018. The question was posed by a member of the independence movement and directed at a visiting spokesperson for the Kanak and Socialist National Liberation Front (FLNKS) of New Caledonia. The simple and poignant response—that France is kind—highlights the fact that governments vary in their willingness to suppress.

2. Bell et al. 2016, 450.

3. On a recent flight to West Papua I sat next to a Swedish engineer who worked at the Grasberg Mine. Although he had worked there for two years, he had never ventured beyond the insulated and highly secure housing complex at the mine. He expressed surprise that I was traveling to Jayapura, the capital, given the rumors of violence. I asked what he thought the cause of the conflict was and he replied that one cause was that the native West Papuans wanted more profits from the mine. When asked for his opinion on the matter, he said that he did not have one but that that the company leadership defended their position by pointing to their existing contract.

4. I noticed the small ways in which these sentiments are expressed when attending a workshop on community activism in West Papua. One session began when the audience held hands and sang a song called "Aku Papua," with the following chorus (translated): "Black skin, curly hair, I am Papua; black skin, curly hair, I am Papua." In the icebreaker that followed the song, we played a sort of musical-chairs game in which the person in the middle would state something true about themselves and participants for whom that was also true would then scramble to find a new chair. The statements were meant to be prosaic—e.g., I have children—so I was surprised when one person stated that they had been beaten by the police, and half the room jumped up and sought a new chair.

5. MacLeod 2015, xvi.

6. Minahan 2002, 2053. Hugh Brody, "December 1, 1961: Fly the Flag of Independence—West Papua and the Indonesian Empire," *OpenDemocracy*, November 30, 2011.

7. Brody, "December 1, 1961."

8. In 1828 the Dutch claimed the coast west of the 141st meridian but extended their claim across the island in 1848 to ward off potential British and German counterclaims (Minahan 2002, 2052). Two interesting adjustments were made to the border between 1893 and 1895. First, there is a section in the middle of the island where the border forms

a jagged westward arc that was meant to account for the curvature of the Fly River and allocate its eastern bank to the British (now Papua New Guinea). Second, the straight line extending south from the Fly River indentation was shifted 1.3 miles east of the 141st meridian to compensate the Dutch for the lost territory east of the Fly River. For further reading, see Frank Jacobs, "Borderlines: Who Bit My Border?," *New York Times*, March 13, 2012.

9. Chauvel 2009; Matsuno 2011.

10. Anderson 1983, 176.

11. See Bone 1958 for records on UN voting results.

12. Minahan 2002, 2055.

13. MacLeod 2015, 50–53; Crawford 2006, 555–556.

14. Saltford 2003.

15. MacLeod 2015, 53.

16. Minahan 2002, 2055. MacLeod (2015, 51, 261–262) maintains that independence was not actually declared on this date, even though it is considered the start of the movement. He records that declarations were made on the following occasions: (1) by Karel Gobai in 1969; (2) by Seth Rumkoren on "1 July 1976 at Markas Victoria, a guerilla camp near the PNG/West Papua border"; (3) by Michael Kareth, "a Papuan leader allied with the West New Guinea National Congress . . . in Brussels in 1997"; (4) by Forkorus Yaboisembut "at the Third Papuan People's Congress on 19 October 2011."

17. https://onwestpapua.com/story-behind-morning-star-flag-brief-historical-review/. Although another source indicated that the seven blue stripes symbolize the seven regions of West Papua (MacLeod 2015, 11).

18. Rutherford 2003; Kirksey 2012.

19. MacLeod 2015, 10–11.

20. Scott 1985.

21. Minahan 2002, 2055.

22. Kingsbury 2011, 492.

23. Vanuatu is regarded by the West Papuan secessionists as a fairly supportive government.

24. MacLeod 2015, 58. Common estimates lie in the 100,000 to 150,000 range (Budiardjo and Liem 1988).

25. Osborne 1985; Budiardjo and Liem 1988; Human Rights Watch 1998; 2006; 2009; Withers and Poulsen 2002.

26. Minahan 2002, 2057.

27. Allansson, Melander, and Themnér 2017.

28. The transmigration program was halted in 2000. However, migration to West Papua continues as Indonesians from other parts of the country come to seek economic opportunity or join already established kin groups. See Upton 2009.

29. Elmslie 2010.

30. William Lloyd-George records that whereas native West Papuans accounted for 99 percent of the population in 1940, they constituted less than half by 2010. See William Lloyd-George, "A Journey through West Papua," *The Monthly*, September 2011.

31. Elmslie 2010; MacLeod 2015. Elmslie and Webb-Gannon 2013 argue that the actions of the Indonesia state vis-à-vis West Papua are tantamount to genocide and can be assessed as such. For a focused debate on this topic see Chauvel 2009; Elmslie 2009; and Upton 2009.

32. Chauvel 2009.

33. Singh 2017.

34. MacLeod 2015, 61.

35. Rohrbach 2020.

36. Walter 2009, 143–148.
37. Walter 2009, 155–156.
38. Walter 2009, 161.
39. Kirksey 2012, 18, 41–54.
40. MacLeod 2015, 108–119.
41. Boix, Miller, and Rosato 2013 code Indonesia as a democracy starting in 1999. The Polity IV index codes Indonesia as a 6 (the usual threshold for democracy) from 1999 to 2003, and an 8 thereafter (10 is the maximum).
42. Reilly 2007; Macdonald 2013.
43. See Weill 2019 on how governments use legal means to block secessionist parties.
44. MacLeod 2015, 125–159.
45. Kirksey 2012, 139; MacLeod 2015, 101, 106.
46. Interview with independence leader, February 14, 2018.
47. Interview with Octovianus Mote, February 24, 2019.
48. Mote pointed that out that while violent methods can be counter-productive, he and other ULMWP leaders are careful not to denounce them. They are proud of the historical OPM-led struggle. Authors' interview, February 24, 2019.
49. Chenoweth and Stephan 2011.
50. MacLeod 2015
51. MacLeod 2015, 100.
52. Sharp 1973; Schock 2005; Chenoweth and Stephan 2011; Vinthagen 2015.
53. Interview in West Papua.
54. Various individuals shared this view with me. For example, Benny Wenda stated that the Indonesian government has made promises of autonomy in the past but never followed through, therefore he is doubtful that tactics of electoral competition would be effective. Author's interview with Benny Wenda, June 8, 2018.
55. MacLeod 2015, 201.
56. See also Aspinall 2011, 460.
57. Kirksey 2013, 90.
58. For example see Human Rights Watch 1998; 2006; 2009.
59. Kirksey 2013, 103, 123.
60. The Melanesian Spearhead Group is an intergovernmental organization that includes Fiji, PNG, the Solomon Islands, Vanuatu, and the FLNKS of New Caledonia.
61. In May 2018, Wenda spoke to the Dutch Parliament. Author's interview with Benny Wenda, June 8, 2018.
62. The film documents the killing of five children by the police on December 7, 2014, in the Paniai District. The film is available on the Free West Papua website: https://www.freewestpapua.org/2015/12/10/1-year-on-still-no-justice-for-paniai-massacre-victims/.
63. Matsuno 2011, 186–187.
64. Interview with Benny Wenda, June 8, 2018.

7. BOUGAINVILLE

1. The statement by Moses Havini that heads this chapter is from his interview with the author on February 6, 2013. The intentionally provocative comment was regularly uttered by Havini on the Australian media during the 1990s.
2. Regan 2013, 120.
3. Nelson 2005, 168.
4. Tryon 2005, 31–32.
5. Regan 2005; Tanis 2005.
6. Minahan 2002, 318.
7. Ratner 1996; Shaw 1996; Griffiths 2016a.

8. Minahan 2002, 319.

9. Premdas 2004, 235.

10. Ghai and Regan 2006, 593–594.

11. Marilyn Havini consulted clan leaders across the island when designing the flag. See Jim Beatson, "Moses Havini: Leader of Struggle for Bougainville's Autonomy," *Sydney Morning Herald*, May 15, 2015.

12. Havini and Havini 2009.

13. Havini and Havini 2009, 2.

14. Wallis 2014, 318.

15. Regan 2013, 120.

16. Tanis 2002.

17. Minahan 2002, 320.

18. Liria 1993, 5.

19. Tanis 2002.

20. Braithwaite et al. 2010, 12–13. Eventually, BCL accepted a 66 percent corporate tax rate. Evidently, one of the reasons for these comparatively generous terms was that the BCL management wanted to keep PNG happy and mitigate the risks of future attempts at nationalizing the mine.

21. Premdas 2004, 233.

22. Braithwaite et al. 2010, 14–15.

23. Liria 1993, 62–65.

24. Tanis 2005, 453.

25. See for instance Premdas 2004, 233; Ghai and Regan 2006, 593.

26. Minahan 2002, 320.

27. Braithwaite et al. 2010, 25.

28. Braithwaite et al. 2010, 30.

29. James Tanis reflected in an interview that Ona was a zealous man, a black and white thinker, and not particularly good with the political aspects of the conflict. He said that at one point Ona outlawed all but three specific Christian faiths in the BRA and insisted that all troops conduct prayer at certain times during the day. As a consequence, this alienated the Pentecostals and the guerrillas who were connected to a local cargo cult. At another point late in the war, the guerrillas captured John Momis, the moderate leader whom Ona viewed as a traitor. Apparently, Ona ordered Tanis to execute Momis but Tanis refused the order because he felt that Momis brought legitimacy to the cause. Taken from author's interview with James Tanis, October 12, 2012.

30. Liria 1993; Braithwaite et al. 2010, 23.

31. According to Liria 1993, 77, these subunits were colloquially known as "Rambos," after the American movie series starring Sylvester Stallone.

32. For a detailed geographic description of the command structure, see Regan 2013.

33. Premdas 2004, 235.

34. Regan 2013, 122.

35. Braithwaite et al. 2010, 24–25.

36. Liria was evidently a friend of Samuel Kauona, having served together in the PNGDF. In a manner that is reminiscent of civil war settings elsewhere (e.g., Robert E. Lee and Ulysses Grant), the two men fought on opposing sides. In his diary, Liria 1993, 179–181, recalls an occasion during the conflict when he spoke with Kauona over the wireless for three hours one night, as numerous soldiers listened in.

37. Liria 1993, 25. The force amounted to an undersized battalion of less than 500 men.

38. Liria 1993, 98, describes a tense standoff in which two PNGDF officers debated whether the soldiers should be allowed to beat a prisoner to let off steam.

39. Regan 2013, 122.
40. Tanis 2002, 12.
41. Regan 2013, 122.
42. Wallis 2012, 29; Minahan 2002, 321. See Regan 2013, 123 for a discussion of the casualty estimates.
43. Braithwaite et al. 2010, 32.
44. Regan 2013, 123.
45. Kalyvas 2006.
46. Tanis 2002.
47. Allansson, Melander, and Themnér 2017.
48. Premdas 2004, 240;
49. Premdas 2004, 240; Regan 2013, 123.
50. Minahan 2002, 320, writes that during the early years of the conflict much of Australia's annual $300 million in aid to PNG went toward equipping and training soldiers to fight in Bougainville and reopen the Panguna mine.
51. Singer 2003, 177.
52. Regan 2011; 2013, 123–126.
53. Tanis 2005.
54. Regan 2013, 124–129.
55. Regan 2005; 2011; 2013; Ghai and Regan 2006; Braithwaite et al. 2010; Wallis 2012; 2014.
56. Wallis 2012, 34.
57. McEwen 2018, 48.
58. Interview with James Tanis, October 12, 2012.
59. It meets the threshold for democracy according to Boix, Miller, and Rosato 2013 and Vanhanen 2000. However, during the years in question it is coded as a 4 by the Polity IV index—the usual democracy threshold is 6.
60. Griffiths and Wasser 2019; Aksoy and Kocacık-Şenol 2020.
61. United Nations Population Division (2018).
62. International Institute for Strategic Studies (2017).
63. This calculation uses the 2018 populations of both regions: 4.3 million for West Papua and 250,000 for Bougainville.
64. Liria 1993, 115.
65. Interview, February 8, 2013.
66. Minahan 2002, 321.
67. Liria 1993, 193.
68. Interview with Moses Havini, February 6, 2013.
69. Interview with James Tanis, October 12, 2012.
70. BRA tactics evolved with the conflict. Liria 1993 writes that in the early days the BRA had few automatic weapons. As such, their ambushes of PNGDF columns were usually head-on or from the rear, rather than at the flank where enemy casualties would have been greater. This is because a flank attack required automatic weapons in order to challenge the broader and numerically greater side of the PNGDF column.
71. Braithwaite et al. 2010, 52.
72. Braithwaite et al. 2010, 53, 61.
73. Kirksey 2012, 96–103.
74. Premdas 2004, 240.
75. Liria 1993, 85.
76. Beatson, "Moses Havini."
77. Interview with Moses Havini, February 6, 2013.
78. Interview with Moses Havini, February 6, 2013.

79. The application of *uti possidetis juris* requires that a critical date be identified: the exact date when administrative ownership should be recognized (Bartos 1997). For cases of decolonization, the critical date was typically the moment when the colony was scheduled to become independent. In 1975 East Timor was a standalone Portuguese colony that declared independence, only to be seized by Indonesia. As such, the East Timorese could make a strong claim for independence via decolonization. In contrast, Bougainville had been a secondary province within greater New Guinea for the entire twentieth century.

80. Havini said in the interview that he initially expected that the Australian authorities would just arrest him—he was slandering the country in public. The fact that they never did underscored, for him, the value of the right to free speech in a society like Australia.

81. Premdas 2004, 241.

82. See for instance Regan 2013.

83. Interview with James Tanis, October 12, 2012. For his part, Kauona said: "We would rather he [Ona] join us in the peace process, but in a way Francis provides the check and balance by staying out. He serves as a warning; as a reminder of the alternative if the peace process fails." (Braithwaite et al. 2010, 61).

84. Chenoweth and Stephan 2011; Fazal and Griffiths 2014; Fazal 2018a; Griffiths and Wasser 2019.

85. Griffiths and Wasser 2019.

8. NEW CALEDONIA

1. The epigraph is from a plaque at the Jean-Marie Tjibaou Cultural Center in Noumea. The words were spoken by Tjibaou at the 1975 Melanesian 2000 Festival, a cultural event designed by Tjibaou that aimed to celebrate Kanak culture and forge a national identity.

2. I use "Kanaks" for the plural case, even though "Kanak" is sometimes used in the literature.

3. United Nations and Decolonization: Non-Self-Governing Territories, http://www .un.org/dppa/decolonization/nsgt.

4. Connell (2003, 126) states that there are twenty-nine languages, but Wikipedia references thirty.

5. Minahan 2002, 890.

6. Minahan 2002, 890. When Rear Admiral Febvier DesPointes came ashore on Grand Terre on September 24, 1853, he read the following proclamation: "I officially take possession, in the name of the Emperor and for France, of the island of New Caledonia and its dependencies, on which I raise the national flag, and I declare to everyone that from this day on this land is French and national property" (Chappell 2013, 24).

7. Chappell 2013, 19.

8. Henige 1970, 48.

9. The term sometimes has a pejorative meaning but in interviews I was told that it is often assumed with pride by the referent group (Chappell 2013, 130). Although the etymology of the term is unclear, it is derived in part from a shared prefix with Caledonia.

10. Chappell 2013, 2.

11. Minahan 2002, 891.

12. Fraser 1990, 65.

13. Connell 2003, 126.

14. Minahan 2002, 891.

15. Stanley 1989, 549; Chappell 2013, 33.

16. Fraser 1990, 65.

17. Griffiths 2014.

18. This is discussed in Fraser 1990, 31, but I also heard the same story anecdotally when I visited both Jayapura and Noumea.

19. Chappell 2013, 38; Griffiths 2016, 34.

20. Smith 1975, 130–138.

21. Interview in Nouméa, May 8, 2018.

22. Chappell 2013, 43.

23. Chappell 1999, 373.

24. Chappell 2013, 92–102.

25. Chappell 2013, 97.

26. Fraser 1990, 65.

27. Fraser 1990, 53, 64.

28. Anderson 1983.

29. Fraser 1990, 42.

30. Chappell 2013, 165.

31. Connell 2003, 157.

32. Minahan 2002, 891.

33. Fraser 1990, 160–162, notes that the flag was first raised at Conception on December 1, 1984.

34. Chappell 2013, 183–194.

35. L'Express, March 1, 1985, 16.

36. Chappell 2013, 202.

37. Chappell 1999, 377.

38. Djubelly Wea favored guerrilla war to end French domination and felt that Tjibaou has sold out the Kanak cause. For more information, see "New Caledonia Radical Kills Nationalist Chief," New York Times, May 5, 1989. In an interview with Wea, Helen Fraser records that he felt bitterness and jealousy toward Tjibaou for not being part of the Matignon Accords (Fraser 1990, 210–211).

39. Connell 2003, 130.

40. MacLellan 1999; http://www.austlii.edu.au/au/journals/AILR/2002/17.html.

41. In 1998 New Caledonia was given the unique distinction of a territory sui generis.

42. MacLellan 1999, 245–246.

43. Crawford 2006, 334.

44. Fraser 1990, 42.

45. Connell 2003, 134.

46. Connell 2003, 158–159.

47. Groupe 1878 was named in honor of Chief Atai's 1878 revolt (Chappell 2013, 179).

48. To be sure, this was not the only cause of division. There were many. One interesting issue arose between those who advocated for a form of scientific Marxism and those who simply aimed for more moderate forms of social justice. One Groupe 1878 leader stated that "all human societies evolved from egalitarian communism, through historical stages of slavery and feudalism, to capitalism, state socialism, and finally economically developed but egalitarian communism." Related debates focused on whether modern notions of development could be fitted to Kanak culture. Such arguments alienated many settlers and drove them to support the RPCR (Chappell 2013, 178–179).

49. Fraser 1990, 102. The LKS had already split from the more moderate Palika in 1981.

50. Le Monde, November 12, 1984.

51. Fraser 1990, 106.

52. Fraser 1990, 124.

53. Chappell 2013, 192.

54. Chappell 2013, 202.

55. Chappell 2013, 195.
56. Fraser 1990, 110.
57. Two such interviewees preferred to remain anonymous, but Sylvain Pabouty stated this on May 11, 2008.
58. See Henningham 2017.
59. Chappell 2013, 115.
60. Chappell 2013, 197–198.
61. Edward Cody, "France Expelling Australia's New Caledonia Consul," *Washington Post*, January 12, 1987.
62. Tjibaou 2006, 235.
63. Fraser 1990, 171.
64. Chappell 2013, 201.
65. Griffiths and Wasser 2019.
66. Fraser 1990, 27.
67. Chappell 2013, 187.
68. One earlier and quite fascinating suggestion from the 1980s was that New Caledonia secede and join the United States as the fifty-first state. This was advocated by a small splinter group on the west coast of Grand Terre (Fraser 1990, 31). On a personal note, the first time I ever heard of New Caledonia was on the radio as a child when the newsperson mentioned this movement and went so far as to suggest that should New Caledonia join the United States as the fifty-first state, it could be renamed New California.
69. Interview with Gomès, May 9, 2018.
70. Comments by Daniel Goa at the University of New South Wales, July 13, 2018.
71. Pabouty stated that his involvement in the Kanak independence effort is both a birthright and an obligation. He earned a degree in public administration in France. He is quite dedicated to issues of social policy and social justice. Author's interview, May 11, 2018.
72. Interview with Gomès, May 9, 2018.
73. Alexandre Dayant, "Worries as New Caledonia's Independence Vote Approaches," *The Interpreter*, Lowy Institute, January 16, 2018.
74. Daryl Morini, "New Caledonia: The Crisis America Isn't Going to Do Anything About," *National Interest*, November 3, 2014.
75. Horowitz 2004; 2009.

9. NORTHERN CYPRUS

1. The epigraph is a question put to me by a Greek Cypriot when I was preparing to cross the Green Line at the Ledra Palace checkpoint in Nicosia on April 12, 2018. The question was imbued with symbolism. I could not tell if the asker was simply using a common term for Northern Cyprus, one that highlights the perceived illegality of the territory, or trying to impress upon me the politics of the Cyprus problem.
2. I use "Northern Cyprus" to refer to the region and "TRNC" when referencing the government.
3. Although "frozen" is a contested descriptor of de facto states (for example, see Kereslidze 2015, 310), I retain it here because they are more static in relation to other secessionist kinds.
4. Ker-Lindsay 2011, 2–11.
5. Geldenhuys 2009, 172.
6. Griffiths 2014; 2016a.
7. Durrell 1957.
8. Minahan 2002, 1395.
9. Ker-Lindsay 2011, 21.

10. Bahcheli 2004, 165.

11. In a personal interview, Mustafa Ergün Olgun, the former undersecretary to the TRNC presidency, related a story of ethnic identity hardening that he experienced in 1955 when he attended an English-speaking international school in Nicosia as an eleven-year-old. Olgun joined the school choir and befriended a Greek Cypriot girl who would sing next to him at performances. However, some time later she distanced herself from him. When Olgun asked why, she replied that her parents had told her to sever her friendship with him because of his Turkish Cypriot identity. Despite his protests that such differences should not matter, she would not continue the friendship. For Olgun, this became one of many bitter experiences regarding his relationship with the Greek Cypriots. Interview with Olgun, April 10, 2018.

12. Ker-Lindsay 2011, 20–22. In the early days, EOKA reached out to Turkish Cypriots for an alliance against the British.

13. Ker-Lindsay 2011, 24.

14. Allansson et al 2017.

15. Ker-Lindsay 2011, 3.

16. Ker-Lindsay 2011, 24, writes that by acknowledging that the Turkish Cypriots have a right to self-determination separate from the Greek Cypriots, the British elevated their status from a minority to a community. Doing so increased the bargaining position of the Turkish Cypriots and angered the Greek Cypriots.

17. Geldenhuys 2009, 172–173.

18. Crawford 2006, 143.

19. Ker-Lindsay 2011, 27–28.

20. Smith 1975, 289.

21. Flags of the World Website: https://fotw.info/flags/cy-trnc.html.

22. Interview with Tahsin Ertuğruloğlu, former TRNC foreign minister, April 16, 2018.

23. Interview with Professor Ahmet Sözen, April 16, 2018.

24. Ken Jennings, "You Can See Northern Cyprus's Flag from Space," *Condé Nast Traveler*, March 26, 2018.

25. The words in Turkish are "Ne mutlu Türküm diyene!"

26. Ker-Lindsay 2011, 26.

27. Plumer 2003.

28. A similar point is made by Bahcheli 2004, 167, in reference to the 1963–1974 period; it created a deep-set anxiety in the Turkish Cypriot community about having security.

29. Wolfe 1992, 229.

30. Ker-Lindsay 2011, 41–42.

31. Horowitz 1985.

32. Ker-Lindsay 2011, 42–45.

33. Bahcheli 2004, 168; Geldenhuys 2009, 177. In truth, the unmixing had begun as early as the 1950s, as villages increasingly became more Greek or more Turkish, but the north-south division took hold after the 1974 invasion. Author's interview with Sözen, April 16, 2018.

34. Minahan 2002, 1397.

35. Ker-Lindsay 2017, 434.

36. According to Mustafa Ergün Olgun, Denktash's "closest aid" for many years, Denktash saw the issue of Cypriot independence in legal terms. Author's interview with Olgun, April 10, 2018.

37. Interview with Sözen, April 16, 2018.

38. Bahcheli 2004, 164.

39. Bahcheli 2004, 170.
40. Ker-Lindsay 2011, 64–68.
41. Denktash was opposed to the Annan Plan, but stepped aside to let others conduct the negotiations. Author's interview with Olgun, April 10, 2018.
42. Geldenhuys 2009, 185; Pegg and Berg 2016; Berg and Pegg 2018
43. Interview with Ertuğruloğlu, April 16, 2018.
44. Geldenhuys 2009, 180–181.
45. Berg and Pegg 2020.
46. Ker-Lindsay 2018, 86–89.
47. See Fazal 2018b and Pavković 2020 on the aversion of the international community to unilateral declarations of independence.
48. Crawford 2006, 144.
49. Crawford 2006, 159; Ker-Lindsay 2017, 432. In the case of Manchuria, the act of nonrecognition was referred to as the Stimson Doctrine.
50. Ker-Lindsay 2017 details the way in which the United Kingdom sought to prevent the unilateral declaration of independence, and then, once it was declared, led the universal condemnation. He writes that Bangladesh may have recognized the TRNC for a brief moment before regretting its decision and pretended that it had not (447).
51. Mustafa Ergün Olgun stated that the EU failed to use its opportunity on this occasion to solve the Cyprus problem. Author's interview with Olgun, April 10, 2018.
52. Interview with Ertuğruloğlu, April 16, 2018.
53. Ker-Lindsay 2011, 55–56.
54. Crawford 1996, 81.
55. Ker-Lindsay 2011, 106.
56. Interview with Olgun, April 10, 2018, and Ertuğruloğlu, April 16, 2018.
57. Interview with Erol Kaymak, professor at Eastern Mediterranean University, April 10, 2018.
58. Interview with Sözen, April 16, 2018.
59. Denktash's declaration of independence in 1983 was partly a bargaining strategy. But over time he became increasingly skeptical that anything short of a confederal solution would be satisfactory. Author's interview with Olgun, April 10, 2018.
60. Fazal and Griffiths 2014.
61. Ker-Lindsay 2011, 72.
62. Bahcheli 2004, 174.
63. According to Erol Kaymak, Northern Cyprus has approximately 100,000 foreign students at its universities, the largest per capita foreign student body of any state in the world. Author's interview with Kaymak, April 10, 2018.
64. Interview with Ertuğruloğlu, April 16, 2018.
65. Crawford 2006, 45–46, 388–89.

10. A MACROANALYSIS OF SECESSIONIST TACTICS

1. Griffiths 2016a.
2. Griffiths and Wasser 2019.
3. Griffiths and Wasser 2019. Also see Toft 2002; Walter 2009; Griffiths 2015.
4. See Griffiths and Wasser 2019, xx on this topic. Also see Toft 2002.
5. Note that these are the same operational criteria that I used in my book Griffiths 2016a. They were originally developed by Coggins 2014.
6. According to David Armitage 2007, 136, declarations have "been primarily assertions of sovereignty, both externally, against any colonizing or occupying power, and internally, as they have defined a new state's source of legitimacy, its claim to territory, and its assertion of international legal personality."

7. Pavković 2020.

8. Pegg 1998; Caspersen 2012; Florea 2014; Pegg 2017.

9. Mampilly 2011, 112–114.

10. Boix, Miller, and Rosato 2013.

11. Singer, Bremer, and Stuckey 1972.

12. Note that while both New Caledonia and French Polynesia (both on the list) possess strong secessionist undercurrents, neither has made a formal declaration of independence and thus neither counts as a movement according to the criteria used in the dataset.

13. Determining eligibility for decolonization via the application of the principle of *uti possidetis juris* requires the determination of a critical date for when administrative status should be assessed. For decolonization, that date was the moment when the colony was scheduled to become independent (see Bartos 1997).

14. Uniquely, Somaliland counts as both a de facto and decolonial strategic type.

15. Minahan 1996, 62.

16. British Somaliland was removed from the UN list when it was joined to Italian Somaliland. British Cameroon was removed from the list after it joined French Cameroon. West Papua was removed from the list when it was joined to Indonesia. East Timor (or Portuguese Timor) was removed when it was acquired by Indonesia.

17. Eritrea was a difficult borderline case that I chose not to code as decolonial. A former Italian colony, Eritrea was seized by the British in 1941 and administered until 1950, when it was federated with Ethiopia. Although Eritrea's administrative path comes close to qualifying for decolonization, it was never included on the UN list of Non-Self-Governing Territories, perhaps because it voluntarily joined a country that was not, itself, a product of decolonization.

18. Interview with James Tanis, October 12, 2012.

19. Minahan 1996, 483.

20. Sheila Tefft, "Indonesian Rebellion Defies Jakarta's Rule," *Christian Science Monitor*, August 14, 1990.

21. Griffiths and Wasser 2019.

22. Content analysis was done on the start year of the movement, and the two years before and after the start.

23. The P-value = .08.

24. The P-value = .01.

25. The P-value = .06.

26. Both variables are taken from Griffiths 2015. The EthnoDistinct variable captures the religious and/or linguistic difference between the secessionist group and the dominant culture of the state, coded as: (0) no difference; (1) either religiously or ethnically different; (2) both religiously and ethnically different.

27. The difference in these averages is statistically significant at the 99 percent confidence level (P-value = .01)

28. For example, the average rate of use for decolonial movements is statistically different from democratized movements (the most common type to use the norm after decolonial and indigenous legal) at the 90 percent confidence level (P-value = .06)

29. The next most likely normative appeal for democratized movements was decolonization, but these rates pass a difference of means test at the 90 percent confidence level (P-value = .07).

30. A difference of means test between the rate of appeal to human rights versus the freedom to choose is statistically significant at the 99 percent confidence level (P-value = .01).

11. THE CAUSES AND CONSEQUENCES OF BAD STRATEGY AND POOR TACTICS

1. The first epigraph is a line uttered by Jyn Erso in the Star Wars spinoff *Rogue One*. It testifies to her belief that hope is necessary for a rebellion.

2. Kirksey 2012, 48.

3. MacLeod 2015, 109–110.

4. Interview with Rashid Nur, the Somaliland representative to the United States, April 1, 2011.

5. Jolly 2015.

6. Younger voters were less concerned over uncertainty but less likely to vote; therefore, calls to them emphasized the need to vote. Author's interview on December 4, 2015 with the political director for the 2015 Catalan election.

7. Interview with James Tanis, October 12, 2012.

8. This is similar in form to Fearon's (1995) argument regarding private information and the incentive to misrepresent.

9. It is also found in other political contexts; see Babad 1997.

10. Kahneman and Tversky 1974.

11. Minder 2017, 300.

12. Interview, May 25, 2017.

13. Interview with Royo, November 20, 2015.

14. Interview with Havini, February 6, 2013.

15. McAdam 1986; Wood 2003.

16. Ahram 2019, 158.

17. "Was the Kurdish Referendum in Iraq a Mistake?" *Al Jazeera*, April 6, 2018.

18. Gellner 1983, 43–44.

19. Roeder 2018, 24.

20. Interview with Fred Hooper, August 10, 2018.

21. Martin Chulov, "Iraqi Kurds Polarised as Region Holds Historic Referendum on Independence," *The Guardian*, September 25, 2017.

22. Connell 2003, 157.

23. Interview on January 20, 2017.

24. Interview with Professor Ahmet Sözen, April 16, 2018.

25. Interview with Quim Arrufat, December 21, 2015.

26. See Cunningham 2014; Seymour, Bakke, and Cunningham 2016; Krause 2017.

27. Roeder 2018.

28. Putnam 1998.

29. Interview with James Tanis, October 12, 2012.

30. Cunningham 2014.

31. Ignatieff 1993; Owen 1995.

12. THE FUTURE OF THE SOVEREIGNTY GAME

1. Jackson 1990.

2. Strayer 1970; Bull 1977; Poggi 1978; Tilly 1992; Spruyt 1994; Ruggie 1998; Plattner 2003; Schmitter 2003; Nexon 2009; Phillips and Sharman 2015; Butcher and Griffiths 2015; 2017; Griffiths 2018.

3. Griffiths and Butcher 2013.

4. Griffiths 2016a.

5. Interview with the New Zealand deputy high commissioner to Rarotonga, November 20, 2012.

6. Gilpin 1981, 40.

7. Fabry 2010.
8. Crawford 2006, 388–389.
9. Fabry 2010.
10. Zacher 2001; Fazal 2007; Atzili 2012.
11. The interwar years were a transition period between the de facto state-based regime and the post-1945 constitutive regime. Self-determination was regarded as a positive right, but the international community was mostly unwilling to support it. Meanwhile, the territorial integrity norm did not have the salience that it has had since World War II. See Griffiths 2016b for a discussion.
12. Norman 1998; Buchanan 2003.
13. Beran 1998; Wellman 2005.
14. Fabry 2010, 220.
15. See Berlin 2009 on how recognition can be used a way to sanction governments that commit human rights violations.
16. See Waters 2020 on this topic.
17. Hirschman 1970.
18. Griffiths 2016b.
19. Snyder and Vinjamuri 2004.
20. Cunningham 2014, 24. For simplicity she models state factions as institutionalized actors and self-determination factions as uninstitutionalized actors, arguing that these assumptions hold most of the time.
21. Interview with representative of the Indonesian government on February 27, 2018.
22. See Beran 1998; Wellman 2005; Pavković and Radan 2007; Weill 2020.
23. Pavković and Radan 2007.
24. Interview with Germà Bel, August 29, 2015.
25. Weill 2020.
26. Weill 2019.
27. Weill 2019.
28. Fazal 2018.
29. Griffiths and Wasser 2019.

References

Abbondanza, Gabriele. 2018. The Republic of Murrawarri and the Debate on Aboriginal Sovereignty in Australia. *Indigenous Policy Journal* 28(3): 1–16.

Agne, Hans, Jens Bartelson, Eva Erman, Thomas Lindemann, Benjamin Herborth, Oliver Kessler, Christine Chwaszcza, Mikulas Fabry, and Stephen D. Krasner. 2013. Symposium "The Politics of International Recognition." *International Theory* 5(1): 94–107.

Agnew, John. 1994. The Territorial Trap: The Geographical Assumptions of International Relations Theory. *Review of International Political Economy* 1(1): 53–80.

Agranoff, Robert. 1996. Federal Evolution in Spain. *International Political Science Review* 17(4): 385–401.

Ahram, Ariel I. 2019. *Break All the Borders: Separatism and the Reshaping of the Middle East.* Oxford: Oxford University Press.

Aksoy, Faruk, and Melike Ayşse Kocacık-Şenol. 2020. Democratic Institutions, Secessionist Strategy, and the Use of Violence: An Empirical Analysis. In *Strategies of Secession and Counter-Secession*, edited by Ryan D. Griffiths and Diego Muro, 103–121. London: Rowman and Littlefield, ECPR Press.

Allansson, Marie, Erik Melander, and Lotta Themnér. 2017. Organized Violence, 1989–2016. *Journal of Peace Research* 54(4): 574–587.

Anderson, Benedict. 1983. *Imagined Communities.* London: Verso.

Anderson, Michael. 2014, Background Evidence to Support a Declaration of Aboriginal Sovereignty. *Carrington Rand Journal of Social Sciences* 1(1): 1–11

Anonymous. 2002. Government Recognition in Somalia and Regional Political Stability in the Horn of Africa, *Journal of Modern African Studies* 40(2): 247–272.

Armitage, David. 2007. *The Declaration of Independence.* Cambridge, MA: Harvard University Press.

Art, Robert J. 1980. To What Ends Military Power? *International Security* 4(4): 3–35.

Aspinall, Edward. 2011. Aceh: The Secession That Never Was. In *The Ashgate Research Companion to Secession*, edited by Aleksandar Pavković and Peter Radan, 459–462. Burlington, VT: Ashgate.

Atzili, Boaz. 2012. *Good Fences, Bad Neighbors: Border Fixity and International Conflict.* Chicago: University of Chicago Press.

Babad, Elisha. 1997. Wishful Thinking among Voters: Motivation and Cognitive Influences. *International Journal of Public Opinion Research* 9(2): 105–125.

Bahcheli, Tozun. 2004. Under Turkey's Wings: The Turkish Republic of Northern Cyprus, the Struggle for International Acceptance. In *De Facto States: The Quest for Sovereignty*, edited by Tozun Bahcheli, Barry Bartmann, and Henry Srebrnik, 164–186. London: Routledge.

Bahcheli, Tozun, Barry Bartmann, and Henry Srebrnik, eds. 2004. *De Facto States: The Quest for Sovereignty.* London: Routledge.

Bakke, Kristin M. 2015. *Decentralization and Intrastate Struggles: Chechnya, Punjab, and Québec.* Cambridge: Cambridge University Press.

Balcells, Laia. 2017. *Rivalry and Revenge: The Politics of Violence during Civil War.* Cambridge: Cambridge University Press.

Barkey, Henri J. 2019. The Kurdish Awakening: Unity, Betrayal, and the Future of the Middle East. *Foreign Affairs* (March–April).

Bartelson, Jens. 1995. *A Genealogy of Sovereignty*. Cambridge: Cambridge University Press.

Bartos, Tomas. 1997. Uti Possidetis. Quo Vadis? *Australian Year Book of International Law* 18: 37–96.

Basta, Karlo. 2020. Business as a Political Actor: Mapping the Role of the Private Sector in Independence Referenda. In *Strategies of Secession and Counter-Secession*, edited by Ryan D. Griffiths and Diego Muro, 161–179. London: Rowman and Littlefield, ECPR Press.

Bel, Germà. 2011. The Concern over Infrastructure. In *What Catalans Want: Could Catalonia Be Europe's Next State?*, edited by Toni Strubell, 68–73. Ashfeld, MA: Catalonia Press.

Bel, Germà. 2015. *Disdain, Distrust, and Dissolution: The Surge in Support for Independence in Catalonia*. Eastbourne: Sussex Academic Press.

Beland, Daniel, and André Lecours. 2010. *Nationalism and Social Policy: The Politics of Territorial Solidarity*. Oxford: Oxford University Press.

Bell, Loren, Stuart Butler, Trent Holden, Anna Kaminski, Adam Skolnick, Iain Stewart, Ryan Ver Berkmoes, and Hugh McNaughtan. 2016. *Lonely Planet Indonesia*. 11th ed. Carlton, Victoria: Lonely Planet.

Beran, Harry. 1998. A Democratic Theory of Political Self-Determination for a New World Order. In *Theories of Secession*, edited by Percy Lehning, 33–60. New York: Routledge.

Berg, Eiki. 2009. Re-Examining Sovereignty Claims in Changing Territorialities: Reflections from "Kosovo Syndrome." *Geopolitics* 14(2): 219–234.

Berg, Eiki, and Scott Pegg. 2018. Scrutinizing a Policy of "Engagement without Recognition": US Requests for Diplomatic Action with De Facto States. *Foreign Policy Analysis* 14(3): 388–407.

Berg, Eiki, and Scott Pegg. 2020. Do Parent State Strategies Matter in Resolving Secessionist Conflicts with *De Facto* States? In *Strategies of Secession and Counter-Secession*, edited by Ryan D. Griffiths and Diego Muro, 52–68. London: Rowman and Littlefield, ECPR Press.

Berlin, Alexander H. 2009. Recognition as Sanction: Using International Recognition of New States to Deter, Punish, and Contain Bad Actors. *University of Pennsylvania Journal of International Law* 31(2): 531–591.

Berlin, Isaiah. 1969. *Four Essays on Liberty*. Oxford: Oxford University Press.

Bob, Clifford. 2005. *The Marketing of Rebellion: Insurgents, Media, and International Activism*. Cambridge: Cambridge University Press.

Boix, Carles, Michael Miller, and Sebastian Rosato. 2013. A Complete Dataset of Political Regimes, 1800–2007. *Comparative Political Studies* 46(12): 1523–1554.

Bones, Robert C. 1958. *The Dynamics of the Western New Guinea Problem*. Ithaca, NY: Cornell University Press.

Borch, Merite. 2001. Rethinking the Origins of *Terra Nullius*. *Australian Historical Studies* 32(117): 222–239.

Boutros-Ghali, Boutros. 1992. *An Agenda for Peace: Preventive Diplomacy, Peacemaking, and Peacekeeping*. New York: United Nations.

Braithwaite, John, Hilary Charlesworth, Peter Reddy, and Leah Dunn. 2010. *Reconciliation and Architectures of Commitment: Sequencing Peace in Bougainville*. Canberra: Australian National University Press.

Bremer, Stuart A., and Faten Ghosn. 2003. Defining States: Reconsiderations and Recommendations. *Conflict Management and Peace Science* 20(1): 21–41.

Brennan, Sean, Brenda Gunn, and George Williams. 2004. "Sovereignty" and Its Relevance to Treaty-Making between Indigenous Peoples and Australian Governments. *Sydney Law Review* 26(3): 307–352.

Brubaker, Rogers. 2004. *Ethnicity without Groups*. Cambridge, MA: Harvard University Press.

Buchanan Allen. 1997. Self-Determination, Secession, and the Rule of Law. In *The Morality of Nationalism*, edited by Robert McKim and Jeff McMahan, 301–323. Oxford: Oxford University Press.

Buchanan, Allen. 1998. The International Institutional Dimension of Secession. In *Theories of Secession*, edited by Percy B. Lehning, 225–254. London: Routledge.

Buchanan, Allen. 2003. The Making and Unmaking of Boundaries: What Liberalism Has to Say. In *States, Nations, and Borders: The Ethics of Making Boundaries*, edited by Allen Buchanan and Margaret Moore, 231–261. Cambridge: Cambridge University Press.

Buchanan, James M. 1965. An Economic Theory of Clubs. *Economica* 32(125): 1–14.

Budiardjo, Carmel, and Soei Liong Liem. 1988. *West Papua: The Obliteration of a People*. Thornton Heath: Tapol.

Bull, Hedley. 1977. *The Anarchical Society: A Study of Order in World Politics*. New York: Columbia University Press.

Burg, Steven L. 2015. Identity, Grievances, and Popular Mobilization for Independence in Catalonia. *Nationalism and Ethnic Politics* 21(3): 289–312.

Butcher, Charles, and Ryan Griffiths. 2015. Alternative International Systems? System Structure and Violent Conflict in 19th Century West Africa, Southeast Asia, and South Asia, *Review of International Studies* 41(4): 715–737.

Butcher, Charles, and Ryan Griffiths. 2017. Between Eurocentrism and Babel: A Framework for the Analysis of States, State Systems, and International Orders. *International Studies Quarterly* 61(2): 328–336.

Butt, Ahsan I. 2017. *Secession and Security: Explaining State Strategy Against Separatists*. Ithaca, NY: Cornell University Press.

Butt, Ahsan I. 2020. State Strategy against Secessionists. In *Strategies of Secession and Counter-Secession*, edited by Ryan D. Griffiths and Diego Muro, 69–83. London: Rowman and Littlefield, ECPR Press.

Buzan, Barry, and Richard Little. 2000. *International Systems in World History: Remaking the Study of International Relations*. Oxford: Oxford University Press.

Cardús, Salvador. 2013. What Has Happened to Us Catalans? In *What's up with Catalonia?*, edited by Liz Castro, 95–100. Ashfield, MA: Catalonia Press.

Caspersen, Nina. 2012. *Unrecognized States: The Struggle for Sovereignty in the Modern International System*. Cambridge, MA: Polity.

Caspersen, Nina. 2015. The Pursuit of International Recognition after Kosovo. *Global Governance* 21(3): 393–412.

Chappell, David A. 1999. The Noumean Accord: Decolonisation without Independence in New Caledonia? *Pacific Affairs* 72(3): 373–391.

Chappell, David A. 2013. *The Kanak Awakening: The Rise of Nationalism in New Caledonia*. Honolulu: University of Hawai'i Press.

Chauvel, Richard. 2009. Genocide and Demographic Transformation in Papua. *Inside Indonesia* 97 (July–September).

Chenoweth, Erica, and Maria J. Stephan. 2008. Why Civil Resistance Works: The Strategic Logic of Nonviolent Conflict. *International Security* 33(1): 7–44.

Chenoweth, Erica, and Maria J. Stephan. 2011. *Why Civil Resistance Works: The Strategic Logic of Nonviolent Conflict*. New York: Columbia University Press.

Coggins, Bridget L. 2014. *Power Politics and State Formation in the Twentieth Century: The Dynamics of Recognition*. Cambridge: Cambridge University Press.

Coggins, Bridget L. 2017. Rebel Diplomacy: Theorizing Violent Non-State Actors' Strategic Use of Talk. *Rebel Governance in Civil War*, edited by Ana Arjona, Nelson Kasfir, and Zachariah Mampilly, 74–97. Cambridge: Cambridge University Press.

Collier, David, and John Gerring. 2009. *Concepts and Method in Social Science: The Tradition of Giovanni Sartori*. New York: Routledge

Connell, John. 2003. New Caledonia: An Infinite Pause in Decolonization? *The Round Table* 92(368): 125–143.

Crameri, Kathryn. 2014. *Goodbye Spain? The Question of Independence for Catalonia*. Chicago: Sussex Academic Press.

Crawford, James. 2006. *The Creation of States in International Law*. 2nd ed. Oxford: Oxford University Press.

Cunningham, Kathleen Gallagher. 2014. *Inside the Politics of Self-Determination*. Oxford: Oxford University Press.

Cunningham, Kathleen Gallagher, and Katherine Sawyer. 2017. Is Self-Determination Contagious? A Spatial Analysis of the Spread of Self-Determination Claims. *International Organization* 71(3): 585–604.

Danilovich, Alex, ed. 2017. *Iraqi Kurdistan in Middle Eastern Politics*. London: Routledge.

Danilovich, Alex, ed. 2019. *Federalism, Secession, and International Recognition Regime: Iraqi Kurdistan*. London: Routledge.

Davies, Norman. 2011. *Vanished Kingdoms: The Rise and Fall of States and Nations*. New York: Viking.

De la Calle, Luis. 2015. *Nationalist Violence in Postwar Europe*. Cambridge: Cambridge University Press.

Downing, Brian M. 1993. *The Military Revolution and Political Change: Origins of Democracy and Autocracy in Early Modern Europe*. Princeton, NJ: Princeton University Press.

Durrell, Lawrence. 1957. *Bitter Lemons*. London: Faber and Faber.

Eaude, Michael. 2007. *Catalonia: A Cultural History*. Oxford: Signal.

Elazar, Daniel J. 1994. *Federal Systems of the World*. 2nd ed. Longman.

Elliott, J. H. 1992. A Europe of Composite Monarchies. *Past and Present* 37(1): 48–71.

Elmslie, Jim 2009. Not Just Another Disaster: Papuan Claims of Genocide Deserve to be Taken Seriously. *Inside Indonesia* 97 (July–September).

Elmslie, Jim. 2010. West Papuan Demographic Transition and the 2010 Indonesian Census: "Slow Motion Genocide" or Not? *CPACs Working Paper No. 11/1*.

Elmslie, Jim, and Camella Webb-Gannon. 2013. A Slow-Motion Genocide: Indonesian Rule in West Papua. *Griffith Journal of Law and Dignity* 1(2): 142–165.

Englebert, Pierre, and Rebecca Hummel. 2005. Let's Stick Together: Understanding Africa's Secessionist Deficit. *African Affairs* 104(416): 399–427.

Erman, Eva. 2013. The Recognitive Practices of Declaring and Constituting Statehood. *International Theory* 5(1): 129–150.

Fabry, Mikulas. 2010. *Recognizing States: International Society and the Establishment of New States since 1776*. Oxford: Oxford University Press.

Fazal, Tanisha. 2007. *State Death: The Politics and Geography of Conquest, Occupation, and Annexation*. Princeton, NJ: Princeton University Press.

Fazal, Tanisha. 2018a. Go Your Own Way: Why Rising Separatism Might Lead to More Conflict. *Foreign Affairs* 97(4): 113–123.

Fazal, Tanisha. 2018b. *Wars of Law: Unintended Consequences in the Regulation of Armed Conflict*. Ithaca, NY: Cornell University Press.

Fazal, Tanisha, and Ryan Griffiths. 2014. Membership Has Its Privileges: The Changing Benefits of Statehood. *International Studies Review* 16(1): 79–106.

Fazal, Tanisha, and Margarita Konaev. 2019. Homelands versus Minelands: Why Do Armed Groups Commit to the Laws of War? *Journal of Global Security Studies* 4(2): 149–168.

Fearon, James. 1995. Rationalist Explanations for War. *International Organization* 49(3): 379–414.

Fearon, James, and David Laitin. 2003. Ethnicity, Insurgency, and Civil War. *American Political Science Review* 97(1): 75–90.

Ferguson, Yale H., and Richard W. Mansbach. 1996. *Polities: Authorities, Identities, and Change.* Columbia: University of South Carolina Press.

Finnemore, Margaret, and Katherine Sikkink. 1998. International Norm Dynamics and Political Change. *International Organization* 52(4): 887–917.

Fishman, Robert M. 1990. Rethinking State and Regime: Southern Europe's Transition to Democracy. *World Politics* 42(3): 422–440.

Florea, Adrian. 2014. De Facto States in International Politics (1945–2011). *International Interactions* 40: 788–811.

Fraser, Helen.1990. *Your Flag's Blocking Our Sun.* Sydney: ABC Enterprises.

Forcadell, Carme. 2013. Catalonia: A New State in Europe. In *What's up with Catalonia?*, edited by Liz Castro, 13–18. Ashfield, MA: Catalonia Press.

Geldenhuys, Deon. 2009. *Contested States in World Politics.* London: Palgrave MacMillan.

Gellner, Ernst. 1983. *Nations and Nationalism.* Ithaca, NY: Cornell University Press.

Generalitat de Catalunya. [n.d.]. *Catalan, Language of Europe.* https://llengua.gencat.cat/permalink/91192f76-5385-11e4-8f3f-000c29cdf219.

Generalitat de Catalunya. 2014. White Paper on The National Transition of Catalonia. http://economia.gencat.cat/web/.content/70_economia_catalana/Subinici/Llistes/nou-estat/catalonia-new-state-europe/national-transition-catalonia.pdf

George, Alexander L., and Andrew Bennett. 2005. *Case Studies and Theory Development in the Social Sciences.* Cambridge, MA: MIT Press.

Ghai, Yash, and Anthony J. Regan. 2006. Unitary State, Devolution, Autonomy, Secession: State Building and Nation Building in Bougainville, Papua New Guinea. *The Round Table* 95(386): 589–609.

Gilpin, Robert. 1981. *War and Change in World Politics.* Cambridge: Cambridge University Press.

Gleditsch, Kristian, and Michael D. Ward. 1999. A Revised List of Independent States since the Congress of Vienna. *International Interactions* 25(4): 393–413.

Gourevitch, Peter. 1978. The Second Image Reversed. *International Organization* 32(4): 881–912.

Grant, Thomas D. 1999. *The Recognition of States: Law and Practice in Debate and Evolution.* Westport, CT: Praeger.

Griffiths, Ryan D. 2014. Secession and the Invisible Hand of the International System. *Review of International Studies* 40(3): 559–581.

Griffiths, Ryan D. 2015. Between Dissolution and Blood: How Administrative Lines and Categories Shape Secessionist Outcomes. *International Organization* 69(3): 731–751.

Griffiths, Ryan D. 2016a. *Age of Secession: The International and Domestic Determinants of State Birth.* Cambridge: Cambridge University Press.

Griffiths, Ryan D. 2016b. States, Nations, and Territorial Stability: Why Chinese Hegemony Would Be Better for International Order. *Security Studies* 25(3): 519–545.

Griffiths, Ryan D. 2017. Admission to the Sovereignty Club: The Past, Present, and Future of the International Recognition Regime. *Territory, Politics, Governance* 5(2): 177–189.

Griffiths, Ryan D. 2018. The Waltzian Ordering Principle and International Change: A Two-Dimensional Model. *European Journal of International Relations* 24(1): 130–152.

Griffiths, Ryan D., Pablo Guillen Alvarez, and Ferran Martinez I. Coma. 2015. Between the Sword and the Wall: Spain's Limited Options for Catalan Secessionism. *Nations and Nationalism* 21(1): 43–61.

Griffiths, Ryan D., and Charles R. Butcher. 2013. Introducing the International System(s) Dataset (ISD), 1816–2011. *International Interactions* 39(5): 748–768.

Griffiths, Ryan D., and Louis M. Wasser. 2019. Does Violent Secessionism Work? *Journal of Conflict Resolution* 63(5): 1310–1336.

Griffiths, Ryan D., and Diego Muro, eds. 2020. *Strategies of Secession and Counter-Secession.* London: Rowman and Littlefield, ECPR Press.

Halperin, Morton H., David Scheffer, and Patricia L. Small. 1992. *Self-Determination in the New World Order.* Washington, DC: Carnegie Endowment for International Peace.

Harris, Simon. 2014. *Catalonia Is Not Spain: A Historical Perspective.* N.p. [Barcelona]: 4Cat Books.

Havini, Marilyn, and Moses Havini. 2009. The Bougainville Flag: The Story of the Flag, https://www.facebook.com/AutonomousBougainvilleGovernment/posts/the-story -of-the-flagthe-bougainville-flag-was-selected-from-a-nationwide-design /1926337757588696/

Henige, James. 1970. *Colonial Governors: From the Fifteenth Century to the Present.* Madison: University of Wisconsin Press.

Henningham, Stephen. 2017. The Limits of Influence: Australia and the Future of New Caledonia, 1975–1988. *Journal of Pacific History* 52(4): 482–500.

Hibbert, A.B. 1949. Catalan Consulates in the Thirteenth Century. *Cambridge Historical Journal* 9: 352–358.

Hirschman, Albert O. 1970. *Exit, Voice, and Loyalty: Responses to Declines in Firms, Organizations, and States.* Cambridge, MA: Harvard University Press.

Horowitz, Donald L. 1985. *Ethnic Groups in Conflict.* Berkeley: University of California Press.

Horowitz, Leah S. 2004. Toward a Viable Independence? The Koniambo Project and the Political Economy of Mining in New Caledonia. *Contemporary Pacific* 156(2): 287–319.

Horowitz, Leah S. 2009. Environmental Violence and Crises of Legitimacy in New Caledonia. *Political Geography* 28: 248–258.

Horowitz, Michael C., Evan Perkoski, and Philip B. K. Potter. 2018. Tactical Diversity in Militant Violence. *International Organization* 72(1): 139–172.

Huang, Reyko. 2016. Rebel Diplomacy in Civil War. *International Security* 40(4): 89–126.

Human Rights Watch. 1998. *Indonesia: Human Rights and Pro-Independence Actions in Irian Jaya.* New York: Human Rights Watch (December).

Human Rights Watch. 2006. *Too High A Price?* New York: Human Rights Watch (June).

Human Rights Watch. 2009. *What Did I Do Wrong? Papuans in Merauke Face Abuses by Indonesian Special Forces.* New York: Human Rights Watch (June).

Huntington, Samuel. 1972. Foreword, in E. A. Nordlinger, *Conflict Regulation in Divided Societies.* Cambridge, MA: Harvard University Press.

Ignatieff, Michael. 1993. *Blood and Belonging: Journeys into the New Nationalism.* New York: Farrar, Straus and Giroux.

Jackson, Robert. 1990. *Quasi-States: Sovereignty, International Relations, and the Third World.* Cambridge: Cambridge University Press.

Jackson, Robert. 1993. The Weight of Ideas in Decolonization: Normative Change in International Relations. In *Ideas and Foreign Policy: Beliefs, Institutions, and Political Change,* edited by Judith Goldstein and Robert O. Keohane, 111–138. Ithaca, NY: Cornell University Press.

Jackson, Robert. 2007. *Sovereignty.* Cambridge, MA: Polity.

Jackson, Robert H., and Robert G. Rosberg. 1982. Why Africa's Weak States Persist: The Empirical and the Juridical in Statehood. *World Politics* 35: 1–24.

James, Alan. 1986. *Sovereign Statehood: The Basis of International Society.* London: Allen and Unwin.

Jo, Hyeran. 2015. *Compliant Rebels: Rebel Groups and International Law in World Politics.* Cambridge: Cambridge University Press.

Jolly, Seth K. 2015. *The European Union and the Rise of Regionalist Parties.* Ann Arbor: University of Michigan Press.

Kahneman, Daniel, and Amos Tversky. 1974. Judgement under Uncertainty: Heuristics and Biases. *Science* 185: 1124–1131.

Kalyvas, Stathis N. 2006. *The Logic of Violence in Civil War.* Cambridge: Cambridge University Press.

Kalyvas, Stathis, and Laia Balcells. 2010. International System and Technologies of Rebellion: How the End of the Cold War Shaped Internal Conflict. *American Political Science Review* 104(3): 415–429.

Kartsonaki, Argyro. 2020. The False Hope of Remedial Secession: Theory, Law, and Reality. In *Strategies of Secession and Counter-Secession*, edited by Ryan D. Griffiths and Diego Muro, 31–51. London: Rowman and Littlefield, ECPR Press.

Keating, Joshua. 2008. How to Start Your Own Country in Four Easy Steps. *Foreign Policy* (February).

Keating, Michael. 2004. European Integration and the Nationalities Question. *Politics and Society* 31(1): 367–88.

Keck, Margaret E., and Kathryn Sikkink. 1998. *Activists beyond Borders: Advocacy Networks in International Politics.* Ithaca, NY: Cornell University Press.

Kereslidze, Nino. 2015. The Engagement Policies of the European Union, Georgia and Russia Towards Abkhazia. *Caucasus Survey* 3(3): 309–322.

Ker-Lindsay, James. 2011. *The Cyprus Problem: What Everyone Needs to Know.* Oxford: Oxford University Press.

Ker-Lindsay, James. 2012. *The Foreign Policy of Counter-Secession: Preventing the Recognition of Contested States.* Oxford: Oxford University Press.

Ker-Lindsay, James. 2015. Engagement without Recognition: The Limits of Diplomatic Interaction with Contested States. *International Affairs* 91(2): 267–285.

Ker-Lindsay, James. 2017. Great Powers, Counter-Secession, and Non-Recognition: Britain and the 1983 Unilateral Declaration of Independence of the "Turkish Republic of Northern Cyrpus." *Diplomacy and Statecraft* 28(3): 432–453.

Ker-Lindsay, James. 2018. The Four Pillars of a Counter-Secession Foreign Policy. In *Secession and Counter-Secession: An International Relations Perspective*, edited by Diego Muro and Eckart Woertz, 85–90. Barcelona: CIDOB (Barcelona Centre for International Affairs).

Kingsbury, Damien. 2011. West Papua: Secessionism and/or Failed Decolonization? In *The Ashgate Research Companion to Secession*, edited by Aleksandar Pavković and Peter Radan, 491–496. Burlington, VT: Ashgate.

Kirksey, Eben. 2012. *Freedom in Entangled Worlds: West Papua and the Architecture of Global Power.* Durham, NC: Duke University Press.

Krasner, Stephen. 1999. *Sovereignty: Organized Hypocrisy.* Princeton, NJ: Princeton University Press.

Krasner, Stephen. 2013. Recognition: Organized Hypocrisy Once again. *International Theory* 5(1): 170–176.

Krause, Peter. 2013–2014. The Structure of Success: How the Internal Distribution of Power Drives Armed Group Behavior and National Movement Effectiveness. *International Security* 38(3): 72–116.

Krause, Peter. 2017. *Rebel Power: Why Nationalist Movements Compete, Fight, and Win.* Ithaca, NY: Cornell University Press.

Kuperman, Alan. 2008. The Moral Hazard of Humanitarian Intervention: Lessons from the Balkans. *International Studies Quarterly* 52(1): 49–80.

Laitin, David D. 1998. *Identity in Formation.* Ithaca, NY: Cornell University Press.

Lake, David A., and Angela O'Mahony. 2004. The Incredible Shrinking State: Explaining Change in the Territorial Size of Countries. *Journal of Conflict Resolution* 48(5): 699–722.

Lecours, André. 2020. The Two Québec Independence Referendums: Political Strategies and International Relations. In *Strategies of Secession and Counter-Secession*, edited by Ryan D. Griffiths and Diego Muro, 143–160. London: Rowman and Littlefield, ECPR Press.

Lieberman, Evan S. 2005. Nested Analysis as a Mixed-Methods Strategy for Comparative Research. *American Political Science Review* 99(3): 435–452.

Lineira, Robert, and Daniel Cetra. 2015. The Independence Case in Comparative Perspective. *Political Quarterly* 86 (2): 257–264.

Linz, Juan L. 1989. Spanish Democracy and the Estado de las Autonomías. In *Forging Unity Out of Diversity*, edited by Robert A. Goldwin, Art Kaufman, and William A. Schambra, 260–303. Washington, DC: American Enterprise Institute for Public Policy Research.

Liria, Yauka Aluambo. 1993. *Bougainville Campaign Diary.* Melbourne: Indra.

Lluch, Jaime. 2010. How Nationalism Evolves: Explaining the Establishment of New Varieties of Nationalism within the National Movements of Quebec and Catalonia. *Nationalities Papers* 38(3): 337–359.

Lukes, Steven M. 1974. *Power: A Radical View.* London: Macmillan.

Macdonald, Geoffrey. 2013. Election Rules and Identity Politics: Understanding the Success of Multiethnic Parties in Indonesia. *IFES Hybl Democracy Studies Fellowship Paper.* Washington, DC: International Foundation for Electoral Systems.

MacLellan, Nic. 1999. The Noumea Accord and Decolonisation in New Caledonia. *Journal of Pacific History* 34(3): 245–252.

MacLeod, Jason. 2015. *Merdeka and the Morning Star: Civil Resistance in West Papua.* Brisbane: University of Queensland Press.

Maddens, Bart, Gertjan Muyters, Wouter Wolfs, and Steven Van Hecke. 2020. The European Union in the Narratives of Secessionist Parties: Lessons from Catalonia, Flanders, and Scotland. In *Strategies of Secession and Counter-Secession*, edited by Ryan D. Griffiths and Diego Muro, 122–142. London: Rowman and Littlefield, ECPR Press.

Mampilly, Zachariah Cherian. 2011. *Rebel Rulers: Insurgent Governance and Civilian Life during War.* Ithaca, NY: Cornell University Press.

Manela, Erez. 2007. *The Wilsonian Moment: Self-Determination and the International Origins of Anticolonial Nationalism.* Oxford: Oxford University Press.

Mansell, Michael. 2016. *Treaty and Statehood: Aboriginal Self-Determination.* Annandale, NSW: Federation Press.

Matanock, Aila M. 2017. Bullets for Ballots: Electoral Participation Provisions and Enduring Peace after Civil Conflict. *International Security* 41(4): 93–132.

Matsuno, Akihisa. 2011. West Papua and the Changing Nature of Self-Determination. In *Comprehending West Papua*, edited by Peter King, Jim Elmslie, and Camellia Webb-Gannon, 177–190. Sydney: Centre for Peace and Conflict Studies, University of Sydney.

Mayall, James. 1990. *Nationalism and International Society.* Cambridge: Cambridge University Press.

McAdam, Doug. 1986. Recruitment to High-Risk Activism: The Case of Freedom Summer. *American Journal of Sociology* 92(1): 64–90.

McCurry, Stephanie. 2010. *Confederate Reckoning: Power and Politics in the Civil War South.* Cambridge, MA: Harvard University Press.

McEwen, Nicola. 2018. Insights from the Scottish Independence Referendum. In *Secession and Counter-Secession: An International Relations Perspective*, edited by Diego Muro and Eckart Woertz, 47–54. Barcelona: CIDOB (Barcelona Centre for International Affairs).

McGregor, Russell. 2009. Another Nation: Aboriginal Activism in the late 1960s and 1970s. *Australian Historical Studies.* 40(3): 343–360.

Meetser, Daniel H. 2012. Remedial Secession: A Positive or Negative Force for the Prevention and Reduction of Armed Conflict. *Canadian Foreign Policy Journal* 18(2): 151–163.

Minahan, James. 1996. *Nations without States: A Historical Dictionary of Contemporary National Movements.* London: Greenwood.

Minahan, James. 2002. *Encyclopedia of the Stateless Nations: Ethnic and National Groups around the World.* London: Greenwood.

Minahan, James. 2016. *Encyclopedia of Stateless Nations: Ethnic National Groups around the World.* 2nd ed. Santa Barbara, CA: Greenwood.

Minder, Raphael. 2017. *The Struggle for Catalonia: Rebel Politics in Spain.* London: Hurst.

Msimang, Sisonke. 2018. All is Not Forgiven: South Africa and the Scars of Apartheid. *Foreign Affairs* (January–February).

Mueller, Dennis C. 1989. *Public Choice II.* Cambridge: Cambridge University Press.

Muñoz, Jordi, and Raul Tormos. 2015. Economic Expectation and Support for Secession in Catalonia: Between Causality and Rationalization. *European Political Science Review* 7(2): 315–341.

Nelson, Hank. 2005. Bougainville in World War II. In *Bougainville before the Conflict*, edited by Anthony J. Regan and Helga M. Griffin, 168–198. Canberra: Australian National University.

Nexon, Daniel H. 2009. *The Struggle for Power in Early Modern Europe: Religious Conflict, Dynastic Empires, and International Change.* Princeton, NJ: Princeton University Press.

Norman, Wayne. 1998. The Ethics of Secession as the Regulation of Secessionist Politics. In *National Self-Determination and Secession*, edited by Margaret Moore, 34–61. Oxford: Oxford University Press.

Oltramonti, Giulia Prelz. 2020. Viability as a Strategy of Secession: Enshrining *De Facto* Statehood in Abkhazia and Somaliland. In *Strategies of Secession and Counter-Secession*, edited by Ryan D. Griffiths and Diego Muro, 180–199. London: Rowman and Littlefield, ECPR Press.

Oppenheim, Lassa F. L. 1955. *International Law: A Treatise.* 8th ed. London: Longmans, Green.

Osborne, Robin. 1985. *Indonesia's Secret War: The Guerilla Struggle in Irian Jaya.* Pandora Press.

Osiander, Andreas. 2001. Sovereignty, International Relations, and the Westphalian Myth. *International Organization* 55(2): 251–287.

Osterud, Oyvind. 1997. The Narrow Gate: Entry to the Club of Sovereign States. *Review of International Studies* 23(2): 167–184.

Owen, David. 1995. *Balkan Odyssey.* New York: Harcourt Brace.

Partal, Vicent. 2011. *What Catalans Want: Could Catalonia be Europe's Next State?* Edited by Toni Strubell. Ashfield, MA: Catalonia Press.

Pape, Robert A. 2003. The Strategic Logic of Suicide Terrorism. *American Political Science Review* 97(3): 343–361.

Pavković, Aleksandar. 2020. In Search of International Recognition: Declarations of Independence and Unilateral Secession. In *Strategies of Secession and Counter-Secession*, edited by Ryan D. Griffiths and Diego Muro, 15–30. London: Rowman and Littlefield, ECPR Press.

Pavković, Aleksandar, and Peter Radan. 2007. *Creating New States: Theory and Practice of Secession*. Burlington, VT: Ashgate.

Pegg, Scott. 1998. *International Society and the De Facto State*. London: Routledge.

Pegg, Scott. 2017. Twenty Years of De Facto State Studies: Progress, Problems, and Prospects, in *Oxford Research Encyclopedia of Politics*. DOI: 10.1093/acrefore/9780190228637.013.516

Pegg, Scott, and Eiki Berg. 2016. Lost and Found: The WikiLeaks of De Facto State–Great Power Relations. *International Studies Perspectives* 17(3): 267–286.

Perales-García, Cristina. 2013. How Did We Get Here? In *What's up with Catalonia?*, edited by Liz Castro, 105–112. Ashfield, MA: Catalonia Press.

Phillips, Andrew, and Jason C. Sharman. 2015. *International Order in Diversity: War, Trade and Rule in the Indian Ocean*. Cambridge: Cambridge University Press.

Plattner, Marc F. 2003. Competing Goals, Conflicting Perspectives. *Journal of Democracy* 14(4): 42–56.

Plumer, Aytug. 2003. *Cyprus, 1963–64: The Fateful Years*. Lefkosa: Cyrep.

Poggi, Gianfranco. 1978. *The Development of the Modern State: A Sociological Introduction*. Stanford, CA: Stanford University Press.

Polity IV Project. Political Regime Characteristics and Transitions, 1800–2013.

Premdas, Ralph R. 2004. Bougainville: The Quest for Self-Determination. In *De Facto States: The Quest for Sovereignty*, edited by Tozun Bahcheli, Barry Bartmann, and Henry Srebrnik, 232–244. London: Routledge.

Putnam, Robert D. 1998. Diplomacy and Domestic Politics: The Logic of Two-Level Games. *International Organization* 42(3): 427–460.

Putnam, Robert D. 2000. *Bowling Alone*. New York: Simon and Schuster.

Quinn, Frederic. *The French Overseas Empire*. Westport, CT: Praeger, 2000)

Radan, Peter. 2002. *The Break-up of Yugoslavia in International Law*. London: Routledge.

Radan, Peter. 2008. Secession: A Word in Search of a Meaning. In *On the Way to Statehood: Secession and Globalization*, edited by Peter Radan and Aleksandar Pavković, 17–32. Burlington, VT: Ashgate.

Ratner, Steven R. 1996. Drawing a Better Line: Uti Possidetis and the Borders of New States. *American Journal of International Law* 94(4): 590–624.

Regan, Anthony J. 2005. Identities among Bougainvilleans. In *Bougainville before the Conflict*, edited by Anthony J. Regan and Helga M. Griffin, 418–446. Canberra: Australian National University.

Regan, Anthony J. 2011. *Light Intervention: Lessons from Bougainville*. Washington, DC: United States Institute of Peace.

Regan, Anthony J. 2013. Bougainville: Conflict Deferred? In *Diminishing Conflicts in Asia and the Pacific: Why Some Subside and Others Don't*, edited by Edward Aspinall, Robin Jeffrey, and Anthony J. Regan, 119–152. Canberra: Pandanus.

Reilly, Benjamin. 2007. Electoral and Political Party Reform. In *Indonesia: Democracy and the Promise of Good Governance*, edited by Ross H. Mcleod and Andrew MacIntyre, 41–54. Singapore: Institute of Southeast Asian Studies.

Relitz, Sebastian. 2019. The Stabilisation Dilemma: Conceptualising International Responses to Secession and De Facto States. *East European Politics* 35(3): 311–331.

Reynolds, Henry. 1996. *Aboriginal Sovereignty: Reflections on Race, State, and Nation.* St. Leonards, NSW: Allen and Unwin.

Rezvani, David A. 2014. *Surpassing the Sovereign State: The Wealth, Self-Rule, and Security Advantages of Partially Independent Territories.* Oxford: Oxford University Press.

Roeder, Philip G. 2007. *Where Nation-States Come From: Institutional Change in the Age of Nationalism.* Princeton, NJ: Princeton University Press.

Roeder, Philip G. 2018. *National Secession: Persuasion and Violence in Independence Campaigns.* Ithaca, NY: Cornell University Press.

Rohrbach, Livia. 2020. Patterns of Strategic Interaction in Self-Determination Disputes: A Comparative Analysis of East Timor, Aceh, and West Papua. In *Strategies of Secession and Counter-Secession,* edited by Ryan D. Griffiths and Diego Muro, 200–221. London: Rowman and Littlefield, ECPR Press.

Ross, Carne. 2007. *Independent Diplomat: Dispatches from an Unaccountable Elite.* Ithaca, NY: Cornell University Press.

Ruggie, John. 1998. *Constructing the World Polity.* New York: Taylor and Francis.

Rutherford, Danilyn. 2003. *Raiding the Land of Leviathan: The Limits of the Nation on an Indonesian Frontier.* Princeton, NJ: Princeton University Press.

Saideman, Stephen M. 1998. Is Pandora's Box Half Empty or Half Full? The Limited Virulence of Secessionism and the Domestic Sources of Disintegration. In *The International Spread of Ethnic Conflict: Fear, Diffusion, and Escalation,* edited by David A. Lake and Donald Rothchild, 127–150. Princeton, NJ: Princeton University Press.

Saltford, John. 2003. *The United Nations and the Indonesian Takeover of West Papua, 1962–1969: The Anatomy of Betrayal.* London: Routledge Curzon.

Sambanis, Nicholas, and Jonah Schulhofer-Wohl. 2009. What's in a Line? Is Partition a Solution to Civil War? *International Security* 34(2): 82–118.

Sandholtz, Wayne, and Kendall Stiles. 2008. *International Norms and Cycles of Change.* Oxford: Oxford University Press.

Schelling, Thomas C. 1966. *Arms and Influence.* New Haven, CT: Yale University Press.

Schmitter, Philippe C. 2003. Democracy in Europe and Europe's Democratization. *Journal of Democracy* 14(4): 71–85.

Scott, James C. 1985. *Weapons of the Weak: Everyday Forms of Resistance.* New Haven, CT: Yale University Press.

Schock, Kurt. 2005. *Unarmed Insurrections: People Power in Nondemocracies.* Minneapolis: University of Minnesota Press.

Schock, Kurt. 2013. The Practice and Study of Civil Resistance. *Journal of Peace Research* 50(3): 277–290.

Seymour, Lee J. M., Kristin M. Bakke, and Kathleen Gallagher Cunningham. 2016. E pluribus unum, ex uno plures: Competition, Violence, and Fragmentation in Ethnopolitical Movements. *Journal of Peace Research* 53(1): 3–18.

Shaw, Malcom N. 1996. The Heritage of States: The Principle of Uti Possidetis Juris Today. *British Yearbook of International Law* 67: 75–154.

Shaw, Malcom N. 2014. *International Law.* 7th ed. Cambridge: Cambridge University Press.

Singer, J. David, Stuart Bremer, and John Stuckey. 1972. Capability Distribution, Uncertainty, and Major Power War, 1820–1965, in *Peace, War, and Numbers,* edited by Bruce Russett. Beverly Hills: Sage.

Singer, Peter W. 2003. *Corporate Warriors: The Rise of the Privatized Military Industry.* Ithaca, NY: Cornell University Press.

Singh, Bilveer. 2017. *Papua: Geopolitics and the Quest for Nationhood.* London: Routledge.

Smith, Whitney. 1975. *Flags through the Ages and Across the World.* New York: McGraw-Hill.

Snyder, Jack, and Leslie Vinjamuri. 2004. Trials and Errors: Principle and Pragmatism in Strategies of International Justice. *International Security* 28(3): 5–44.

Solozábal, Juan José. 1996. Spain: A Federation in the Making? In *Federalizing Europe?*, edited by Joachim Jens Hesse and Vincent Wright, 204–265. Oxford: Oxford University Press.

Sorens, Jason. 2012. *Secessionism: Identity, Interest, and Strategy.* Montreal: McGill-Queen's University Press.

Spruyt, Hendrik. 1994. *The Sovereign State and its Competitors.* Princeton, NJ: Princeton University Press.

Staniland, Paul. 2012. Organizing Insurgency: Networks, Resources, and Rebellion in South Asia. *International Security* 37(1): 142–177.

Staniland, Paul. 2014. *Networks of Rebellion: Explaining Insurgent Cohesion and Collapse.* Ithaca, NY: Cornell University Press.

Stanley, David. 1989. *South Pacific Handbook.* Chico, CA: Moon.

Stanton, Jessica A. 2013. Terrorism in the Context of Civil War. *Journal of Politics* 75(4): 1009–1022.

Sterio, Milena. 2013. *The Right to Self-Determination Under International Law: "Selfistans," Secession, and the Rule of the Great Powers.* London: Routledge.

Stewart, Megan A. 2018. Civil War as State-Making: Strategic Governance in Civil War. *International Organization* 72(1): 205–226.

Strayer, Joseph R. 1970. *On the Medieval Origins of the Modern State.* Princeton, NJ: Princeton University Press.

Swenden, Wilfried. 2006. *Federalism and Regionalism in Western Europe: A Comparative and Thematic Analysis.* Basingstoke: Palgrave.

Tanis, James. 2002. In between: Personal Experiences in the 9-Year Long Conflict on Bougainville. *State, Society and Governance in Melanesia Project Working Paper.* Canberra: Australian National University.

Tanis, James. 2005. Nagovisi Villages as a Window on Bougainville in 1988. In *Bougainville before the Conflict*, edited by Anthony J. Regan and Helga M. Griffin, 447–472. Canberra: Australian National University.

Tarrow, Sidney G. 2011. *Power in Movement: Social Movements and Contentious Politics.* Cambridge: Cambridge University Press.

Tilly, Charles. 1975. *The Formation of National States in Western Europe.* Princeton: Princeton University Press.

Tilly, Charles. 1992. *Coercion, Capital, and European States.* Revised 2nd ed. Cambridge, MA: Blackwell.

Tjibaou, Jean-Marie. 2006. *Kanaky.* Translated by Helen Fraser and John Trotter. Canberra: Pandanus.

Toft, Monica Duffy. 2002. *The Geography of Ethnic Violence: Identity, Interests, and the Indivisibility of Territory.* Princeton, NJ: Princeton University Press.

Toft, Monica Duffy. 2010. Ending Civil Wars: A Case for Rebel Victory? *International Security* 34(4): 7–36.

Tremlett, Giles. 2006. *The Ghosts of Spain: Travels through Spain and Its Silent Past.* New York: Walker.

Tryon, Darrell. 2005. The Languages of Bougainville. In *Bougainville before the Conflict*, edited by Anthony J. Regan and Helga M. Griffin, 31–46. Canberra: Australian National University.

Upton, Stuart. 2009. A Disaster, but not Genocide. *Inside Indonesia* 97 (July–September).

Utomo, Ario Bimo. 2019. The Paradiplomatic Role of the ConIFA in Promoting Self-Determination of Marginalized Entities, *Global and Strategis* 13(1): 25–36.

Vanhanen, Tatu. 2000. *The Polyarchy Dataset: Vanhanen's Index of Democracy.* https://www .prio.org/Data/Governance/Vanhanens-index-of-democracy/.

Van Dyke, Vernon. 1977. The Individual, the State, and Ethnic Communities in Political Theory. *World Politics* 29(3): 343–369.

Van Houten, Pieter. 2007. Regionalist Challenges to European States: A Quantitative Assessment. *Ethnopolitics* 6(4): 545–568.

Vinthagen, Stellan. 2015. *A Theory of Nonviolent Action: How Civil Resistance Works.* London: Zed.

Visoka, Gezim. 2018. *Acting Like a State: Kosovo and the Everyday Making of Statehood.* New York: Routledge.

Wallis, Joanne. 2012. Ten Years of Peace: Assessing Bougainville's Progress and Prospects. *The Round Table* 101(1): 29–40.

Wallis, Joanne. 2014. Nation-Building, Autonomy Arrangements, and Deferred Referendums: Unresolved Questions from Bougainville, Papua New Guinea. *Nationalism and Ethnic Politics* 19(3): 310–332.

Walter, Barbara. 2006. Information, Uncertainty, and the Decision to Secede. *International Organization* 60(1): 105–135.

Walter, Barbara. 2009. *Reputation and Civil War.* Cambridge: Cambridge University Press.

Waters, Timothy William. 2020. *Boxing Pandora: Rethinking Borders, States, and Secession in a Democratic World.* New Haven, CT: Yale University Press.

Weber, Max. 1964. *The Theory of Social and Economic Organization.* Edited by Talcott Parsons. Translated by A. M. Henderson and Talcott Parsons. New York: Free Press.

Weill, Rivka. 2018. Secession and the Prevalence of Militant Constitutionalism Worldwide. *Cardozo Law Review* 40(2): 905–990.

Weill, Rivka. 2020. Global Constitutional Strategies to Counter-Secession. In *Strategies of Secession and Counter-Secession*, edited by Ryan D. Griffiths and Diego Muro, 84–100. London: Rowman and Littlefield, ECPR Press.

Weinstein, Jeremy M. 2007. *Inside Rebellion: The Politics of Insurgent Violence.* Cambridge: Cambridge University Press.

Wellman, Christopher Heath. 2005. *A Theory of Secession.* Cambridge: Cambridge University Press.

Williams, Paul R., and Karen Heymann. 2004. Earned Sovereignty: An Emerging Conflict Resolution Approach. *ILSA Journal of International and Comparative Law* 10(2): 437–445.

Williams, Paul R., and Francesca Jannotti Pecci. 2004. Earned Sovereignty: Bridging the Gap between Sovereignty and Self-Determination. *Stanford Journal of International Law* 40(2): 347–386.

Withers, Lucia, and Signe Poulsen. 2002. *Grave Human Rights Violations in Wasior, Papua.* Amnesty International Report. London. AI-Index: ASA 21/032/2002.

Wolfe, James H. 1992. The United Nations and the Cyprus Question. In *Cyprus: A Regional Conflict and its Resolution*, edited by Norma Salem, 227–243. New York: St. Martin's.

Wood, Elisabeth. 2003. *Insurgent Collective Action and Civil War in El Salvador.* Cambridge: Cambridge University Press.

Wutzke, Jeffrey. 1998. Dependent Independence: Application of the Nunavut Model to Native Hawaiian Sovereignty and Self-Determination Claims. *American Indian Law Review* 22(2): 509–565.

Zacher, Mark. 2001. The Territorial Integrity Norm: International Boundaries and the Use of Force. *International Organization* 55(20): 215–250

Index

Tables are indicated by t; figures are indicated by f

Lafleur, Jacques, 117, 119
Latin America secessions, 22, 26, 91
Libya, 21, 121, 123
Liria, Yauka Aluambo, 99–100, 101, 105, 107, 200n31, 200nn36–38, 201n70

Machoro, Eloi, 121–122
Macron, Emmanuel, 46, 125, 192n57
Makarios III (archbishop), 131, 133–134
Mas, Artur, 55, 57, 59–60, 62, 63, 162
Merkel, Angela, 61, 156–157, 195n72
microstates, 16, 18, 32, 143, 189n40, 196n33, 197n44
Momis, John, 97, 200n29
Montevideo Convention, 13–14, 77, 140
Mote, Octovianus, 89, 199n48
Murrawarri Republic, 195n12; Australian government response to, 77–78; compellence tactics, 69, 76–77, 79; electoral capture use of, 9; flag design and symbolism, 72–73, 72f; geography, maps, and boundaries, 69, 70f, 71, 195nn4–6; inherent sovereignty appeal of, 76–77, 79; name history and meaning, 71; normative appeal tactics of, 76–77; state consent importance for, 78–79; strategy and tactics, 76–79, 157, 160–161; terra nullius claim of British rejection by, 9, 38, 73, 76–77

Nagorno Karabakh. See Artsakh
Naisseline, Nidoïsh, 116, 121
New Caledonia, 112f, 203n41, 203n48; compellence tactics mixture in, 120–121, 126; decolonization principle and approach in, 9, 15, 40, 114, 116–117, 120, 122–126; flag, 114–115, 115f, 203n33; France response to secessionist efforts in, 118, 122–123, 125, 192n57, 197n1; French colonial history in, 110, 111, 113–115, 202n6; geography, 111; institutionalized movement evolution in, 120–121, 123–124, 126; international support and awareness of, 122–123; Kanak Awakening of 1970s in, 113, 116–117, 120–121; Kanaks as minority in, challenges with, 110–111, 124; Nouméa Accord in, 110, 115, 119–120, 123–125; Ouvéa Massacre in, 118–119, 122, 123, 125; penal colony history in, 111, 117; referendum on independence in, 110, 124–126; strategy and tactics in, 41, 110, 120–126, 157; United Nations recognition history for, 114, 118, 123; uti possidetis juris principle and, 114; violence with secessionist movement in, 118–119,

121–122, 123, 125, 203n38; white settlers/ Caldoches in, 111, 113, 117
normative appeal tactics: analysis of, 151–154, 152t, 153f; dataset for, 148–149; distribution and rate by secessionist kind, 152–153, 152t, 153f; overview of, 4, 30–31; purpose and character of, 34, 35, 148; setting and local conditions role in, 8–9, 154; by state and movement, 180–185t
Northern Cyprus, 129f, 206n63; Annan Plan negotiations and failure in, 136, 138, 206n41; Black Christmas 1963–1964 unrest for, 133, 138, 140; British colonial history in, 128; countersecession efforts against, 44–45, 137, 140; earned sovereignty as focus of, 127; ethnic divisions and conflict in, 3, 10, 128, 130–131, 130t, 133–134, 138–139, 140, 205n11, 205n33; flag design and adoption, 131–133, 132f; geography and demographics, 128; independence declaration, 134, 137, 206n59; militarized boundary/Green Line in, 3, 69, 127, 133–134, 135–136, 138–139, 204n1; strategy and tactics, 127, 135–140, 162; Turkey/Turkish Army support and role in, 131, 132, 134–135, 138–140

Olgun, Mustafa Ergün, 205n11
Ona, Francis, 35, 100–102, 104, 108, 162, 200n29, 202n83
Oppenheim, Lassa, 11, 17

Pabouty, Sylvain, 116, 119, 125, 204n71
Papua New Guinea (PNG), 46, 82f, 96f; civil war with Bougainville, 35, 39, 99–103, 105–109, 159, 162, 200n31, 200nn36–38, 201n50, 201n70; human rights abuses on Bougainville, 94, 99–100, 103, 105, 107–108. See also Bougainville; West Papua
Partal, Vicent, 57, 58, 164
Pedret i Santos, Ferran, 48, 193n1
political parties, secessionist: scholarship on, 5, 6, 36–37, 36f
primary rights theory/appeal, 4, 207n30; application of, considerations in, 172–173; Catalonia use of, 62–63; challenges and controversy with, 25, 28–29; comparative analysis of games focused on, 169, 169t, 171–173; by state and movement, 180–185t
Puigdemont, Carles, 63–64, 162
Pujol, Jordi, 53, 194n40

Rajoy, Mariano, 53, 63–66, 156–157, 195n72
rebel diplomacy, 5, 107

Wahid, Abdurrahman, 88, 92
Wasser, Louis, 7, 109, 142–143, 147, 176
Wea, Djubelly, 119, 203n38
weak combative movements, 4; counter-
secession tactics with, 46–47, 93; examples
of, 9, 38t, 39, 40, 80, 88; human rights abuses
showcased by, 141, 152–153, 152t, 153f;
nonviolent civil resistance of, 141, 149;
normative appeal tactics for, 152–153, 152t,
153f; tactical variation for, 38t, 39–40. *See
also* West Papua
Wenda, Benny, 92–93, 199n54
West Papua, 9, 82f, 197n3, 198n30; Aceh
independence efforts contrasted with,
91–92; Biak Massacre in, 88, 156;
Bougainville contrasted with, 94, 105;
colonial history and impact in, 81, 83, 85,
197n8; compellence tactics history and
evolution, 89–90; countersecession response to, 15, 46, 90, 198n31; declaration
of independence, 86, 198n16; decolonization principle and recognition for, 15, 40,

92, 93; electoral capture inability for, 88,
91, 199n54; flag of, symbolism of and
conflict with, 1, 46, 84–85, 85f, 87, 88, 156;
geography, 80; human rights appeal from,
68, 80, 90, 92–93, 198n31; New York
Agreement and, 83–84; nonviolent civil
resistance in, 2, 39, 47, 89–90, 91, 93,
199n48; normative appeal tactics, 92; social
marginalization and racism experience for,
81, 86–87; strategy and tactics, 40, 47, 80,
89–93, 157, 159, 161–162; transmigration
program and, 86–87, 198n28; United
Nations history with, 83, 93; *uti possidetis
juris* principle application in, 83, 93, 157;
violence and casualties in secessionist
history of, 86, 86f, 89, 199n48, 199n62
Wilsonian (Woodrow) moment, 14, 23
World War I, 12, 14, 22, 23, 97, 168
World War II, 23, 52, 106, 114, 142, 209n11

Yeiwene, Yeiwene, 119, 121
Yugoslav dissolution, 26–27

Printed in the USA
CPSIA information can be obtained
at www.ICGtesting.com
CBHW031426080424
6580CB00009B/56/J